Matabeleland and the Victoria Falls

The letters and journals of Frank Oates 1873-1875

MATABELE LAND

AND

THE VICTORIA FALLS

A NATURALIST'S WANDERINGS IN THE INTERIOR
OF SOUTH AFRICA

FROM THE LETTERS & JOURNALS OF THE LATE

FRANK OATES, F.R.G.S.

EDITED BY C. G. OATES, B.A.

LONDON
C. KEGAN PAUL & CO., 1 PATERNOSTER SQUARE
1881

Cover design copyright © Chris Eason 2007. Front cover shows *Ox-hide shield*, from a drawing by W. E. Oates; and (left to right*) Shoshong, Bamangwato*; *Tati Settlement*; and *Hunters Camp on the Semokwe River*, all from water-colours by W. E. Oates. Back cover shows *Acræa acontias*, litho print by Mintern Brothers, from a specimen collected by Frank Oates at Victoria Falls in January 1875; *Head-dress of zebra-skin and feathers*, from a drawing by W. E. Oates; Victoria Falls photograph by Chris Eason, 2005.

First published 1881 as *Matabele Land and the Victoria Falls: A Naturalist's Wanderings in the Interior of Africa*, C. G. Oates (ed); C. Kegan Paul & Co., London.

This edition published by Jeppestown Press, 10A Scawfell St, London, E2 8NG, United Kingdom.

Editing, arrangement, notes and introduction copyright © David Saffery 2007

ISBN 978-0-9553936-4-8

All Rights Reserved. No part of this publication may be reproduced, stored in a retrieval system, or transmitted, in any form or by any means, electronic, mechanical, photocopying, recording, scanning or otherwise, except as described below, without the permission in writing of the Publisher. Copying is not permitted except for personal use, to the extent permitted by national copyright law. Requests for permission for other kinds of copying, such as copying for general distribution, for advertising or promotional purposes, for creating new collective works, or for resale, and other enquiries, should be addressed to the Publisher.

Matabeleland and the Victoria Falls

The letters and journals of Frank Oates

1873-1875

Edited by C. G. Oates
Introduction and notes by David Saffery

JEPPESTOWN

Contents

Contents	vii
Introduction to the 2007 edition	xi
Preface	15
Memoir	19
Chapter I	33

    Departure from England—St. Helena—Cape Town—Arrival at Durban—Pietermaritzburg— Start up country— Pretoria; its climate and vegetation—The High Veldt—Dutch Boers—The Crocodile River—Bamangwato.

Chapter II	47

    The journey resumed—Halt on the Seruli—Bushmen on the Gokwe—The Shashe—The Tati settlement—Adventure with a lion—W. E. Oates returns to the coast; particulars of his journey.

Chapter III	60

    Frank Oates proceeds to the King's Town—Crosses the Ramaqueban—Dutch hunters on the Impakwe—The Inkwesi's picturesque scenery—John Lee's farm—Manyami's kraal—The Shashani— Fine country—Kumala River.

Chapter IV	71

    Arrival at Gubuleweyo—Interview with the King—Start for the Zambesi—Hope Fountain—Inyati—Difficulty of obtaining bearers—The Zambesi abandoned—Hunting expedition on the Umvungu and Gwailo Rivers—Experiences of a half-caste—Birds' nests—The indunas' tree—Hunting—A lunar eclipse—Return to Gubuleweyo—Wild fruit.

Chapter V	92

    Stay at Gubuleweyo—New Year's Day—The Great Dance—Cattle slaughtered—Departure of the king; the royal procession—A dispute referred to him—Lobengula's court.

Chapter VI	107

    Return to Tati—Changed aspect of the country—Constant delays—The Mashonas—At Manyami's again—John Lee's—Letter home—The

Inkwesi—Wild fruit—A hornbill's nest—The Ramaqueban Rivers—Graves of Englishmen—White Ants—Bushman remains—The Tati reached.

CHAPTER VII   121

Hunting trip on the Semokwe—A native musician—Gigantic baobabs—Return to Tati—Journey to Shoshong—The Bamangwato and Matabele nations—Fighting amongst the natives—Start back for Tati—Misadventures and delays—Fresh arrangements.

CHAPTER VIII   136

Again at Tati—Fresh causes of delay—Lions on the Motloutsi—Threatened by natives—Forthcoming prospects.

CHAPTER IX   143

Fresh start for the Zambesi—The Ramaqueban again—A lion Singular building—Wild fruit—First kraal of the Makalakas—Stopped by the induna—Return to Tati—To Gubuleweyo back—Fresh leave obtained—Altered arrangements for journey.

CHAPTER X   155

Third start for the Zambesi—Again stopped by natives—Fresh leave from the king—The journey resumed—Frank Oates's companion obliged to leave him—He goes forward alone—Breakdown of his waggon—Annoyances from the natives—Help from Tati—Return there—Letters home—Future plans.

CHAPTER XI   177

Final start from Tati—Bushman remains—A game-drive—Wild dogs—The Makalakas again—The Matengwe River—English hunters met with—The Nata River—The Pantamatenka—Christmas Day—Start on foot for the Zambesi—The goal at last.

CHAPTER XII   192

Main features of the Falls—The return commenced—Frank Oates attacked by fever—Course of the illness; improvement and relapse—His death—Dr. Bradshaw takes his effects to Bamangwato—His favourite dog—Arrival of W. Oates and Mr. Gilchrist in Natal—Conclusion.

BIBLIOGRAPHY   205

INTRODUCTION TO THE 2007 EDITION

On New Year's Eve 1874, the British explorer and naturalist Frank Oates became one of the first Europeans since David Livingstone to view the magnificent Victoria Falls. A month later, aged just 34, he died from malaria during his trek south from the Falls, and is buried at a drift by the Shashe River near Kgari Macheng in north-eastern Botswana; an hour's ride from the spot where he died.

In 1881 Oates' younger brother, Charles, a barrister living in Yorkshire, compiled this book from the original diaries, letters, paintings and sketches of Frank Oates to paint a vivid picture of the Victorian exploration of Central Africa. His hope appears to have been that the scientific data collected by Oates would thus be preserved; this was echoed by the book's somewhat lukewarm review in *Proceedings of the Royal Geographical Society*, which expressed the suggestion that 'the permanent value of the book [would] rest upon the scientific appendices' which included the dimensions of a number of skulls of dead 'Bushman' people, enthusiastically gathered by Oates from the spot where a massacre of a band of 'Bushmen' had taken place a year or two earlier, and carefully despatched to Oxford University for examination after his death.

A century later, the scientific value of measurements "of crania of races low in the scale of human life"[1] is perhaps a little less certain (hence the omission of these appendices from this edition). So what value does this book have to a twenty-first century reader?

Without doubt, a large portion of this book's importance lies in the historical first-person accounts that Oates recorded, both in his journal and—usually in a more jocular tone—in his letters to his family in England, of the trek north to the Tati goldfields; his contact with prominent historical figures such as Lobengula of the Ndebele and Sekgoma of the Ngwato, and the hunters John Lee and Frederick Selous; as well as his carefully-observed accounts of life at Lobengula's capital, Bulawayo. Ironically, despite being one of the first Europeans to see the cataract of Victoria Falls in full spate, Oates never wrote a full account of it, or any description of the five weeks he spent in the area, confining himself to the singularly unhelpful sentence, "After breakfast, I visited the Falls—a day never to be forgotten."

---

[1] Rolleston G., 'Ethnology', Appendix to 1881 edition of *Matabele Land and the Victoria Falls*. DS

Oates is not always an easy guide, particularly for a modern reader. Even by prevailing standards of nineteenth-century racism some of his language is offensive, and unsettling in its vehemence. Nevertheless, I have left even his cruder outbursts as originally published.

I have tried where possible to add explanatory footnotes to Oates' text and his brother's commentary.

D.S.

Preface

IN offering to the public the following pages, I feel, as editor, that I owe a few words of apology and explanation to the reader by way of preface— apology for the imperfections of the volume; explanation how such imperfections have arisen.

The traveller whose journey to the Zambesi is here recounted died of fever a few days after he had left that river on his way homewards, and the book has been compiled from his note-books, and letters home. The latter were written with no view of publication; the former were intended only for the writer's own subsequent use and as suggestive guides to memory.

It is always a question in such a case how far the surviving friends of the deceased writer or traveller do well in publishing the unfinished labour of his pen. What his own wish would have been cannot be known, or even guessed at, unless specially expressed; and the reflection forcibly presents itself to the mind that perhaps a certain injustice may be done to the memory of the dead by publishing, in a form which may fairly challenge the criticism of the general reader, a few hasty jottings by the wayside, written under circumstances the least favourable to literary composition, and a limited number of letters home, meant merely for the perusal of the writer's nearest and most indulgent friends. On the other hand, however, it must be borne in mind that, much as must inevitably be lost in editing pages such as these for want of the inspiring touch which the writer himself could alone have finally given them, there will probably be a directness and freshness of the expressions which a traveller makes use of on the spot, hampered as he then is by no oppressive consciousness that he is addressing that imaginary "public"— consisting after all but of a number of individuals like himself, all with the same human heart and interests—which might be wanting in his more matured work.

Guided, then, by the latter consideration, and by the reflection that every day the number of our countrymen is increasing who look to South Africa with a growing interest—whether as a land for colonization, exploration, or scientific research—I venture to add another to the long list of already published books upon that country, hoping that the reader may find therein matter of some general interest, and that, if not, he will look leniently on the error of judgment which has led me, together with those who have here shared my responsibility, to offer for his perusal pages prepared at first mainly for private friends, but which it was afterwards thought might possibly prove of interest to a somewhat wider circle.

Further, with reference to the length of time which has elapsed between the date of the writer's death and the publication of this volume, I can only claim in extenuation of this circumstance the fact that a considerable period necessarily intervened before the traveller's journals and papers reached this country, that they required on their arrival much care in their disposal, and that the whole of the natural history collections had to be gone through systematically before being finally placed in competent hands for arrangement and classification. The delay, then, has enabled me to include in the volume the papers in the appendix on the latter subject, contributed by such able hands, which I believe will add interest to the whole; and that not only in the case of scientific readers, but of all those who would realize in a measure what it is which makes up the life and experiences of the naturalist traveller in his wanderings in distant lands. I may add, moreover, that the general state and condition of the country of which these pages treat would appear, from the accounts of those who have recently visited it, to remain substantially the same, or only changed in points of minor interest. The abandonment, however, of the Tati Gold-mine and the establishment of Kama in the Bamangwato sovereignty perhaps demand attention.

In editing this work it has been my object to preserve, wherever possible, the writer's narrative in exactly his own words; and this plan has been steadily adhered to throughout, those passages only being omitted which appeared little likely to interest the general reader, or in which—as several times occurred—old ground was re-traversed. In such cases the intervening periods have been bridged over by a short narrative of my own, intended merely to connect the story and weld the whole together. The maps, it may be added, are all of them the result of the traveller's own special observations, recorded as he went along.

Of the illustrations in the body of the work, I may remark that they are all from original drawings taken on the spot, or from the objects they purport to represent. Some are from sketches by the late Frank Oates; the remainder—and these the larger number—from those of his brother, W. E. Oates[2], who accompanied him during a portion of his journey. It may therefore perhaps be fairly claimed for them that, whatever their artistic merits, these drawings are—what alone they claim to be—faithful representations of the scenes and objects they depict.

It may be proper to add, before concluding—what I have failed elsewhere to mention—that a considerable number of specimens in my brother's collection were destroyed at Shoshong in his lifetime by the unroofing, during a gale, of the hut where they were stored, and that some of the spirit jars of reptiles and beetles were afterwards left behind when the collections were conveyed to England; circumstances which led in all probability to the loss of many valuable specimens.

There are not many who will need to be reminded that to "inspan" and "outspan," words of frequent occurrence in the traveller's journal, mean, in South African parlance, to "yoke" and "unyoke," and that "spoor" means "footprints" or "track." All other words of Dutch or native origin introduced into the text are explained, I believe, where they occur. The accent in the word "Matabele" falls, it may be added, on the third of its four syllables.

My task is ended—in many respects a very mournful, yet a very pleasing one; and if there be found but a few readers who derive either pleasure or profit from a perusal of these pages, I shall feel amply rewarded for my trouble.

May 1881

C. G. O.[3]

---

[2] William Oates was Frank Oates' junior by two years, and joined him on his expedition to southern Africa in 1873. Returning to Britain in January 1874, William Oates only learned of Frank's death three months later at Durban, while preparing for a hunting trip in Zululand. William Oates died of typhoid in Madeira in 1896, on his way to South Africa. DS

[3] Frank Oates's brother, Charles Oates, a barrister. DS

Memoir

"To be able to give one's name to a bird, or a flower, may seem to many but poor ambition; and yet, materially considered, it is quite as likely to be perpetuated as to give it to a street or town, and is much more likely to define the tastes and individuality of the *giver*."—*Bret Harte*.

THE saying has seldom been truer of any one than of the writer of the succeeding pages, that "the child is father of the man." His love of nature generally, and of natural history in all its branches, was one of Frank Oates's earliest instincts; and to the study of our English wild-birds—their ways and haunts, their comings and their goings—he was especially devoted from boyhood. The pages of Waterton and Buffon, treating of wider fields of study, supplied his imagination at that period with richer food; and the plates of Audubon's Birds, when access could be had to them, were turned by him with feelings little short of reverence. From his earliest days he had resolved to visit those distant, and, to him, still mysterious lands, where the page of nature was yet to the white man in great part an unread book; and those who, after his death in the full prime of manhood, witnessed the arrival at his English home of his large collections of natural history specimens, brought from the interior of South Africa by the devoted service of a friend, realized strangely how the boy's ambition had been fulfilled in after life, and felt that, though cut off in the very perfection of his powers, the purpose of his being had not wholly failed. Those even who knew him best were surprised indeed, when these evidences of his work abroad arrived, to see how much he had accomplished in the brief period—a little short of two years—of his absence. As, one after another, the packing-cases were opened, each in its turn afforded to the looker-on some fresh illustration of the untiring determination of the deceased traveller to make the very utmost of his opportunities whilst abroad. The voice that could alone have told the story of those collections, the hand that had brought them thus together, were silent and still in a far distant grave; but an utterance—the more pathetic because it was inaudible—seemed to go forth, unbidden, from those speechless records of devoted work and enterprise, and tell the secret tale of a life in earnest sympathy with nature curtailed—the hand, as it were, yet warm from its labours.

There, on the one hand, lay the opened cases of rare and brilliant bird-skins, each specimen with its separate label, in the collector's writing, carefully recording its habitat, and other particulars useful to the student, accompanied in many instances by examples of nests and eggs. There, on the other hand, were lesser boxes, filled with varied specimens of insects, some from those very Victoria Falls of the Zambesi, the rich and almost untried harvest-ground of the naturalist, whose attractions had lured the wanderer to his untimely grave. And there, again, were those large wide-necked bottles, familiar to the collector, containing, some of them, strange-looking beetles, others still stranger reptiles; there the packets of botanical drying paper, each sheet enveloping its floral treasure. Turning again to other cases, were found in numbers the singular implements of savage warfare, or industry, and with them many of those rude yet tasteful attempts at ornamentation suggested by native fancy; evidences—the whole of them—of that untutored skill and delicate refinement of workmanship which characterize many of the finer races of unlettered savages. Whilst further, the mighty tusks of the huge African elephant, the skins of the lion, the leopard, and the cheetah—for it was these beasts of prey that the traveller had especially loved to hunt—besides those of many an African antelope, with horns and heads of equal grace and beauty, told silently of stirring adventures in the bush. Lastly, but yet not least, were those scientific instruments he had used in taking observations of his journey with so much faithful perseverance; the note-books; the letters of friends (some of these unopened, containing those trifling items of home news, so sweet to the far-off traveller, which his eyes had never seen, for they had arrived after his decease); the pencilled outlines of the country's scenery; the water-colour drawings of those fatal Falls; how much did not these records breathe to the silent bystander, how much suggest of what had been, and still more what *might have been!*

Poor fellow! not there himself to speak to us, those records of an earnest life, those cared-for and well-worn letters which he *had* received and treasured, how far more eloquent they were to us than any words could have been! They told us all, more than all, than any words which he could, or at least would, have spoken—so lightly did he ever treat his own achievements—and seemed to leave the world and ourselves poorer and yet richer by his death!

But the subject has led me, in my capacity of editor of these pages, beyond the proper limits of my duties, and I must crave the indulgence of the reader for this long digression. My object is merely to relate, as briefly as I can, such simple facts of Frank Oates's earlier life as may serve to illustrate the scope and bearing of the ensuing pages, and bring to view the motives which led him to enter on his life of travel., What I have said, indeed, may perhaps it is true, help to show—what I was anxious early to point out—how very catholic were the interests of the deceased, How great the hold each separate department of the world's life, and history, and daily growth, had laid upon him, Devoted to the study of natural history, as I have already pointed out, and especially to that of birds—the pursuit of which might be called his ruling passion—yet never did he close his eyes to all those varied interests of other kinds, which were constantly opening round him in his life of foreign travel. "He was not" indeed, as has lately been said of the young French naturalist Jacquemont, who, like Frank Oates himself, died early and in harness—"He was not at all one of those specialists who shut themselves up in a narrow speciality, and become blind and deaf to the great interests of human life."[4]

Rather may it be said of him, that his interests were perhaps too wide, and that he overtaxed his strength and powers in following the promptings of his nature. Speaking indeed in homely phraseology, whilst out in Africa, he admitted himself that he had "too many irons in the fire," and some of the difficulties and vexations which beset him upon his journey must be attributed to embracing every opportunity which presented itself: not only of adding a new specimen to his collection, but also of noting any fresh fact with regard to the country and its inhabitants which came before his notice. For, in addition to his natural history pursuits, he was, as above intimated, engaged on this journey in taking observations of the country which he passed through, and laying down his route, and also, wherever possible, in seeking intercourse with the natives, and gaining knowledge of their character.

This same tendency of his—to attempt too much—had once before also served him in evil stead when at the University in earlier life. Born on the 6th of April 1840, a son of the late Mr. Edward Oates, of Meanwoodside, near Leeds—himself a lover of nature, and a man of literary tastes—Frank Oates entered at Christ Church, Oxford, at the close of 1860. And here his love of nature and her teachings soon displayed itself by his choice of reading for a class in the Natural Science Schools. His work, however, in this direction did not keep him from study in many other departments of knowledge; and, besides his studies, all out-door pursuits had each their respective fascination for him. Of

---

[4] Mr. P. G. Hamerton, *Lives of Modern Frenchmen*, p. 95.

these, riding held with him, as it had always done, the foremost place; and when the time of year or incidental circumstance kept him from an occasional gallop with the hounds, he would have a long day's ride into the country instead, drinking in, the while, deep draughts of enjoyment from the scenes he passed through. One such ride, still showing him faithful to his love of birds, he describes himself in a letter to one of his brothers on May Day, 1864, as follows:

"I had a jolly ride," he writes, "to Wychwood Forest a few days ago, with S—of Wadham. We both enjoyed it, as we both entered into the loveliness of the scene. Unfortunately the day was cold, and few birds were seen, though we did hear the nightingale once, and the cuckoo once or twice. We were riding about the forest in the dark, with some prospect of being lost, and did not get back to Oxford till eleven o'clock, having ridden about thirty-six miles."

The exhilaration of these long rides was almost a necessity to him, counteracting, as they did in a measure, the strain of mental work. He also loved bathing, swimming, and sailing, the first two of which Oxford supplied him with in liberal measure, whilst even the last-named he found occasional opportunity of indulging his taste for on the Isis.

Then there were cricket and rowing, to both of which he gave a share of his attention, with rifle-shooting at the butts, and fencing at the gymnasium. This is a tolerable list of occupations, in addition to which Oxford had also its social attractions for him; for, besides the undergraduates of his own standing whom he knew, he was further privileged with the acquaintance of a few such men as the present Dean of Westminster—then Regius Professor of Ecclesiastical History in the University—the present distinguished Master of Balliol, the late Sir Benjamin Brodie, and Professor Henry Smith; whilst the nature of his studies brought him into frequent pleasant intercourse with Professor Rolleston and others at the museum. The second year of his residence he sustained a loss, which he long felt, in the death of his young tutor, Mr. G. R. Luke, Senior Student of Christ Church, to whom he had formed no slight attachment. Of this event, rendered doubly sad by the circumstance under which it occurred, he wrote to a friend the day afterwards (March 4, 1862) as follows :— "Oxford," he says, "has just lost one of its brightest lights, and I a valuable friend, whom, I fear, I did not sufficiently appreciate in his lifetime—poor Luke! It would be too much to say that there was not so good, but I can confidently that I do not think there was a better man in Oxford. He was such a genuine, worthy, and conscientious fellow as is rarely met with; and his kindness was equalled by his noble spirit—his modesty by his high learning and abilities. And this valuable life, difficult as it is to realize it, has been cut short;—Luke was drowned in the river yesterday, having gone alone quite contrary to his custom, in a skiff. It seems that he was near half an hour in the water, and dead when taken out. This sad accident, coming so suddenly, must throw a damp over the feelings of many; and if there is any gratitude amongst men, there must have been many a sigh for him last night. I heard the news before six o'clock, and it had reached Christ Church some time before, the accident having happened about four. You may imagine my horror when, on entering my rooms to put on my cap and gown for hall, I was met by my scout, and asked if I had heard that Mr. Luke was drowned. In an hour or two I should have been reading with him."

And now enough may have perhaps been said to give some insight into Frank Oates's life at Oxford, and with one more quotation from his letters, this period of his history shall be closed. His first year at college an attack upon his chest in early spring had prevented his residence during the summer term at the University, and led to his spending as much of the succeeding winter as the Oxford terms admitted of in Italy, where he gathered many pleasant reminiscences. The following spring, too, he was late in coming up, owing to a return of his ailment during the Easter vacation, when he was again a prisoner to his room at home. Writing on April 23rd (1862), during this period of confinement, he says, "I see the tree-tops tipped with green, and hear the thrush's voice, telling me of old times, and asking me why I keep house, and I've no doubt spring is here. So I want to be out again, and to greet her as an old friend." And presently he was out again, revelling in the spring sunshine with his friends, the birds. But this is not the intended quotation. Sufficiently recovered from this illness for the journey back to Oxford, he returned there on May 9th to find the place. "shaded with its great green trees, and with its gray old walls looking almost joyous." It was not, however, till two evenings later that he "came in for the full benefit of the May aspect of things," as he describes it, when he took a long ramble into the country to Wytham, and first saw the rich pastoral country which surrounds Oxford in its summer dress. His account of this walk, written (again to the same friend) on May 12th, tells forcibly of his appreciation of all country sights and sounds.

"... Your letter arrived yesterday morning," he says, "and of course my evening was at once laid out for me, and now I come to what I ought to have begun with—my ramble of last night. You perhaps thought, as it grew dusk, that I was still lingering about the scene you describe; and so I was. It was with really joyous feelings that I set out at six o'clock, and trudged along the Sevenbridge Road. It was Sunday evening, and the road was crowded with Oxford folks and the militia. The floods which surrounded the road seemed an object of interest to them, but I pushed on, bestowing a hurried glance now and then at the tufted willows, and islands, and shores of long grass, which dotted over and surrounded the lake-like fields, with the dappled sky reflected on their watery surface. Botley reached, I inquired the way to Wytham. A shady green lane was pointed out to me, and I was soon away in thought, all alone in that quiet place; and so on I strolled, through the fields, past the wood, through the village, and, as night closed in, back again. If I were a word-painter I might describe my walk; but not being one, should any attempt of mine thereat be intelligible to you, it will only be because you know what I would describe, and can realize my feelings.

"There had been some little rain, and it was still rather dull and damp when I set out; but I should have gone if it had been worse, and really the evening ended almost brightly. I enjoyed the freshness of everything, and the wild-birds seemed to enjoy it; they did not appreciate it as I did, but they enjoyed it more. The notes of many a songster rang out from the thick cover of the wood on my left, and amongst the well-known notes some strange music was mixed, now and then becoming louder and more distinct. These must have been the wonderful soft strains of the nightingale. The woodpeckers were laughing wildly, and the rooks returning to the tops of the elms, and talking as is their wont; the youngsters responding eagerly, and seeming as if they were chattering and being fed at the same time. The cows were placidly grouped about the hedges, or wandering leisurely to and fro, favouring the passerby with a whiff of their scented breath. On the other side, flooded fields were rich in the most luxuriant vegetation; whilst continually, and, as it grew later, more continually, the cuckoos answered one another from many a deep shade. I was glad to think that you would be thinking me there, and hoped you would not fancy that I should give up the excursion."

Nor, passing now from reminiscences of his Oxford life, was his love of the country and its associations, here sufficiently evinced, confined to one particular sort of scenery; and the wild moor-lands of his native county attracted him as strongly as the quiet and peaceful beauties of Oxfordshire, or even more so. During the Easter vacation of 1864 he had been on a short walking tour into the Yorkshire dales with one of his brothers and some other friends.

"There is always a sense of freedom," he writes from near Leeds soon afterwards, "in getting away to the moors and mountains which surround us, and lie so near that they seem to invite Leeds men to visit them. For though the river at Kirkstall is sadly changed from the stream that leaves Malham Tarn, and the mountain air has lost somewhat of its freshness when it sweeps over this place, the sight and sound of railways are a constant reminder that a few minutes' consignment to the train, and the payment of a few shillings, are sufficient charm to place one in the world of nature. May those moors and valleys long continue desolate, if desolation may be understood to mean no presence but that of the spirit of nature. I care not what that spirit may be, but I feel a breathing life and an unsurpassable harmony, where man has not utterly defiled the face of the country. What I long for," he concludes, "is a fishing tour in the neighbourhood of Kilnsey or Wensleydale. I must be incorrigibly idle, and born to hate anything that even looks like work; and yet I want to be active, to do something, to find a field for my energies, such as they are."

In the last passage the writer did himself some injustice, and what he seems to have taken for "incorrigible idleness," was in reality nothing else than the demand of nature within him for some real rest and relaxation from his Oxford studies. His scrupulous conscientiousness, moreover, was already beginning to cause him much anxiety with regard to his future life, as the time for his leaving Oxford was approaching. That warning voice of nature, however, unhappily was not attended to. He would hate entered the Schools for his final examination the succeeding autumn, or at latest the following spring; but in the latter part of the summer of this year (1864), under the strain of overwork, his health broke completely down, and for a period of some years he was obliged to live in a state of enforced, and to him scarcely endurable, inactivity. A great portion of this time he spent in the retired parts of Wales, and the English Lake District, and some part of it in Ireland. On one occasion, during this period, writing to one of his brothers on his experiences of overwork, he says—

"Let me advise you earnestly not to try *to do too many things*. I killed the goose with a vengeance, and got no golden egg. I was expecting in a few weeks [when taken ill] a degree with honours, and a good start in life, and … had to leave Oxford without even an ordinary degree, which I knew more than enough to have taken the Easter before, if it would have satisfied me. I should have been surprised to have been told that season, when I was riding H—'s little cob in Rotten Row, in the glory of summer and all the hope of youth, that before the leaves had all left the trees that very horse would have been H—'s death[5], and that I should be a hundred times worse than dead."

---

[5] His friend here referred to was killed by a fall from his horse late that autumn.

Throughout the whole of this weary time, however, he never relinquished—so indomitable was his spirit—the hope of a better time approaching. Once at Liverpool, indeed, for a short stay in 1869, he writes upon this subject, "I like to be where I can be amused and see life without having to take part in it, though I would fifty times rather be at work at something. I wonder," he adds, "whether I ever shall be again." And he *was* at work again, not quite two years later, once more restored to health, and busily preparing for a trip across the Atlantic, which had been recommended to him for the thorough re-establishment of his health, and which accorded happily with the early fancies of his boyhood. It was by this time almost too late for him, even had he now wished it, to have thought seriously of adopting one of the recognized professions. A few years earlier he had thought both of the army and the bar; but with the love of adventure and research so strong within him, it is scarcely probable, had he adopted either, that he would have endured their trammels long. Once, too, it had seemed not unlikely that his strong love of painting, which held with his passion for natural history divided sway over his earlier years, might have proved the more powerful impulse of the two, and led him ultimately to the definite pursuit of art. In choosing against it, however, he probably selected well, as the somewhat sedentary life thereby involved would not so well have harmonized with his constitutional need for physical activity.

On this expedition to America he was absent about a year, a considerable portion of the time being spent in Central America—chiefly in Guatemala—and a part of it in California, camping out amongst the Rocky Mountains. Unlooked for circumstances brought his journey to a speedier close than he had intended; but if unaccompanied by other results, he was at least successful in forming a collection of birds and insects of some interest and value, and contracted several valuable friendships. "His manliness and irreproachable conduct and kindliness," wrote Sir Henry Scholfield, the British Consul at Guatemala, after his decease, "gained for him, during his short stay here, a friend in every one he met." And wherever else in the country he made any sort of stay, he appeared to have been scarcely less fortunate in this respect.

Soon after his return from America in 1872 he began to make arrangements for a more extended journey—the one of which this volume treats, and on which he started in March 1873. His plan on this occasion was to reach the Zambesi from Natal, and if possible visit some of the unexplored country to the north of that river. In the latter hope he was destined to disappointment, and the number of obstacles he met with in realizing the former serve to illustrate some of the ordinary difficulties which may be encountered in African travel. Of the results, however, such as they were, of this journey, in which he lost his life, the reader must be left to form his own judgment from the perusal of the ensuing pages. He had at least acquired much of that needful experience of rough travel and adventure, without which little can be accomplished in the way of exploration or research. It is almost certain that, had he lived, his next journey would have been of a more ambitious kind, remarkable as he was for that love of enterprise which characterizes the true explorer; of this he spoke merely as a "little trip." His experiences, moreover, in this two years' travel, must still further have convinced him, if in a different manner, of those evil effects of attempting too many things, which his Oxford career had previously warned him of. The diversity of his pursuits led him into many delays, each one of which no doubt contributed its share, together with the obstructiveness of native tribes, to that long detention on his journey which finally threw his visit to the Zambesi into the unhealthy season of the year. It must be granted, however, at the same time, that his love of adventure led him into places where the field for inquiry was especially inviting, and offered exceptional advantages; and also that his devotion to natural history beguiled throughout his journey what might otherwise have proved many a weary march. It is more than probable—so fully had the need of this now been brought home to him—that on another journey, had he been spared to make one, he would have concentrated his chief energies upon fewer objects. What these might have been must remain, indeed, matter of conjecture; but whatever else he had abandoned, the pursuit of ornithology would certainly have held a place second only to that of exploration.

In character and temperament Frank Oates was admirably fitted for his work. "I like anything," he once wrote when at Oxford, "that seems difficult of attainment,"—the very zest of the pursuit proving in such cases its own reward to him. So too, in disposition; he had just the one which recommends itself to strangers. "There was something singularly winning about him," wrote a friend, upon his death; "that peculiar combination of courage and gentleness, which is one of the finest traits of character." It was, in fact, this very association of a genial nature with a remarkable openness and candour of disposition, that won for him friends, especially amongst his own countrymen, wherever his lot was cast, and so smoothed his way over many difficulties. And if, as would sometimes happen, he fell amongst unfriendly natives, he preserved himself on such occasions by a seeming show of condescension, and a coolness under danger which commanded their respect. A faithful and accurate observer, but little was lost that came before his notice; and if at the time of his death—in February 1875—he had not realized all that he had hoped from his expedition, he may at least be said to have justified the choice that he had made, and had contributed a measure of faithful labour to the causes of progress and research.

On hearing of his death, the Dean of Christ Church, who had always particularly regretted the illness which in earlier life had prematurely closed his University career, wrote of the untimely termination of his later efforts in a spirit of no less concern. "His name," wrote the Dean at this time, "must be added to the list of those devoted and enterprising Englishmen, who 'scorn delights and live laborious days,' who by their frank love of truth and justice have made our name respected from one hemisphere to the other. I retain a dear memory of him," he concludes, "and grieve to think that so much manly spirit has so soon been quenched."

This manly love of truth here noticed, his zeal in action, and energy for work, had marked Frank Oates conspicuously from a boy. Life was for him no lounge, merely to be dreamed through, but an active, burning reality, from which the fruit that the hour yielded was to be plucked and harvested. From his earliest days, when he watched at springtide the coming of the swallow, or lurked in autumn by the hedgerow, to note the flocks of redwings as they passed—from the time when those authors whom he loved had given him his first glimpses into that distant realm of nature where his imagination loved to wander, and he hoped one day to follow them—till the arrival of the period when that desire was at length destined to be realized, and he had threaded the forests of tropical America, and roamed through the thorny wastes of Southern Africa, was he ever adding something to his knowledge of nature, something to his love of science, or something to his appreciation of the beautiful. With him, indeed, were no half measures. His interest once fairly roused in any subject, he gave to it the strength of his whole soul; a purpose once formed rarely failed in its fulfilment; and such was the elasticity of his temperament that he would turn from one subject to another, each as a mere refreshment from the last. To this was added, in no common measure, a certain freshness and buoyancy of the spirit, which enabled him in a moment to throw off the spell which bound him, and join on occasion in the frolic of the hour. A peculiar brightness characterized his being, and rendered the common incidents of life attractive to him; and should any be found who regard as incongruous the lightness of spirit which occasionally manifests itself even in the ensuing pages, in connexion with more serious subjects, such ones may read with interest the following extract from the writings of the late Charles

Kingsley, with reference to this very tendency, as manifested in another posthumous author, whose book was edited by a friend.

"With a reverence for the dead," he says, "which will at once be understood and honoured, he [the editor] has refrained, perhaps here and there too scrupulously, from altering a single word of the documents as he found them, respecting even certain scraps of Cambridge and Winchester slang, which may possibly offend that class of readers who fancy that the sign of magnanimity is to take everything *au grand sérieux,* and that the world's work must needs be done upon stilts; but which will be, perhaps, to the more thoughtful reader only additional notes of power, of that true English '*Lebensglückseligkeit,*' as the German calls it, which makes a jest of danger and an amusement of toil. Jean Paul makes somewhere the startling assertion that no man really believes his religious creed unless he can afford to jest about it. Without going so far as that, I will say boldly," adds the writer, "that no man feels himself master of his work unless he can afford to jest about it; and that a frolicsome habit of mind is rather a token of deep, genial, and superabundant vitality, than of a shallow and narrow nature, which can only be earnest and attentive by conscious and serious efforts."

There were few circles of society where Frank Oates was not welcome; and once received in any of them, a place was ever after reserved for him in their midst. Whatever raciness or originality of character was to be met with where his lot for the time was cast, he failed not to find it out; and he eagerly availed himself of every opportunity which enabled him to see life in its less conventional aspects. A certain chivalry endeared him to the weak, his fearlessness attached to him the strong, and no act of kindness was ever lost upon or forgotten by him. He wandered far afield; but at home or abroad it ever was the same with him, and he had friends, go where he would: for the intellect, in his case, never overruled the affections; and perhaps it has fallen to the lot of few, dying at his comparatively early age, to leave so many sorrowing hearts behind them.

And now, but one word further. The late Charles Kingsley—again to quote his writings, still in the same connexion as before, with reference, that is, to his friend, Charles Mansfield, traveller, ornithologist, and devotee of science, the posthumous writer above referred to—has said some touching words, which the editor of these pages, too partial, it may be, in his estimate of the deceased, would fain transcribe, and apply to the subject of the present memoir. "He was one of those rare spirits," writes Charles Kingsley[6],' "to whom this life and this world have been, as far as human minds can judge, little beyond a schoolhouse for some nobler life and world to come. Cut off at the very climacteric of his years, just as he was beginning to give the world evidence of his faculties, and just as he had acquired the power of using them in an orderly and practical method, he has left little behind but the *disjectca membra philosophi*. ... Never have I met a human being to whom as clearly as to him the thing which seemed right was a thing to be done forthwith, at all hazards, and at any sacrifice. ... He had gathered round him [ere he died], friends, both men and women, who looked on him with a love such as might be inspired by some being from a higher world. ... Oh, fairest of souls!" concludes the writer, "Happy those who knew thee in this life! Happier those who will know thee in the life to come!"

C. G. O.

" Nor yet quite deserted, though lonely extended,
For faithful in death, his mute favourite attended."– SCOTT.

---

[6] *Paraguay, Brazil, and the Plate.* By C. B. Mansfield, MA. with a sketch of the author's life by the Rev. C. Kingsley, pp. xi.-xvi, *Fraser's Magazine*, November 1856.

Matabeleland and the Victoria Falls

The letters and journals of Frank Oates 1873-1875

Chapter I

Departure from England—St. Helena—Cape Town—Arrival at Durban—Pietermaritzburg— Start up country— Pretoria; its climate and vegetation—The High Veldt—Dutch Boers—The Crocodile River—Bamangwato.

ON the 5th of March 1873, Frank Oates and his brother, W. E. Oates, sailed from Southampton for Natal on board the Union Company's steamship *African*. It was the intention of the former, as already explained in the introduction to this volume, to make a journey to the Zambesi, and, if possible, push on thence to some of the unexplored country northwards. His brother contemplated a shorter trip in the same direction, which was to occupy about a year.

The only land sighted, after leaving England and passing the Needles, were the islands of Porto Santo, Madeira, and Tenerife, and one of the Canaries besides Cape Verde on the African coast, until on March 25th the vessel reached St. Helena, where she touched and remained a few hours. The fruit in the island at this time (including figs bananas, and very fine peaches) was in perfection, whilst scarlet geraniums, fuchsias, and petunias—all growing wild—were in full bloom. Head winds, after leaving St. Helena, considerably delayed the vessel's progress, and Cape Town was only reached on the 3d of April. Here passengers for Natal were transferred from the *African* to a coasting steamer, the *Zulu*, which sailed five days later, and reached Durban on the 19th of the month. The view here across the bay was pretty enough, with ships lying at anchor inside and out, and the lighthouse, a marked feature on the green headland opposite. The brothers left Durban for Pietermaritzburg to prepare for their expedition into the interior soon after landing, the journey, in a six-horse waggon, occupying about twelve hours. The country passed through was for the most part hilly, with very little timber. Here and there some fields of Indian corn *(*'mealies'*)* were seen, and also some pretty bits of mountain scenery with abrupt crags, but the land is chiefly pasture, and, the general aspect of the country not unlike that of the American prairie. A number of ox-waggons were met and passed upon the road. Near Maritzburg a few trees were seen; the approach is pretty, and the place has an English air about it.

At Maritzburg the brothers remained about three weeks, making preparations for their journey northwards. Their plan was to go by the usual trade route through the Transvaal, and then on to Shoshong, the town of Sekomi, chief of the Bamangwato, from here either taking the direct route towards the Zambesi by the Tati River, or making a circuit in a north-westerly direction by way of Lake Ngami. They accordingly each purchased a waggon and the requisite number of oxen for the journey, and engaged some native attendants. Before leaving Maritzburg, W. E. Oates wrote home as follows:—

"*May 4th, 1873.*

"We only stayed a few days in Durban, and came on here, as this is a much better place for getting an outfit for the interior. It is 54 miles from Durban, and not a particularly interesting place. There are hills all round, without much vegetation, and covered with long coarse grass. It is much cooler than it is at Durban, as it is 2000 feet above the level of the sea. It is winter now, and rather cool at night, but still very hot during the day. We arrived here three weeks ago to-morrow, and tomorrow we intend making a start up country. We have each got a waggon and fourteen oxen, besides five ponies between us, and three Kafirs to each waggon. We are going with a man called Gray[7], who is going up to Lake Ngami to trade. He is quite a young fellow, and has only been out here four years. He knows the country through which we are going, and says it is extremely healthy, and the native tribes all friendly. He has taken five waggons, and left on the 11th instant, but as his waggons are heavily laden, we expect to overtake him in a week.

"Buckley[8] and Gilchrist started with their waggon yesterday, but Frank is not ready, he has so many things to get.

---

[7] Mr. Gray died of fever at the above Lake a few months afterwards.

[8] Mr. T. E. Buckley, the gentleman here alluded to, had come out from England in the same ship as Frank Oates and his brother, on a shooting expedition, and had been joined at Maritzburg by Mr. Gilchrist, of Ospisdale, Sutherlandshire, who had already been out upwards of two years, travelling and hunting in South Africa. These gentlemen both accompanied the brothers as far north as the Tati River, whence Frank Oates went on alone towards the Zambesi.

"We have got some blankets, beads, knives, etc., as there is no good taking money, and everything you want you must pay for in that way. The waggons are very comfortable and hold a great deal, including a mattress which lies on the top of the boxes. We are taking coffee, sugar, tea, flour, oatmeal, pickles, some brandy, and several other things for our own use. The Kafirs are supposed to get nothing but meal, which they boil in a large pot and eat with the help of pieces of stick. They occasionally get a little coffee also. . . . There is very little here in the way of fruit and vegetables. The only fruit now is oranges, though there are peaches and apricots in the season. Altogether, there seems very little pains taken to cultivate the land, as the niggers are too lazy to work, and white labour is expensive."

On May 15th the waggons of the two brothers started, with W. E. Oates's servant, Thomas Bell, who had accompanied him from England, and made their first halt about four miles from Maritzburg.

Frank Oates, still at Maritzburg, writes the following day, May 16th :—

"Our waggons left yesterday, and we went with them on horseback, Willie remaining to sleep with them, and I returning here for the night. W. has ridden in here this morning, and we shall both go on again to the waggons, which travel very slowly. I think we have been fortunate in getting good oxen for them. We have also a young horse, a very pretty bay, which had only begun to be broken a fortnight when we got him, but which is four years old, and likely to turn out very well. We have also another bay horse, which W. rides. These two are about 14½ hands high. We have three smallish ponies—one a very pretty brown one, and two little rough black ones. Of course we are taking dogs also. We bought four pointers, and have likewise had a rough dog given us, and another promised, and shall try to pick up as many as we can as we go along, for they are invaluable to have about the camp ... We go with Gray as far as Bamangwato, and shall then either go on with him to Lake Ngami, or visit the Victoria Falls direct, or we may go first to the Lake, and make little explorations to the north and north-west, and in the May following go on to the Victoria Falls, and thence return here Gray is on excellent terms with the King Lecheletebe, a good native, who would assist us in every way in his power. If we go to the Falls we pass through the country of Lobengula, the son of Mosilikatze, whose name you will see in maps. Lobengula is reported to be a 'decent chap' by a friend of ours, a doctor here, from Dewsbury, whose Christian name is Oates. We go by Mooi

River, Colenso, Ladysmith, Newcastle, Pretoria, Crocodile River, and Bamangwato. ... This country is not to be compared with America. The most of it about here is hilly, the hills in places becoming mountains, and all covered with coarse dry grass, and scarcely a stick of timber. There is nothing to compare with the lovely tropical scenery of Central America, or the magnificent mountains, prairies, lakes, and rivers of the United States. I never expect to admire any country so much as I do the western world. Perhaps one reason that the North American Indians were for savages a superior race was their fine scenery."

Again, from the Umgeni River, a few miles upon the journey, he writes, May 17th:—

"We are now fairly on our way. Last night was my first night in the waggon, and W.'s second. We are 13 miles on our way. Our waggons are most comfortable. We have a wooden framework in each waggon, surmounted by a substantial mattress and lots of blankets. We have tin wash-hand basins, cups, and plates, and fare luxuriously. Bell is now cooking some chops. I am reminded of some very pleasant days in the wilds of America."

Ladysmith was reached on the 24th of May and Newcastle on the 3ist, a halt of two or three days being made at each place. On the 23rd of June the party arrived at Pretoria, and Frank Oates writes from that place, June 27th :—

"We have now been 'trekking' *(i.e.* travelling in waggons) for six weeks from yesterday. We have, however, gone slowly, and have been delayed once or twice. We stayed a few days at Ladysmith and Newcastle, two towns, as they are called here (we should call them small villages); we then got into the Transvaal Republic, and had a very bad tract of country to cross, the high veldt. This country is very high, about 5000 feet above the sea, and as it was dead of winter when we crossed it the cold at night was rather severe. One of the coldest nights I think we had, was that of the 8th of June, when the thermometer showed 8 degrees of frost Fahrenheit. This may not seem very much, but the days being hot you feel the cold a good deal, and are glad of a good lot of blankets. In this respect I had taken care that we should be all right. The morning after the night I speak of my hand was numb with the cold, and I dropped and smashed my only thermometer[9]. My aneroid barometer,

---

[9] This instrument was afterwards kindly replaced by Mr. Lys of Pretoria.

which tells me the height above the sea really very accurately as far as I can judge, is still all right, but my sextant suffered so much on board the *Zulu* that I have some difficulty, being a novice, in making use of it.

"In crossing the high veldt the cattle suffer not only from the cold nights but the poverty of the grass, which will get worse and worse till the rainy season, which will be about September. The disease called 'red water,' which is so bad on the coast, and which has caused so many oxen to die and the price to rise so much, does not seem to extend beyond Natal. Out of twenty-eight oxen we lost only three, which is considered a very small percentage. A few of our oxen got into low condition, and we have got seven new ones coming along the road. We shall try to leave the poor ones at some farm, or exchange them for fat ones.

PRETORIA, TRANSVAAL.

"We arrived here (at Pretoria) on the morning of the 23d of June. It is very different from what it was in crossing the Drakensberg. There is scarcely ever ice here, and now (the coldest season) the temperature is perfection—neither hot during the day nor cold at night. There are orange-trees with fruit on them in the gardens, and high hedges of monthly roses in flower; there are also a few large trees (blue gums), something like poplars in mode of growth, but with dark foliage. These are planted here, for the country does not seem to bear much timber naturally. There is plenty of scrub on the slopes of the high land as you descend, and I believe there is a large extent of bush country round here, and when we get into the regular bush, plenty of timber, I imagine, such as it is; but this part of Africa is no timber country. On the high veldt there is nothing but parched grass, in many places burnt for a whole day's trek, as fires are of every day occurrence. On one occasion we had £5 to pay a man in front of whose house our men had set fire to the veldt whilst lighting our camp fire. The farms are few and far between in that desolate region; they grow Indian corn and a few peaches, and have a few cattle and sheep. The Boers are rather good sort of people, and though trying to get every penny they can in a bargain, honest, I should say, on the whole, and hospitable. I cannot speak any Dutch yet, so communication is limited, having to be carried on through an interpreter.

"Here in Pretoria are a great many English. The English keep stores; the Dutch Boers stick to farming. The latter come in with their waggons of grain, wood, and other produce, which is sold by auction at 8am in the market-place. 'Mealies' (unground Indian corn) fetch fifteen shillings a *muid*, which is about 200 lbs. This the Englishmen buy, get ground for two-and-sixpence a *muid*, and ask twenty-two and sixpence, or even twenty-five shillings for, and make a good thing of the numbers of people passing through here to the Marabastadt and Leydenburg gold-fields. The latter fields were newly discovered and much talked about when we were at Durban and Pietermaritzburg, but do not seem as good as the Marabastadt. No one thinks much of the Tati or Baines's gold-fields in Mosilikatze's country.

"I fear the English who are here are a bad lot, with few exceptions. One man who cheated me I asked if he had a conscience. He replied that no one here had them.

"Though here and there you see a garden with a few trees in it, and, as I mentioned, orange-trees and rose-bushes, do not imagine a scene of the least beauty. The town itself, the seat of the government, does not contain a single good building. It is like some little frontier town in America. There is not even a book-shop in it. The country immediately around is flat and devoid of trees, though in the distance are some ranges of hills. The day we reached Pretoria, the mail, a fortnightly one, arrived from Pietermaritzburg with a paper containing English news, very bare items though, up to May 15th. It seems dreadful that we were nearly six weeks in coming here, and the mail came in six days. The mail brings passengers also, but they are allowed hardly any baggage. It goes out again today to Pietermaritzburg, so I am writing this letter by the light of my lantern as I recline in my waggon. I think it is now about 6am., but the sun does not rise till after 7.

"Gray, the trader, left us at Newcastle, and had left here before we arrived for Bamangwato, *en route* for Lake Ngami, where our programme was to accompany him[10]. We are not certain whether we shall follow him or alter our plans. I will write again, letting you know what we have decided. If I leave a second letter here, it will go to Pietermaritzburg a fortnight hence, so you will get it in England soon after you get this."

BOER'S FARM, HIGH VELDT, TRANSVAAL.

---

[10] Strictly speaking, Bamangwato is the name applied to the district north of the Transvaal inhabited by that branch of the Basuto race, and Shoshong the name of the king's town or residence; but the latter also is more frequently spoken of, in common parlance, as Bamangwato or Mungwato.

Four days later W. E. Oates writes, also from Pretoria, "We have now been here a week, and are going to start off again to-day for Bamangwato. Buckley and his friend Gilchrist came up on Saturday, and we have decided to keep together. Gray, the trader we talked about, left here for Bamangwato about a fortnight since. ... I fear we are now too late to get to the Victoria Falls, as the country is not healthy after September. We have been rather more than six weeks in getting from Maritzburg here, and a more wretched country can hardly be conceived—not a tree to be seen, and half the country burnt black, as, if the grass is set on fire, it burns for weeks. The days are intensely hot (not a drop of rain since we left Maritzburg); the nights very cold, with sharp frosts. Countless herds of antelopes are to be seen every day; wildebeest (gnu), blesbok, springbok, and many others called by Dutch names. There are also hyenas, jackals, crows, and vultures.

"The Dutch Boers have farms at intervals. They seem miserably poor; no milk, eggs, meat. I don't know how they live. It is much warmer here, and after to-morrow we get into what is called the bush veldt, where there are lots of trees, and then it begins to get hot. The country we have passed over is from 4000 to 6000 feet above the level of the sea, and on the high veldt there is scarcely any water; the road in many places very bad and strewn with the bones and skeletons of oxen, wildebeest, and other animals, which have been picked clean by the vultures. How people can pass their lives in such dreary solitudes it is difficult to conceive. We, however, are very comfortable and well. We have large supplies with us, more than necessary, I think; but we can sell at Bamangwato what we do not want for nearly double what we gave for it at Maritzburg. This is the last place where there is a regular mail, though traders go from Bamangwato, and will take letters. The waggons make snug dwelling-houses. The mattress goes at the top of the things, and you have the canvas all round. You get in at the front, and let a canvas curtain down. There are canvas pockets at the sides, where you put what you want handy.

"We have been exceedingly lucky with our oxen, as many people have lost nearly all they had from the epidemic which is raging in Natal. One man lost his whole span of eighteen. We have only lost three; partly, I think, because we haven't hurried them. They have got poor, owing to the wretched grass on the high flats. They say, however, they fatten immediately they get into the bush veldt.

"Pretoria is a miserable little place, though the capital of the Transvaal, The store-keepers are English, or Africanders (as the native whites are called). ... The niggers are idle and insolent. It is said the only way to treat them is to thrash them well, and though we have never resorted to this, I have often felt inclined to do so. We have five with us—three Hottentots and two Kafirs. The Kafirs who are total savages are much better to get on with. ... It seems odd that I have such a little to tell you about after so long an absence, but one day here is almost exactly like another, and the country hitherto the same day by day."

The travellers left Pretoria for Bamangwato on the 3oth of June, and after three days' trekking to the north-west, crossed the Crocodile River, keeping for some time afterwards at no great distance from its banks. "On leaving the waggon, to shoot," writes Frank Oates on the 5th of July, "I rode up to the river, which is far the most beautiful thing I have yet seen in South Africa. Trees of various kinds—some resembling willows and oaks, the former in leaf, the latter bare—fringed the river's banks, which are steep. Long grass and bush grew in the country round, and where we outspanned at breakfast there was some very fine grass, tall and drooping, with a tassel. Here too," he concludes, "we got amongst plenty of birds, and to-day is the first that I have felt the country cease to be disappointing."

The following day the road again continued in close proximity to the river. The country was level and covered with trees like those in a fine park, none of them, however, very large. The Hex and Eland's Rivers, tributaries to the Crocodile, were crossed near together the day after, and on the 12th a halt of twenty-four hours was made at Holfontein, a good watering-place upon the road, where many birds were met with, including parrots, doves, and hoopoes. Two days later the Crocodile, which had now for some time been lost sight of, again came in view—a grand stream—and a fine blue distant mountain range stretched to the right and right rear. A halt of two or three days was made by the river's bank, to give the oxen time to rest. Here buffalo, blue wildebeest, springbok, and other game was found, including wild pigs and *pallah*[11]; and a little further north eland was met with, and many of the lesser antelopes. About, this time the dews, which had hitherto been heavy, ceased altogether; possibly, in part, owing to the change of locality. The road now for some time again continued near the left bank of the Crocodile, until the 24th, when, soon after crossing the Notuani, another of its tributaries, the course of the river was finally abandoned, and on the 27th the blue tops of the Bamangwato 'kopjes' (low hills) came in sight. The place itself was reached two days later.

---

[11] Impala antelope (*Aepyceros melampus*). DS

Here a short halt was again made for a few days, to engage fresh Kafirs and prepare for the continuation of the journey northwards. Owing to the want of water in the country between here and Lake Ngami, the part of the proposed expedition which included a visit to the lake had to be abandoned, Frank Oates resolving to proceed, if possible, direct to the Zambesi, the rest of the party accompanying him north as far as the Tati river in search of sport, to return thence by the same route as they had come. Mr. Gray, the trader, had arrived at Bamangwato a few days earlier, and decided to wait there till the rains should come before proceeding on his journey to the lake. The following extracts from letters, sent home about this time by Frank Oates and his brother from Bamangwato, give some further details of the journey up to this point, and of the future plans and arrangements of the party.

LIMPOPO OR CROCODILE RIVER.

W. E. Oates writes as follows on July 30th:—

"We got here yesterday afternoon all right, though for the last four days there has been scarcely any water on the road. When we left the

Crocodile River (on the 25th) we filled our water-casks, and the next night got to some brackish water, which the oxen drank. We trekked all the following day and half through the night, when we reached some water-pits made by the Kafirs, from which the water had to be ladled out in buckets for the oxen. We had then about 25 miles to go without water to get here, which took us two days, all through heavy sand, through which the oxen go about two miles an hour. This is a wretched place; an immense number of Kafir huts, and a few stores belonging to white men. The name of the place is Shoshong, and the king, Sekomi[12], lives here. He is a hideous old nigger, and this morning came down to our waggons, to beg coffee and sugar. He had about a dozen dirty old wretches with him, who carried jackals' tails, and attend him whenever he goes in state. He jumped up on Frank's waggon, and refused to depart until he had had some coffee given him, which Frank gave him to get rid of him. I offered him a bright green scarf I had, but after examining it carefully he returned it to me.

"This is a most uninteresting country—all thorns and sand. The whole way from Pretoria here it is thick bush, composed mostly of stunted thorn trees, whose thorns are white and about four inches long. We stayed four days on the Crocodile River, as our oxen wanted rest. The lions were roaring round the waggons at night, in hopes of getting at the oxen. We have the latter carefully tied up to the waggons at night, and two or three immense fires lighted, to keep them off.

'It is impossible, we find, to get to Lake Ngami now, as there are a hundred miles to go through heavy sand without water to get there. Frank still thinks of going to the Victoria Falls, through Mosilikatze's country, by way of the Tati River, and I intend to go as far as the Tati. ... Every morning here lots of women go out to collect locusts, which swarm a short distance off, and are the only food the natives get now, as their crop of corn has failed, and they are half starving. They have a few little goats, but there is hardly any grass, and only one very small stream of water about two miles off."

Frank Oates also writes the same day as follows: —

"You have, I hope, got our letters written from Pretoria, the capital of the Transvaal. Since then we have not come more than 250 miles, if as much, and have been about a month in doing it. Buckley and Gilchrist have accompanied us, making, with our Waggons, three waggons

---

[12] King Sekgoma I. DS

in all, and I think we shall probably go on together for some time at any rate. The present idea is for us all to go together to the Tati, a river marked in the recent maps, where gold is being found. From here I may go on to Mosilikatze's Town, the residence of the King of the Matabele, in the north-east, and thence be able to get on to the Zambesi and Victoria Falls, though I hardly hope it now, on account of the lateness of the season.

"The country we have passed through so far may be divided into two distinct regions—the high veldt and the bush veldt. The former I described in my last letter. At Pretoria we entered the second, and are still in it. The former is high land, covered with grass, and with scarcely a bush on it. The country since then has been covered with bush, and contains many fine rivers. The Crocodile (or Limpopo) is a really beautiful river, its banks covered with fine trees. The 'bush,' as it is called, consists for the most part of smallish trees, most of which are thorny, with park-like glades here and there. In other places there is a great deal of thorny bush, through which you can hardly force your way. The great want here is water, the smaller streams being now dry, and in travelling it is often necessary to go many miles before reaching water. Still, the road is so well known that one can calculate almost to a certainty where and when to get water, and make a push when necessary, taking one's time both before and after it. Water for our own use can be carried easily in our casks, and it is for the animals we have to travel quickly on such occasions. Meat is rather scarce, but we generally manage to get enough, and, with bread and porridge, coffee and sugar, make out very well. We shall be glad to get away from here, as it is difficult to get anything in the shape of food except what we have with us, and what Gray gives us. There has been a scarcity of corn this year, and the people are very hard pressed, living principally on locusts, which are brought in every day in immense sacks carried on people's heads. We buy water of the women, which has to be brought some distance.

"This is a large town of Kafir huts. The people are of the Basuto branch. The king, Sekomi, visited me this morning, and seating himself on the front-box of my waggon, commenced a conversation, which one of our drivers interpreted, the end of which was that he wanted some coffee and sugar. I gave him five pounds of gunpowder, worth fifteen shillings. He accepted it, and then returned it, asking for coffee instead. I then gave him two or three pounds of coffee, worth perhaps five shillings, which afforded him great satisfaction, and after thanking me he walked off in a stately manner, followed by his train, his right-hand man carrying the coffee in his robe of skin. During the interview the latter produced a huge sort of bodkin from a sheath, and extracted a thorn from Sekomi's finger with the utmost gravity. There are a good many white men living here to trade, and also a missionary, on whom I intend to call.

"I cannot more fully describe the country at present, or our journey. It has not the charm for me that the western world has, but I think further north there must be far more attractive scenery than anything we have yet encountered. The days are hot, though there is often a refreshing breeze. The thermometer is about 82° in the shade during the hottest part of the day, and one hot day in the sun it rose to 100°. The nights are cold, and we have yet had no insect pests, but our animals are infested by ticks. ... It is very annoying never to be able to get letters from home. Mr. Hathorn, of the Standard Bank at Pietermaritzburg, has promised to forward all letters sent to his care for us, and to assist us in every way he can. We found him most kind and obliging in every way in Pietermaritzburg."

On August 4th, the writer, still at Bamangwato, adds:—

"Willie, Buckley, and Gilchrist have gone on. They started yesterday, and I intend to start to-morrow, and shall overtake them. I believe the prospects of the journey are very satisfactory. I have had a long talk to-day with Mr. Mackenzie[13], one of the missionaries here. He is a very nice fellow, and knows all the country well, and has written out for me a long list of the various watering places on the road to the Tati and on to Mosilikatze's. He is the author of a book called *Ten Years North of the Orange River*, and is now instructing some natives for missionary work—some six or eight, I think, living in a sort of college. The other missionary is a Mr. Hepburn[14], who gave a little service in his house yesterday. I am certain they will both do anything they can to help us."

Three years later, one of these missionaries, the Rev. John Mackenzie, left Shoshong for Kuruman, where suitable buildings had been erected by the London Missionary Society for the embryo

---

[13] Mackenzie later served for some months as Deputy Commissioner for Bechuanaland and was attached to the Warren Expedition, before returning to Britain in 1885. In 1891 he began work at the Hankey Mission Station in the Western Cape, where he remained until his death in 1899. DS

[14] James Hepburn spent most of his career in Botswana, and served as an adviser to Khama, leader of the Tswana people. In 1891, following a serious bout of malaria, he quarrelled with Khama and returned to Britain, where he died two years later. DS

theological institution he was at the time of the events now narrated conducting at the former place. His loss must have been felt by many, both travellers and others, to whom he was ever ready to lend a helping hand. On the present occasion, Frank Oates felt strongly sensible of what he owed him for his friendly aid and counsel, and some time later, after the traveller's decease in 1875, it was again this gentleman's good services and sympathetic words that first softened the sorrow of his friends at home when they received the unexpected intelligence of his death in the interior.

SNUFF-BOXES MADE FROM GOURDS.

CHAPTER II

*The journey resumed—Halt on the Seruli—Bushmen on the Gokwe—
The Shashe—The Tati settlement—Adventure with a lion—W. E.
Oates returns to the coast; particulars of his journey.*

FRANK OATES left Bamangwato on the 7th of August, and the following day joined his brother, who had been waiting for him a little way out of the town. In the evening the Makalapsi[15] River was reached, where were a number of Dutchmen just returned from hunting on the Motloutsi, to the north of the Limpopo. They had got a number of rhinoceros, but no elephant. Continuing their journey the following morning, and subsequently crossing the Touani[16] and Lotsani[17] Rivers, the brothers reached the Palatswe River on the 12th. "The scenery here," writes Frank Oates, "is very pretty. A row of low kopjes on the right, with large stones piled on one another, forms a natural terrace to the eastward, from which you look over a sea of green bush, with a few kopjes standing out from the midst." Here goat's milk was brought in a large tortoiseshell from a kraal somewhere near, and exchanged for a small piece of tobacco. Most of the natives carried guns, and game was scarce and wild.

Starting again the ensuing evening, and continuing their journey during the following day, they arrived early on the morning of the 15th at the Seruli[18] River, where a water-pit, sunk in the dry sandy bed of the river, was found for watering the oxen. Here were a party of natives, living in the bush, hunting. They were said to be Bushmen. One of their number, who came to the waggon the following day, looked very striking—a leopard-skin thrown gracefully over his well-formed person, and a necklace of large lavender beads round his neck. Four days were spent by the brothers at the Seruli, whence they proceeded on their journey on the evening of the 19th, making a halt about midnight. From

---

[15] Mahalapye. DS

[16] Tewane. DS

[17] Lotsane. DS

[18] Serule. DS

this point Frank Oates's Journal takes up the story for the next few days—till their arrival at the Shashe on the 24th—as follows:—

"*August 20th.*—Have coffee, and hear the monotonous call of the night-hawk, as we rest and let the cattle feed. W. called my attention yesterday, at close of day, to another (a clucking) note, which he says proceeds from the hornbill. We have been living, whilst at the Seruli, on ostrich eggs. Fried with a little meal is the best way we have had them, or made into a pudding with maizena. They are strong, unless nicely cooked. Started again at 2.30am and trekked for three hours. Horned moon and bright morning star in the east; horizon dark against the sky, already glowing with the pale orange of approaching morning, fading into the dark violet of the upper firmament. Notes of birds are heard.

"What a loss not to be able to appreciate beautiful things, as must be the case with our men, and how much less they affect me even than they used to do, when I seemed to find the world more full of hope and high ends to be attained than it looks now.

DOUBLE-BANDED SAND-GROUSE.—*Pterocles bicinctus.*

"Inspanned again about 8, and crossed the dry bed of a large stream, which continued to keep near the road on the right. It was full of sand, with plenty of bush and trees about it. Francolins abundant, also hornbills, and many other birds in numbers, so I think there must be water somewhere in it, or very near. Reached the Gokwe about noon, having gone nine miles. The trek was a slow one, and part of it being when the sun was getting high, the oxen were tired. Found good francolin shooting where we passed the last spur of the range along the river, and where we outspanned; sand-grouse coming to drink in the evening at the latter place. There was fresh giraffe spoor where we crossed the 'spruit'[19] by the kopjes, and further on fresh lion spoor. . . . The people at the Gokwe are a sort of outcast race under the Basutos, called Bushmen. Men, women, and children came to the waggon. They have fine pack-oxen. They live in the bush, Hendrik says, having a sort of temporary abode near the bed of the river to the left of the road. They were ornamented with beads, and had on necklaces of blue cut ones and skins. They always ask for tobacco, making signs that they want snuff. They are hunting here. They brought ostrich eggs, exchanging them for a cheap knife, mirror, or handkerchief. I had great difficulty in buying an ostrich feather for about three or four pounds of lead. They wanted a whole bar, and on no other terms would bring more feathers."

"*August 21st.*—Calm day, after a very windy night. . . . Started at 7.15pm, and went about seven miles, crossing two spruits, and outspanned for the night about 11."

"*August 22nd.*—Cool morning. Trekked from 6.30 to 10am, the road twisting a good deal; say seven miles. . . . Stopped to rest, and inspanned again about 4pm, the road now winding through stony crags, and numbers of kopjes appearing to our right, to our left, and in front. Going a fair pace. Crossed the dry bed of the Seribi, apparently a very large river. Deep descent, sand very heavy, banks of river picturesquely wooded. We had seen lots of fresh lion spoor on the road before crossing the Seribi, and on this side I see more. Delicious fragrance from a sort of sallow-like blossom. Later, approaching the Motloutsi, we saw large numbers of sand-grouse flying both towards us and the opposite way—to and from the water. Finished trekking about 7, but did not outspan till much later, as when we entered the broad bed of the Motloutsi we stuck

---

[19] Small stream.

in the deep sand, and made many fruitless efforts to get out before outspanning. There was a little pool of water at which the oxen drank, and which the grouse resorted to. The sand around it was covered with feathers of birds.

"Sunset scene very lovely. In the foreground, brown bushes. Two little violet kopjes appear against the sky, behind one of which the sun has set. A lovely rose hue, deepest around the position of the sun, is on the horizon; this fades into violet, and this again into a pale greenish blue. Some very small, clearly defined, deep violet clouds, edged with gold, stand out from the sky."

"*August 23rd*.—Before daybreak the little sand-grouse were flying round, and a few settled to drink. I did not disturb them. The Motloutsi is a large river, with a very sandy bed, and here and there large rocks, and a twisting course. Hendrik says all these sandy rivers become dry or nearly so in winter. Both yellow and cream-coloured acacia blossoms very beautiful and sweet. Pleasant breeze where W.'s waggon is outspanned, mine being hot in the river-bed. Some people came here, but had neither eggs nor feathers for sale. As usual they carry muskets. It is a wonder they find anything to shoot, as they seem to be spread all over the country. At the Gokwe we were told that the Bamangwato hunters were hunting about in that district, but could get nothing. At this time of year the people seem to come out to hunt from all the kraals, leaving only those unfit for that work at home. A giraffe was killed near here by some Bushmen, who gave us meat in exchange for tobacco. When out this morning I saw some kind of melon, which at first looked like ostrich-eggs, growing by the river-bed—the kind, I think, which the oxen eat in times of drought."

"*August 24th*.—Trekked for three hours, then rested, and started again at 11am. ... Reached the Shashe about two, and outspanned. We had come extremely slow; sun hot, sand heavy, road bad, bullocks tired. Ground broken and stony, and falling towards the Shashe. Many crags crop up around, and in front of us are some kopjes—Hendrik says where the Tati is. The Shashe is very broad river, all deep sand, with water in one place where it has been dug for, both for cattle and people. We enlarge the hole (hard work under the heat of the sun), and let the cattle drink. There is an old Bushman here, destitute and alone. He says the Mungwato men took his gun. The other side of the river, he says, is under Lobengula, this under Sekomi, and Hendrik says the Makalakas[20] are not independent, all here belonging to the Matabele and Mungwato sovereignties. These Bushmen are, I suppose, the original inhabitants. Hendrik says they are slaves to the others. They certainly are outcasts. This man does not beg, takes what is given him, and lies naked with his head on a stone by the fire at night. He has no blanket.

Watched the Bushman make his fire with two sticks. He took off his sandals, placed a stick on one of them, and holding it firm with his foot, twisted the other stick rapidly between both hands, working it in a little hollow of the first stick, till black dust began to form. This soon turned red-hot, and there was fire like that in a pipe."

Continuing their journey on the 26th, the brothers reached the Tati[21] the same evening, where a small English settlement of a few huts has collected round the gold mines, which are being worked by Sir John Swinburne. "There is nothing remarkable in the scenery here," writes Frank Oates soon after their arrival; "a few kopjes only, with low scrub and trees. Everything is very much dried up. The river is broad, with deep sand in its bed. Yesterday Nelson[22] gave me a live fish, four or five inches long, something like a perch. He says they live in the sand now. Water is got by digging in the river's bed. … The veldt where we are outspanned," he concludes, "is quite ploughed up with the spoor of elephants which used to come here five years ago, and have been found quite near here since."

At this point Frank Oates and his brother remained a few days before separating, and on the 29th the former wrote home the following letter, giving some account of his future plans, and adding some particulars to his experiences above related :—

"… When we left Bamangwato," he writes, "whence I last wrote, Buckley and Gilchrist went on with W. I followed two or three days later having been busy seeing people and making arrangements. I soon picked W. up, who was waiting for me, the others having gone on in advance—of

---

[20] A generic term for people defeated and subjugated by the Ndebele; Oates probably refers specifically to the Shona-speaking Kalanga people of Western Zimbabwe. DS

[21] Known nowadays as Old Tati. DS

[22] Mr. Nelson of the mine. [C. J. Nelson was a Swede, hired to manage the gold mine at Tati on behalf of the South African Gold Fields Company. DS]

course, as we thought, to Tati. We, however, met a trader with a note from Buckley saying they had turned off at the Seruli River. ... We have been here now two or three days,. and tonight Buckley and Gilchrist arrived, having abandoned their new route.

BOERS' FARMS, CROCODILE RIVER.

"The road we have come crosses a number of sandy river-beds. These rivers are large streams in summer, but are now dry, except occasionally there is a little pool in some, or water may be sometimes obtained by digging. This tract of country through which we have come is called by the Dutch the 'thirst land,' and is now at its worst. On return it will no doubt be easy enough to cross, now it is hard work, especially for the oxen. We trek about three hours at a time, doing perhaps seven or eight miles in a trek. Generally two treks are enough in the twenty-four hours, one in the morning and one in the evening, but in going through the 'thirst' we have to push on and trek as much by night as possible.

"I was in advance of W. when I reached the Shashe, and, as it happened, had then only one man, Hendrik, my black servant, with me; for my driver and his boy had decamped, though they afterwards returned—as of course they were likely to do—the same evening. They will not have their wages paid till they return to Maritzburg, and then not unless they have behaved properly, and they would have had a miserable time if they had actually deserted me. Hendrik can drive, and knowing, as I did, the hold I had on the others and the folly of giving way, I let them go, telling them the sooner they left me the better, and the result of this treatment proved satisfactory. The difference originated in the driver asking me for tobacco when I told him to inspan, and refusing to comply till I had supplied him, which of course I would not do, as I treat them quite liberally enough, and indeed too well. Hendrik was a little poorly at the time, but behaved very well, and we reached the Shashe, where we dug for water.

"Being rather tired, we returned to the waggon after watering the oxen, without driving them away from the river first, which I know now we ought to have done on account of lions, but I have never yet thought it necessary to take such precautions except at night, when we tie them up and light fires. Soon after reaching the waggon I heard the loud cries of an ox in distress, and exclaiming to Hendrik that I thought a lion must be the cause, locked up my medicine chest, from which I was taking medicine for Hendrik, and seized gun. Hendrik followed me, and we both ran to river. As we peered over the bank, there we the ox, the largest and fattest in my span, lying in the grass at the bottom of the bank with a tearing him. He was only a few yards below and before I could distinguish the lion properly it lay upon his prostrate form, the brute leapt the ox and retreated across the river. I fired ran, and hit him hard, for he rolled over, and I ought to have given him the second barrel at once, but thinking him mortally wounded, I hesitated a moment, and in the next he had disappeared dry reeds. I did not like to follow him at once, and Hendrik would not accompany me, but tried to dissuade me from following him at all. However, in about half-an-hour I went in search of the brute, but never found it, and do not know what became of it[23].

"I have yet been brought very little into contact with wild beasts, and have had few stirring incidents but I have been pretty fully employed one way another, and continue to persevere in my journey I found on reaching here that it was too late to go to the Victoria Falls without risk of sickness, in which case I had long before decided to travel in a north-easterly direction to Mosilikatze's country, the country of the Matabele,

---

[23]The body of the dead lion was found soon afterwards by natives—for the shot had proved fatal—and the skin taken by them to the Tati settlement. The ox had sustained so severe an injury he had to be shot the following morning.

over whom Lobengula, son of Mosilikatze, now reigns. I am told I shall see some very beautiful scenery on my way there, and I am now interested in pursuing my journey as far as I can. From here to the King's Town they call six days, but it will probably take me more.

"Here I have met two very nice fellows. One of them, Nelson, a Swede, is managing the mine of the Tati Gold Company. It is on a very small scale, and there are, I think, only seven white men here altogether. Brown[24], the other I refer to, has also some office connected with the mine, and keeps a store. They are both extremely kind, and willing to do anything to help one, and I expect to find more friends at the King's Town—especially Mr. Thomson, the missionary, for whom I have a letter from Mr. Mackenzie, and another from Mr. Hepburn. I likewise carry the mail.

"A flower is almost an unheard-of thing at present, everything being dried up; but the thorny shrubs (mimosas), with their yellow sweet-scented blossoms, are an exception, and a sign of approaching spring. The shrubs they grow on are covered with long sharp thorns, and there are no leaves on them, but blossoms are appearing. There is another kind with hooked thorns and whitish sallow-scented blossoms, which attain the size of a good-sized English fruit-tree. The thorns which defend nearly every tree here are a great impediment in travelling through the bush.

"The nights are now cool, though not so sharp as they were a while ago. The thermometer seldom falls much below 50°. It is coolest just before sunrise. At midday and in the afternoon it gets considerably above 80° in the shade, in fact I should set the point reached at nearer 90°. As I sit writing in my tent, I hear the engine working—an odd sound up in these remote regions."

Three days later, September 2nd, W. E. Oates supplements this letter:—

"I am just adding a line to the above, to leave it before I go. Frank left the day before yesterday, to go to the King's Town. The king (Lobengula) is the great nigger chief here, and behaves very well to all white men. I am staying with Buckley and Gilchrist, and we are now going to the Shashani River, about five days' journey. I think Frank will

---

[24] Alexander Brown was a Scot who managed the Glasgow and Limpopo Company store at Tati; he married the daughter of the hunter Piet Jacobs in 1876, and he and his wife moved to Klerksdorp, in the Transvaal. DS

be all right. He has a Cape Colony black man with him, who knows this country well, and speaks excellent English[25]. He was up here with Sir John Swinburne, who owns the gold-mine, so I am not afraid for Frank if he takes care of himself.

SOUTH AFRICAN WART HOG.—*Phacochærus æthiopicus.*

"The country here is regularly burnt up now, and will continue so until the rains fall in November. The river is nothing but a dry bed of sand, with a little pool of water in it about three miles off—the only water near for miles. You may imagine the luxury of a bath, under such

---

[25]This refers to Hendrik, the man of that name above alluded to.

circumstances, out of the question. There are two men here who have been very kind, one sending us milk twice a day—and, I can assure you, milk is exceedingly scarce. The country is most uninteresting; nothing to see but thick bush, composed chiefly of low thorn-trees with immense spikes, which hold you fast if you get amongst them.

"The only pleasant part of the day is from sunrise (about half-past six) to half-past eight. After that, the less you do the better until 5pm, when it is moderately cool again. At half-past six it is dark. The flies are a perfect plague all day, and get into everything. Towards the end of October there are some heavy thunder showers, and then summer begins, but the regular rains don't fall until November. There are great numbers of hyenas and jackals, which prowl about the waggons all night. Last night one of Buckley's oxen was ill, and the hyenas knowing it attacked him, and this morning we found they had actually eaten part of him alive. Of course the poor brute had to be shot. Unfortunately the hyena escaped, though fired at by Buckley's driver. The people are very glad when anybody shoots these animals, as they are constantly killing goats, and sometimes oxen. They are, however, so wary, that it is difficult to get them.

"Mr. Nelson, the manager of the mine, lent us some newspapers up to the 24th of May, the latest news we have seen from England. He also sent me a small bottle of beer, worth about five shillings here. Nelson is getting the king, Lobengula, some furniture from England, as he told the latter that a king ought not to sit on the ground. Lobengula's country extends from here to the Zambesi, and he is an absolute despot, having the lives of all his people in his own hands. They say if one of the Matabele is found stealing from a white he has him executed."

Soon after writing the above, W. E. Oates left Tati in company with Messrs. Gilchrist and Buckley to hunt on the Semokwe[26] River, where they had very good sport. Returning thence in due time to the coast, they took the same route as that by which they had travelled north, the change of season, however, from winter to summer producing, as they returned, a remarkable change in the entire aspect the country. By the end of October they were at Bamangwato, and reached Pietermaritzburg the 2nd of January. A few extracts from Oates's letters, written as they proceeded, may here be read with interest. He writes first from Bamangwato on November 3d as follows:—

---

[26] Simukwe. DS

"I arrived here with Buckley and Gilchrist about a week since, and shall probably make a start for Pretoria to-night. The spring has now commenced and the grass is beginning to grow. There have been heavy thunderstorms, and the lighting is wonderful, never ceasing for a moment during the storms. The heat also is very great... There has just been a row here. The old chief's eldest son has left the place, and nearly the whole of Mungwato went with him. The chief himself, Sekomi, is still here, and often comes down to the waggons begging. He got quite drunk the other night, and tumbled under my waggon. We had to see him home. He thinks his son means to kill him. He himself killed two or three of his own brothers when he came to be chief, but his two eldest sons are both Christians, and Mackenzie thinks Sekomi is in no danger from them. ... There are some nice flowers of the lily sort sprung up since the rain began, but very few flowers of other kinds yet. The rains, however, have only just commenced, and we shall have all the summer heat going down."

Again, from Pretoria, he writes on December 5th:—

"I got here on the 2nd instant, and great was my delight on receiving letters from home—the first I have had since leaving Pietermaritzburg. ... It seems quite strange to be in a civilized place again. It is very pretty here now, just the height of summer. We are indulging in fruit and vegetables, eggs and milk, to all of which we have long been strangers. The peaches are hardly ripe yet, but apricots are to be bought for a shilling a hundred. ... In coming from Mungwato we had to stop a week at the Meriko[27], as the river was very high with the rains and we couldn't cross. I had some thoughts of taking my waggon in pieces, and floating the things across on rafts, but the water kept subsiding, and at last we got over, the water only just taking the oxen off their feet. In dry weather there is hardly any water, but after the rains the river gets tremendously swollen, and there are very steep banks. Whilst waiting there Dawnay[28] came up with two waggons. He has been out two years, and been to the Victoria Falls. He says it would be worth walking from Durban to see them. He showed me some little sketches he had

---

[27] Marico. DS

[28] The Hon. G. C. Dawnay, on his way home from the Zambesi. [Dawnay was an English aristocrat who spent four years (1870-1874) hunting and travelling in southern Africa; he returned to Africa to fight with the British Army in Zululand and Egypt, and was killed by a buffalo in 1889 while hunting in East Africa. DS]

made, but said it was almost impossible to draw on account of the flies. The tsetse-fly, which kills everything except men, wild beasts, and donkeys, swarms there, and bites so furiously that your hands and face are puffed up in no time. He describes the scenery on the Zambesi as lovely.

"The country is much prettier now than it was when we went up. The grass has sprung up and is quite green, and all the trees are in leaf. The Transvaal, from the Crocodile River here, is beautiful. All along the banks of the river are farms, belonging to the Dutch Boers, surrounded with orange and peach trees. At most of these you can now get milk, butter, and eggs. We have had heavy thunderstorms, which, seen at night, are most gorgeous lightning all round, all colours, and darting in all directions at the same moment. It is just like a display of fireworks. It is much cooler now than we have lately had it, the thermometer seldom being above 90° in the shade, and the last few days there has been a nice breeze.

"My Kafir driver, who came up with me from Maritzburg, ran away when we were staying at the Meriko, and Bell and I had to drive the waggon down here. Fortunately they are very good oxen, so there has been no difficulty, and I have managed to get another driver here. Bullock-driving is quite a business in itself, and a very difficult thing in the bush with refractory beasts. This fellow, Solomon, stole a horse which we had found straying. It belonged to the old chief at Mungwato, and when I was going to hand the horse over to a Dutchman, whom Sekomi had authorised to take charge of the horse if he found him, Solomon went to the waggon where he was tied up, jumped on him, and galloped away. He will probably be caught, as the horse is well known.

"A 'salted,' or seasoned, horse is worth a great deal, as there is a sickness in the bush which is generally fatal to horses which are not 'salted.' It commences when the rains begin to fall. I much regretted losing my little horse. I was told, when I got him, he was salted, but he died after a few hours' illness. There is no cure known for it. He was looking beautiful; his coat shone like satin, and he was getting quite fat with the young grass and some corn which I got for him at Mungwato. The oxen are thriving tremendously, and, since the grass has grown, from wretched skeletons they have become regular Tichbornes[29].

---

[29] Arthur Orton, a butcher from Wagga Wagga who impersonated the English baronet Sir Roger Tichborne in an attempt to claim the Tichborne estates, was extremely fat. DS

"I shall write to you again from Maritzburg, if there is a ship sailing before I go, for I expect I shall have to stay a fortnight or three weeks there, to sell the waggon, oxen, etc. ... I mean to trek to-night when the moon gets up. We get into the high veldt now, where there is no bush. My waggon looks very seedy, the cover torn in many places by mimosa bushes, and the paint worn off. It is infested with beetles, and occasionally a lizard or scorpion is detected. Ants, too, occasionally pay me visits, to which I greatly object, as they bite uncommonly hard in this country. At night, if you are outspanned near water and have a lanthorn in the waggon, the candle is put out by numberless little beetles which creep in; and the frogs literally yell all night long. It is very pretty to see the fireflies."

On January 2nd, as already stated, W. E. Oates reached Pietermaritzburg, where he found the heat very intense. Three weeks later he sailed from Durban, accompanied by Mr. Gilchrist, and landed in England early in the following March.

CHAPTER III

Frank Oates proceeds to the King's Town—Crosses the Ramaqueban—Dutch hunters on the Impakwe—The Inkwesi's picturesque scenery—John Lee's farm—Manyami's kraal—The Shashani— Fine country—Kumala River.

RETURNING now to follow Frank Oates's journey to the King's Town, Gubuleweyo[30], we find the greater portion of his route described at some length in his Journal. Leaving the Tati, as has been mentioned, on the 31st of August, and advancing slowly, he crossed the Ramaqueban[31], Impakwe, and Inkwesi[32] Rivers, and reached John Lee's farm on September 6th. This John Lee is a noted Dutchman, who farms a large tract of country under the king. From here proceeding after a night's rest on his journey, he was detained four days at Manyami's kraal[33], a few miles further on, till leave had been obtained for him from the king to complete the distance, Gubuleweyo being reached by the middle of September. The Journal of this period is as follows :—

"*August 31st.*— ... Left Tati in the evening. About midnight, whilst trekking, Hendrik calls me, saying that the bullocks which are being driven can't be got on, but keep going into the bush. 'Donker' and 'Wildeman', too (the little red wild ox) are getting tired. This is miserable work, and I wish I had brought more bullocks from Mungwato, as I could so well have done, and a far lighter waggon. It is a mild, breezy night, and as we outspan, and 'Rail' and 'Rock' come up in their couples, I am reminded of our first trekking on the high veldt, when we were

---

[30] The Ndebele capital, now often called Old Bulawayo, located about 20km south-west of the present city of Bulawayo, 5km south-west of the Hope Fountain mission. DS

[31] Ramaquabane. DS

[32] Ingwezi. DS

[33] Manyami was the Ndebele induna, or local chief, responsible for admission to the Ndebele kingdom through the waggon-road that ran between Shoshong and Bulawayo. In the early 1870s, he was stationed at the Mangwe Pass. DS

together in force, starting with a good equipment and high hopes. This is an open space where we outspan, with long grass."

"*September 1st.*—Mild, cloudy morning. ... I had been much discouraged by the oxen being so tired last night, and this morning was pleased to find ourselves arrive at the Ramaqueban River at least an hour sooner than I had hoped. Petersen's waggon was on the opposite side[34]. However, we stuck in the drift. Poor 'Weiman', with his blind eye, was in front, and proved awkward, and little 'Vinal' lay down. Petersen, however, sent his driver and two good oxen, and we came out easily and had breakfast. Here some Dutchmen[35] squatted last season to hunt, and took the fever—men, women, and children. Petersen says about half-a-dozen of them died. He thinks it was in January. The trees along the river's bed show a faint budding of green, as I have now seen for some time. The girl who came with us to Tati was travelling on with Petersen, and her brother had come on with us last night to join her. The cool breeze to-day was very pleasant. Petersen's boys had dug for water. Petersen went on, as he usually makes one short trek during the day. I followed in the evening, and shortly after midnight crossed the drift of the Impakwe and outspanned. There seems plenty of water in the river. Barking of dogs; encampment of Dutch hunters. Petersen had turned in. Part of this trek was through somewhat sandy country, but on the whole we are on a much firmer road than we were before reaching Tati. Pitched into marmalade; it is wonderful how much one enjoys such things here, where coffee is without milk, the bread without butter, the meat dry as chips."

"*September 2nd.*—Pleasant breeze. Petersen called me. I find I am likely to have great luck. Here lives the Dutchman whose family suffered so from fever on the Ramaqueban. He has a straw hut, cool, roomy, and snug, with a high entrance than the Kafir huts, but shaped like them. His wife and family are with him, his eldest married daughter, and members of the next generation. He has cattle and goats, does his own smith's work, and hunts. They go as soon as the unhealthy season begins to John Lee's. They intend, in four years I think, to return to their farm on the Meriko. Petersen acted as interpreter, and it is arranged that I

---

[34] Mr. Petersen was a trader whom Frank Oates had met at Tati. [Petersen was German or Danish; he later owned stores at Bulawayo and Hope Fountain. DS]

[35] The party of a hunter, De Smidt, from the Marico District of the Transvaal. DS

wait for the Dutchman, who intends going to-morrow in my direction to get wood and hunt. He will lend me some oxen. I believe it is nothing but the brackish water, especially the Seruli water, that has made such a mess of my oxen. The Dutchman says there is plenty of game along the road. ... Noticed when out in the afternoon, and we crossed the river-bed, how easily the water rose, when one of the boys scooped out a hole with his hands; very different from the dry river-beds the other side Tati."

"*September 3rd.*—Morning felt very chilly. Breakfast on 'biltong'[36] and butter; the fresh butter excellent. We branded and left 'Rondeberg,' 'Engeland,' and 'Vinal.' The Boer put twelve of his bullocks into my waggon, eight of mine in his, and 'Donker,' 'Wikieman,' and 'Spot' were driven. ... Trekked about twelve miles, from the Impakwe to the Inkwesi River, and outspanned about 6pm."

"*September 4th.*—Cup of coffee, and went out about 8am, I and the old man riding, his son walking ahead, and two of their men (Makalakas) accompanying us. ... I do not admire the Matabele particularly. They are independent-looking and well made, but I do not like their countenances. The day following there were a great many about the waggons, attracted by the flesh. They eat like dogs, greedily. Beyond this river, which the Dutchman calls Makobi's, there was a tribe of Mungwato people massacred some thirty or forty years ago by the Matabele; Makobi, the chief, being amongst the slain. They were killed—men, women, and children—to obtain possession of their land. A few only escaped.

"The scenery about our camp is picturesque. The kopjes rise abruptly, and the river has steep craggy banks. There is an approach here to American scenery. What a wonderful difference is made in one's feelings by the constant impression caused by fine scenery! South Africa is sadly dull and monotonous, and I believe the influence is a bad one, and the loss of scenery has a depressing effect on the spirits; one's imagination is never called into play. ... I still admire the scenery, as we ride along home amongst the kopjes by the river. Here and there the large fleshy-leaved shrub,[37] standing boldly out amongst the bare crags, is

---

[36] Meat dried in the sun.

[37] Doubtless a species of Euphorbia, many varieties of which are met with in South Africa.

very striking. There is something here which might remind one a little of Central America, but somehow the charm is wanting."

"*September 5th.*— ... Inspanned at 7pm, and crossed the river. Stony and deep descent and ascent, with very deep sand; very hard work. I feel deeply indebted to the Dutchmen, who not only helped us through it—the young fellow driving and the old one helping—but, having lent us four oxen for the journey, sent for some more, to help us through this drift, after which they say all is right. Lovely moon as we trekked, but after all it is South Africa, and one cannot feel poetical. Picturesque kopjes on either side the road; the scenery, however, not so striking as it was almost beginning to be at Makobi's. Outspanned at 10.30pm, having gone about six miles. Excellent supper on wildebeest steak, fried."

"*September 6th.*—Dark cloudy morning, with a little rain. Started at 7am, and trekked six miles. The country where we stopped had been much burnt, and looked very desolate, with bare ground and bare trees, but there was a fine cool wind and a cloudy sky. I could fancy it a sea breeze. They say at the king's place you get the sea breeze. Started again at 12.30pm. Here one enters on a bit of really fine rugged country. Out of the level, scantily covered with dry brown grass and with a thick growth of leafless trees (small for the most part), rise huge boulders, so piled on one another, with here and there a huge stone so nicely balanced on the top, that one wonders how they ever got there. We are in a populous country, strings of people carrying things on the road. Outspanned at 2.30pm. Here the Dutchman, Smith[38], had been located, as there is a straw house, and water, the road crossing a spruit. Here, too, is John Lee's[39] first kraal. People come round the waggon to beg meat. One is a warrior, handsomely adorned with black ostrich feathers and white ox-tails. Went on again at 5pm, the ground rising a little. Then as we descend a range of kopjes appears in front. In about an hour a pretty white farm is seen to the right, towards which the road winds, and the wild view makes the farm seem to welcome one.

---

[38] De Smidt. DS

[39] A legendary hunter and trader, Lee was born in Somerset East in the Cape in 1827 and settled in the Ndebele kingdom in about 1866, acting as the King's agent and advisor. He retired to the Transvaal in 1891, and his land was subsequently confiscated by the British South Africa Company after he refused to support their war against the Ndebele in 1893. DS

"Lee came to meet me, and asked me in. He is a fat, red-faced man; his wife very young. His house had an air of comfort, and some luxury about it, owing to some handsome leopard karosses on couch and chairs. There was a picture, too, by Baines[40], of Lee shooting three elephants. The horse here represented, which I think cost him £100, was the making of him, he tells me. Lee was a Transvaal Boer, but speaks English. He was about five years hunting. I had supper with him, and chat afterwards. Garland[41], he says, lost seven unsalted horses, and had to send for two salted ones. A good salted horse costs £100. Lee describes how his old favourite used to snuff when game was near, and when it was elephant his manner was mistakable. He has tried donkeys in the tsetse-fly country, but the fly has always killed them. He says all horses, with scarcely an exception, must have the sickness, but he has known an exception. This, however, does not apply to stock bred of salted parents, which often live and never have the sickness. This is better, as the sickness breaks a horse down.

"Lee has just sold twelve red oxen—African with white faces—for £100, unwillingly. His other oxen are all in the hunting veldt. He has, however, let me have Smith's as far as Manyami's, with a boy to bring them back. I think he calls it ten miles to Manyami's, and from his (Lee's) house to the King's fifty odd miles. He says he saw some eland today but game is not plentiful just here. However, it is worse along the road to the King's, as kraals abound. Lee does not wish to have kraals near him, and the king does not permit any to be made in his neighbourhood. Most of the hunters, he says, make great deal of money, but spend their money as fast as they get it, saying, 'There is more ivory where this came from.' Lee himself was careful. His place he says, is very healthy, and it has got so good a name that in unhealthy times people stay about here, and it has been like a town, so that he opened a store. He is trying peaches, apricots, and pomegranates. Potatoes grow well here, and he is seldom without vegetables. He is trying several wild fruits. He has always water in the spruit close by, and waters by hand. He showed me a small wild grape.

"Lee tells me that a lion may often be stopped by throwing your hat at him, when you may have time to shoot. He says an elephant gun

---

[40] The artist Thomas Baines, who had visited the Victoria Falls in 1863. DS

[41] A hunter and trader, originally from Port Elizabeth. He travelled extensively in partnership with Christoffel Schinderhutte, whom Oates calls 'Stoffel Kennedy'. DS

should never be longer than 27 inches (25 is better), nor weigh over 9 lbs. He shoots 8 drams of powder, and an 8 to the lb. ball. The recoil is avoided by the barrel being strong, and nearly as thick at muzzle as at breech. His clothing in hunting is as light as possible; veldtschoen, and he says not even a shirt if he could help it. He carries needles and thread in his hat.

"For trading with the Matabele he recommends white, blue, and, I think, red beads. Selampore is much liked, or strips of coloured calico. Beads, he says, seem going out, and printed calico being preferred. The Matabele country, he says, was formerly under a queen. There were, I think, other queens before. An old man has told him the traditions, which he possesses. A famine caused the people to break up; then Kafirs came and conquered the country. Mosilikatze[42] came next, and conquered these first Kafirs. Makobi's were Mungwato people, but the old inhabitants of the Matabele country were a distinct race with a distinct language. The Bushmen have nothing to do with either. They seem an altogether different race, speaking a different language, and seem, Lee says, to be scattered all over the country of South Africa, a race apart from the regular inhabitants, and having no connexion with them.

"Lee has a young sable antelope, which goes with the cattle, about a year old. It is a rich deep chestnut colour. Lee says they get darker every year, till they become black. He once had a young elephant for some days; perhaps nine months old. He describes it as having been a most sensible and amusing pet. When first taken he made it put its trunk under his arm, and after smelling him, it was satisfied and became friendly. It always first smelt at strangers before making friends, and if once repulsed would not be friendly afterwards. It would climb in at the back of the waggon, and out at the front by the wheels, and was accompanying the waggon when it died from diarrhoea, caused by improper food. It would pick up a pin or a needle, placing it first with its foot at the right angle for its trunk to grasp, and then hold it up and examine it with wonderful sagacity. It was excessively mischievous, and would upset everything. It could not bear to be left alone for a moment, and would cry like a child in such a case. The company even of a little child would content it.

"*September 7th.*—Breakfast with Lee; dinner also. One of his boys caught some barbel and a curious-looking fish in the river. Talked with Lee, and afterwards saw his garden. Inspanned about 8pm, and soon

---

[42] Also Mzilikazi: the founder of the Ndebele nation. DS

crossed a river with sand and reeds, and a good deal of water in its bed. It was a fine moonlight night, the road winding through picturesque kopjes. Went about six miles, and then halted for the night."

"*September 8th.*—Started at 7am, and went four miles through flat land, with but few trees, and hemmed in by craggy, bush-covered kopjes. Came in sight of cultivated land and natives, and reached Manyami's kraal at 9am. The country here is really pretty, and presents a pleasing variety to the eye. The ground is open mostly, and covered with long yellow grass; here and there groups of trees, some of a very fair size, some bare, some brown, and a few green or in blossom. Large stones crop up from the ground, and everywhere rugged kopjes rise round us.

MANYAMI. MANYAMI'S ATTENDANT.

"Soon after our arrival Manyami came, attended by another old fellow, each in a shabby old hat, and vying with each other in squalor and dirt. He refused firmly to send to the king till to-morrow, saying the king had not sent for *me*, but I had come of my own accord, and must not be in a hurry; the oxen could feed and rest. I gave him a bar of lead. Two messengers were to be sent, and I wrote a note to Fairbairn[43] for oxen, and the boy was directed to bring them back. Manyami insisted on their being paid beforehand, and intimated that they might not carry out their message properly unless I paid them. I was angry at their exorbitance, one demanding two coils of wire; to the other I gave half a bar of lead. The old fellow hung about begging. Women brought mealies and Kafir corn. Milk and beer were also brought, and I told them to bring Kafir corn meal next day, which they did, but were very fanciful in their demands, one wanting beads, another must have brass wire, another a handkerchief, and so on. I find they don't care for mirrors; look at themselves, and are highly amused, but refuse them as payment. Common knives are likewise refused, but gun caps taken eagerly. They like printed calico better than white, which they affect to despise. The outcry was for long strips of coloured stuff, and they preferred the quarter of two handkerchiefs *(i.e.* half a handkerchief in quantity), cut lengthwise, to one whole one. Stayed about waggon all day. Pitched tent, and got things out."

"*September 9th.*—The night had been very mild, Old Manyami came bothering early. In the course of the day he kept on coming, and I gave him twenty gun caps. Wonder of wonders, he afterwards presented me with a pumpkin, and I felt less hostile to the old creature. He is really a miserable-looking, ugly, and filthy creature. Stayed about waggon again to-day."

"*September 10th.*—Early breakfast, and then out with the Kafirs to shoot. One carried my ten-bore, one led the dogs, which I am taking out to help to hunt. Went in a north-easterly direction, through very fine picturesque kopjes, with blue distant ranges; the grass long and yellow, and the trees grouped prettily; some kopjes with craggy tops, and partially covered with evergreens, others show- ing more of their stony formation. A good many trees are covered with bunches of cream-coloured blossoms something like 'may,' but have no leaves. They remind

---

[43] Mr. Fairbairn was agent at the King's Town for a Mr. Cruickshank, with whom Frank Oates had had business dealings at Bamangwato. [Their partnership was terminated in 1875, after which Fairbairn traded in Bulawayo. In 1884 he and two partners obtained a mineral concession from Lobengula, which they subsequently sold to the British South African Company. Fairbairn stayed at Bulawayo until the king fired the settlement and fled the BSAC's forces in October 1893. DS]

me a little of 'snow-balls.' Here and there we see a tree whose leaves are brown or scarlet with decay. In places where the grass has been burnt, fresh green blades are springing. There are numbers of little burns here with moist oozy banks, and in many places with water in them, that I suppose find their way to the Shashani. We had to go through a burning patch of country. The flames appeared orange-red, and presented a rather formidable phalanx, writhing in the wind, and with wreaths of dun-coloured smoke rising from them, which indeed filled the air with lighter clouds of the same colour, here and there the wreaths appearing bluish, whilst a dusky haze hung over the horizon. As the flames devoured the yellow grass, they left a blackened track behind. The trees, however, seem to escape; some in blossom, some in autumnal tints, but the greater portion leafless. … One of the boys who came to the waggon had a charm of bone suspended from his breast. It consisted of four pieces of bone, carved and strung together. By them he professes to foretell what luck will befall a hunter or any one else. They are unstrung and shaken in the hand, and then thrown on the ground. The person going to hunt must spit on the ground, and as he throws he must say, 'My gun! May I shoot something.' The bones, as they are hung, appear about the size and shape of a swallow-tail butterfly. I like the Matabele better than I did. They are good-natured and jovial, and seem to understand a joke. There were great firings and noises at the kraal in the evening, in honour, it appears, of a man returned from the diamond-fields."

"*September 11th.*—Fair, pleasant, windy day. Eight oxen and a note from Fairbairn, who says I have missed a dance at Gubuleweyo. The king says I am to come and make haste. A letter from Gubuleweyo to forward to the Tati excites more exorbitant demands for payment. Two boys must take it, and each have a pannikin of powder. Manyami said he must see the powder before he would send the boys. Great noises at the kraal again to-night."

"*September 12th.*—Manyami brought a small elephant tusk for sale, weighing a little over a pound, and asked five coils of wire for it. I offered 1 him two, which he accepted. He is an extremely ugly little old man, and simply filthy. Packed the waggon and started at 11am, the road winding amongst kopjes. We crossed several spruits, and stopped at the Shashani River about 1pm. Beans and guinea-fowl for dinner. Dick went back to look for screw-jack, and we lost a trek in consequence."

"*September 13th.*—Inspanned at 3am; most villainous jolting. Really fine country here; kopjes on every side, rising into fine crags, with huge stones strewed on the ground. In the distance more ranges of kopjes are to be seen, becoming blue against the horizon; and though the kopjes themselves are too stony to give growth to many trees, trees intervene. One could make a picture here. Country a good deal burnt in places, and fresh grass springing up green. Later in the day, after a long rest, we went through ordinary flat bush veldt, and then through an open undulating country, covered with yellow grass; a few trees and detached kopjes in the distance. Passed several kraals, and went through mealie stubble-fields, fenced from the waggon-track by branches rudely stuck in the ground. A crowd of Kafirs, making a fearful noise, appeared, and accompanied the waggon to where we were going to outspan, so we went on a little further past the kraal. There was a perfect Babel. A few men came after us when we had halted— swarthy fellows, with splendid teeth. One had a fine leopard-skin he was anxious to sell; others a wooden dish, beans, Kafir corn, tobacco, and beer. The men's head-dresses were various and becoming. One man we passed had on a skull-cap of spotted tiger-cat skin, with feathers sticking out behind like eagles' or *pauws*'[44]. Others wore round masses of feathers (one was of guinea-fowls') nearly as big as their heads, and one had a jackal's tail sticking straight up over his fore-head. They were not at all an unpleasant-looking or unfriendly set, though noisy and forward.

FEATHER HEAD-DRESS.

"*September 14th.*—Fine bright morning; clear sky. Two hours' trekking brought us to Kumala River, now dry, which we crossed, outspanning a mile or two further on. The country here is open, park-likes and undulating, extending away in a nearly level plain to the right.

---

[44] *Paauw*, or kori bustard (Otis kori). DS

69

After we had stopped, a number of impudent Kafirs crowded round the waggon. One made a fearful row, at last coming to entreaties, saying we had set the veldt on fire.

"Starting again at 4pm, we next went over rising ground, the country getting very clear of timber, and at half-past six stopped at a small spruit with water in it, having crossed two previously. A long, dry, treeless plain here stretched before us, with kopjes rising into ranges against the horizon. It seems the spruit we are now out-spanned at is the head-waters of a river flowing into the Limpopo, and where we were outspanned this morning is the head-waters of Kumala River, which flows into the Zambesi."

The day afterwards a short trek of about three miles brought the traveller to the King's Town, as related in the ensuing chapter.

HEAD-DRESS OF ZEBRA-SKIN AND FEATHERS.

CHAPTER IV

Arrival at Gubuleweyo—Interview with the King—Start for the Zambesi—Hope Fountain—Inyati—Difficulty of obtaining bearers—The Zambesi abandoned—Hunting expedition on the Umvungu and Gwailo Rivers—Experiences of a half-caste—Birds' nests—The indunas' tree—Hunting—A lunar eclipse—Return to Gubuleweyo—Wild fruit.

THE account of Frank Oates's present stay at Gubuleweyo, and his first impressions of the town and its inhabitants, taken from his Journal, is somewhat scanty. This was one of those more striking episodes in the journey, which needed no written record to impress their details upon his mind, and the narrative of which in this, as in other similar instances, is consequently the most wanting, where the reader would naturally expect and desire to find it the fullest. The account, such as it is, of his arrival at the town, and the first two days spent there, is taken as follows from his Journal:—

"*September 15th.*—Another trek of about an hour and a half brought us, about 9am, to Gubuleweyo. There is not much timber as the kraal is approached. The scene is picturesque but desolate, the road winding and steep. Some of the peculiar-looking trees[45] are here of great size. Strings of women were carrying vessels of water on their heads as we arrived. It was bitterly cold, and there was both wind and rain. Fairbairn and a number of others were standing about the kraal. Petersen was there, and introduced me. They asked me in, and I drew up my waggon to Fairbairn's *scherm*[46] and had breakfast with them. Fairbairn and Petersen took me to the king, whom I called on out of compliment, telling him that I had not yet unpacked my waggon—a hint that I should have a present for him. He was very gracious, and placed meat and plates before me, and inquired what sport I had had coming up, noticing the dilapidated state of my dress. I was going out of the hut legs first, when

---

[45] Probably the Euphorbia above referred to, which frequently attains the size of a small tree.

[46] The term applied to the small fold or enclosure made round a hut or waggon, for shelter and protection, by means of branches rudely placed in the ground.

he pulled me back and made me go head first. He sent me to look at his new house, of which he is very proud. It is being built of brick by an Englishman.

"In the afternoon Fairbairn and I rode over to see Mr. Thomson, the missionary. He will act as interpreter if I wish, but does not think it necessary. As we returned at sundown, we met a party of natives. They were Umtegan's troop, returning from an 'impey',[47] or raid, with cattle taken from the Mashonas, a tribe not altogether subject to the king, though a part of them are. Umtegan was in European clothes, and on horseback. They stopped to go through the exercise of certain rites before entering the town. They had only a few hundred bullocks with them. Lately some thousands were brought in by an impey of a similar kind. At supper I had a young lion to pet; it belongs to the king, and roams about amongst the traders. There is a waggon at Fairbairn's made at Beverley, in Yorkshire, which was brought out here in separate pieces, and fitted together afterwards. Fairbairn says it is a capital one. The poor man who brought it from England died before landing.

"*September 16th*.—Took the king my present— a central fire shot gun with ammunition. As I approached, with men carrying it, he took me by the hand and led me to a waggon, and sat on the 'dissel-boom'.[48] We all sat on the ground. He was much pleased with the gun, and thanked me. The men with me would ask for beer, and he sent us to his sister for it. She was lying on a rug at her hut door, and I was introduced."

It was now ascertained from those here who knew most about the matter, that it was not even yet considered too late to reach the Zambesi that season, by taking a more direct route from this place, to be accomplished for the most part on foot, instead of proceeding along the usual trade route by way of Tati, which is available for waggons, but a good deal further round from the King's Town. On hearing this, Frank Oates at once determined to try and reach the river by the shorter road that season, and the remainder of the time he spent on this occasion at Gubuleweyo was chiefly occupied in obtaining information for the expedition, and making the necessary arrangements for it. The early part of the journey could be accomplished with the waggon and oxen; after that it would be necessary to go on foot.

---

[47] *iMpi*, Ndebele, 'fight, engagement'. DS

[48] *i.e.* The pole of the waggon.

On the evening of the 24th of September he accordingly started with his waggon, remaining the night with Mr. Thomson, the missionary, at Hope Fountain, a short distance from the kraal. The night was very close—the first which had been so— and on the following evening, after they had trekked some miles from Mr. Thomson's in the direction of Inyati[49] to the north-east, there was heavy rain and wind, accompanied by thunder and lightning. This rain, the first there had yet been, was said to be earlier than usual in its commencement by about two months. The other conditions, however, of the projected journey to the Zambesi, all of them, still appeared favourable. It was the traveller's long-cherished desire at least to reach the Zambesi, and see the Falls, if he found it inexpedient on the present occasion to cross the river and penetrate into the less known territory to the northward. But there were difficulties, not only of climate, but from the obstructiveness of native character, to be encountered, and endless was the opposition which he met with from the latter cause. Four distinct attempts did he make at various times from this date to reach the river, and in each of the first three was he destined to disappointment.

His present effort, made in September, was the first of these; his fourth and last attempt was made at the end of the succeeding year, nor was it till the last day of 1874 that he actually beheld the white spray of the great cataract breaking through the trees upon the river's bank. That effort truly was rewarded with success, yet a success how dearly purchased—with his life!

Before leaving Hope Fountain, to resume the journey, he wrote home the following letter to his mother :—

"MR THOMSON'S, NEAR GUBULEWEYO,
"*September 25th, 1873.*
"You will, no doubt, have more recent news from Willie than from me. I left him with Buckley and Gilchrist at the Tati, meditating a short journey in the neighbourhood before leaving, and came on myself to the King's. Town, Gubuleweyo, the site, or somewhere near the site, of the place marked in the maps as Mosilikatze's Town. Mosilikatze was the father of the present king, and conquered this country. The name of the nation is the Matabele, which is always shown in the maps. The former inhabitants of the country were divided into various nations, but it is all

---

[49] A London Missionary Society mission founded by Robert Moffat in 1859, located 80km north-east of modern Bulawayo.

called the Matabele country now from the name of its powerful owners. The country reaches to the Zambesi, and produces a great deal of ivory and ostrich feathers. There are a good many white men at Gubuleweyo, trading. Mr. Fairbairn, a young Scotchman, is my agent there.

"I cannot give you a detailed account of my stay of nine days at the King's Town. It is really to a stranger a most curious place. The king, Lobengula lives in royal state. He is absolute monarch, and feared and obeyed far and wide. The people inhabiting the country we have passed through in coming here are altogether of an inferior race. At Bamangwato there is a king, but he is thought nothing of. I called on 'Bengula, accompanied by Fairbairn, the day I arrived here, and found him the picture of a savage king, just as one might have imagined, and coming quite up to the standard. The day I first saw him he was nearly naked, and lying on a skin inside his hut, to enter which you have to crawl in on your hands and knees through a little aperture in the front; in fact it is like a beehive entrance. He took me by the hand, and placed meat before me, and asked a few questions about my journey. I told him I should come again next day. Of course I had to make him a present, and I knew he would expect it next day, after which I should ask his leave and assistance to go through his country to the Victoria Falls if possible. I gave him a gun and ammunition, which pleased him very much, and he has done everything he could for me. It appeared that I was still in time to reach the Falls by going on foot, after leaving my waggon at the place marked on the map as Inyati. The king said it was possible to get to the Falls in ten days, and I suppose at my rate of travelling it ought to b done in a fortnight or three weeks at most, and the king says I have still two months of favourable weather, but so anxious is he that no white man should come to grief in his country, that he has been urging on me all possible haste from the moment the subject was first mentioned. He has given me two excellent men as guides; these two, having the king's authority, will carry all before them.

"I left Gubuleweyo last night, and came on as far as here, the house of Mr. Thomson the missionary, for my first trek. Mr. Thomson has kindly interested himself in me, and done all he could to assist me. He has a nice wife and children, and this morning I have had the luxury of a civilized breakfast, including tablecloth, bread and butter and eggs, and milk to one's coffee—things that I don't often see now. I am now availing myself of one of his rooms to write to you in.

"One of the men appointed by the king to guide me—himself a man of high character and good family, as Mr. Thomson tells me—left Gubuleweyo with me, and this morning hurried on to get bearers for me at the kraals ahead. I shall want from twenty to thirty, and as it will take some time to collect them, and my oxen want rest, I shall follow slowly, making a three or four days' journey of what is usually done in two days. At Inyati, where I am to leave my waggon, are two white men trading. These are the last outposts of civilization, but up to that point there is regular communication all the way—that is to say, all the way my waggon takes me. If I find that I am delayed and cannot reach the Falls as quickly as I had hoped, I shall very likely turn back without accomplishing my object, as I am desirous not to run any foolish risks, and have been at great pains in collecting all possible information.

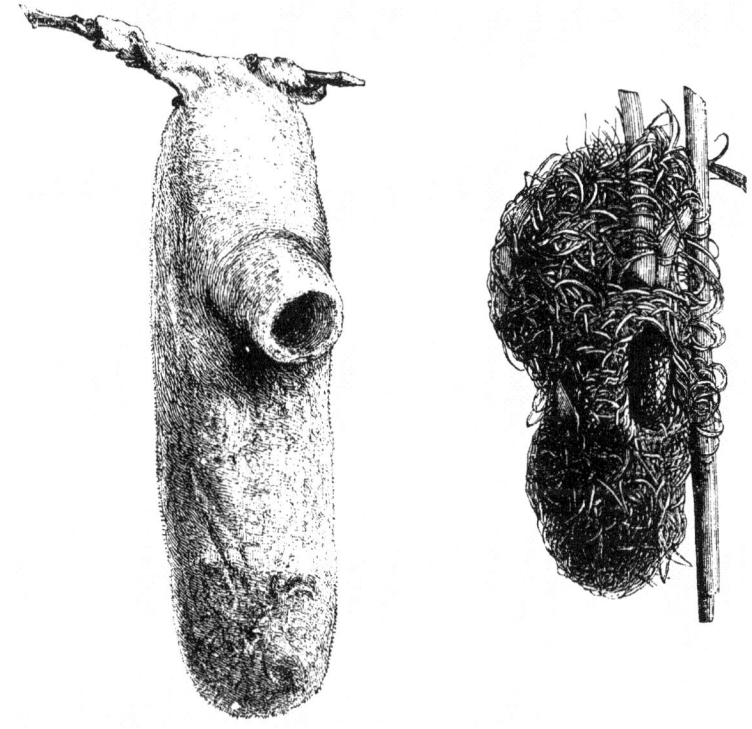

BIRDS' NESTS.

"The men who carry my things will be most of them of the conquered population, and the two guides appointed by the king (one of whom, as I have mentioned, left me this morning to go on in advance, the other being now at Inyati) are able to do what they like. No one dare oppose the king, and the Matabele men he gives me renders any fear of desertion or disobedience superfluous. Besides, these two men know that they must carry out the king's orders to the letter. I have also got an interpreter, a man who speaks English and Kafir perfectly, my own servant Hendrik, and my driver and his boy[50]. I shall take my tent if possible, plenty of ground sheets and bedding, meal, tins of biscuits, and coffee. For meat we have to rely on the guns carried by the party, but there seems not the slightest fear of scarcity, in fact the bearers are expected to live entirely on meat, having guns and ammunition allowed them for the purpose. No beast of burden or dog can accompany us, as it is the tsetse-fly country.

"Had it been earlier in the season I should have gone from the Tati, by which route you can take your waggon to within a few miles of the Falls, but as I should have had to see the king first, to get his permission, by the time I could have returned to the Tati it would have been too late. I have not a map before me now, but suppose it may be 200 miles or thereabouts from Inyati, my starting-point, to the Victoria Falls. I shall hurry on to the Zambesi so as to leave the river as soon as possible. I can then take my time in returning, as when I leave the river the worst is over, and I soon get into a healthy country again, but, as of course every one knows, the Zambesi at certain seasons of the year is unhealthy. All this I have carefully studied, and have been guided by what I consider reliable evidence. I shall be further guided by circumstances that may occur, and shall exercise my judgment as to how far I carry out my original project."

Leaving Hope Fountain after writing the on the 25th of September, the traveller went a distance that night, and continued his journey early on the following morning. Here the Journal for next two days resumes the story:—

"*September 26th.*—Cool, cloudy morning; the wind in our faces. Started about 7.30am, went six miles. The country we passed through was bush veldt; trees small, and in most places thinly scattered; grass very dry. One of the boys was running wildly about to keep himself warm—a hint for me to give him a shirt. The wind was high, and where we outspanned the boys made a fire in the hollow bed of a spruit. Starting again at 1pm, the country assumed rather a fresh aspect, with a green verdure like that of a young cornfield, where the grass had been burnt. The trees here were not close, and some were a good size, with young foliage of a vivid green. Passing next between two kopjes, we descended

---

[50] The interpreter here spoken of was a native from Graham's Town, who remained with Frank Oates till July the following year.

into a fine, bushy, undulating tract, misty-looking in the distance under a lowering sky. Outspanned at 3.40pm at the Cokhé River, and had tea. Here they told me there was a kraal close by, presided over by 'Bengula's brother, Bolinlila; and as some of the oxen were tired, I sent over to see if I could leave them here. The reply being favourable, and a present requested, I sent the oxen—five in number—with a small strip of coloured calico.

"The boy sent me by the king, who was running about so vigorously this morning, now showed me a small scratch on his heel, and asked to be doctored. I put on some glycerine, but believe it was a ruse, as he afterwards got on the sacks at the back of the waggon, and rode instead of walking. The other man who was sent me by the king is the thinnest mortal I think I ever saw, his legs literally like those of spiders. It was dreadfully cold, and I gave all the poor wretches some hot tea. Towards evening we advanced again four miles further. It was like a cold trek on the high veldt—front sail drawn down, candle lighted, myself in the blankets. Outspanned at 7.40pm. Windy and rainy night.

"*September 27th*. Dark windy morning; Scotch mist. Hendrik woke me soon after six, to say they were inspanned. We made two treks—about twelve miles in all—and stopped about 3pm at the Bembesi[51] River, where some boys herding cattle brought us sour milk curdled for sale, which was very good. During the morning we passed some very striking-looking trees, leafless, but covered with large clusters of bright scarlet flowers on straight, brittle, thorny stalks. At a distance they looked like naked trees covered with scarlet berries, such as one sees in winter at home. Before night we went on four miles further, and stopped one trek they say from our destination."

At ten o'clock the following morning the Inquinquesi[52], a larger river than the Bembesi, with plenty of water in it and a sandy bed, was crossed, and a halt made upon its banks. Here was Inchlangin[53], the kraal where the traders were, Inyati itself being a short way off. Thither a messenger was at once despatched to ascertain what success the king's man, who had gone on in advance, had had in obtaining bearers. Soon

---

[51] Bembezi. DS

[52] Inkwenkwesi. DS

[53] Probably eNhlangeni (Ndebele; 'the meeting place'). DS

afterwards this man presented himself at the waggon, saying that the boy required for the journey would be forthcoming they following morning. When the day arrived, however, they were not brought in sufficient number to be of any service, and the start had to be postponed a day or two longer, pending the results of further efforts. The following is the day's entry in the Journal :—

"*September 29th*.—Fine warm day; heavy rain in the evening. The King's man came again; this time accompanied by the induna of the kraal (I suppose only the acting induna, as the real one is the man I met at the King's). He brought with him two other chief men, given me as well as himself by the king, and to all three I gave some limbo[54]. The induna said he would rather have a shirt, and I told him I would give it him when he had got me the boys. He only brought three today. Two volunteers, whom I told to wait, also presented themselves from another distant kraal.

"After this, as no more could be done, I went out shooting with Mandy[55] (one of the traders here) in the afternoon, and got some birds. We had a pleasant walk, and saw the wild cotton growing. We also saw a beautiful tree with delicate green leaves and wreaths of violet-coloured laburnum-like blossoms; also a very sweetly-scented flower, white and star-shaped, growing in small clusters upon a tree of some size. Mandy says there are crocodiles here, but the king does not allow them to be killed, as it is thought that any one possessing the body can work spells. It is death to a native to kill one. A white man on one occasion shot one here eighteen feet long, which had been destroying calves and goats, and the king sent to have it buried, and had men to watch the place.

"It seems that lately, during a ceremony previous to the king's marriage (circumcision), it was thought inauspicious for any guns to be fired in the neighbourhood. They say a Kafir who fired one some where in the veldt at the time was impaled for it."

The greater part of the following day (September 30th) was spent in packing and arranging things for the walk to the Falls, and it was not till the day after this that the induna reappeared, now stating that he

---

[54] Coarse cloth. DS

[55] Frank Mandy, a trader from Grahamstown. In 1881 he was managing an ostrich farm near Port Elizabeth, but he returned to Zimbabwe in 1890 as a lieutenant in the Pioneer Column. He died at Kimberley in 1903. DS

could not get bearers. The natives, it is likely enough, were afraid of fever on the Zambesi at this season, and did not want to go, but it afterwards appeared that the induna of the kraal and the headman sent by the king had made no proper efforts to obtain the staff required for the journey. The upshot of the matter was that the Zambesi had to be abandoned, and the traveller obtained instead permission from the king to go for a few weeks' hunting into the country to the north-east, where good sport was likely to be had. Before starting on this expedition he wrote home from Inyati, on October 5th, as follows:—

"You will not be much surprised to hear that I have had to give up the Zambesi. I got here just in time to do it, if the carriers had been forthcoming, but the people in authority threw so many difficulties in my way, that I had to send back to the king, and so much valuable time has been lost that I have given up the expedition. I am, however, going a little way into the country with my waggon, and shall probably be a month or two before I am back again here.

"There are three Englishmen living here, trading. Two of them, in whose house I am now writing, are very obliging to me. This is a mission station, but there is no missionary here now. It is the last post of white men in this part of the world. When you reach the Zambesi you come to the outposts of the Portuguese traders from the east coast, but between these points are no Europeans settled. The rain is beginning, though the regular rains have not set in yet. It is after the first heavy rains that fever begins to annoy people on the Zambesi, but I believe, generally, even then only slightly, but after the next downfall—when there is much rain and the rain is beginning to dry up, about January, February, and March—the really bad season sets in. However, I am now avoiding even the former risk, and where I am going I shall be so near here all the time that I can return almost when I choose. I don't exactly know where I *am* going, but it will be somewhere in a north or north-easterly direction from here.

"I hear that Cruickshank, my agent at Bamangwato, is now at the King's Town, but I am three days' journey from there, and he will shortly be returning to Bamangwato. Fairbairn, his agent at the King's Town, will, however, in all probability, be there when I return and here I am in good hands too, so that I have friends all along the road, and letters always come and go as surely, if more slowly, than where there a regular post, for waggons are constantly coming and going, and everybody helps everybody else in this part of the world. I have been pressed into the service as postman myself before now. Only delays must be expected, and are often very vexatious."

On the 7th of October Frank Oates started his projected expedition in the north-east, on which he was absent from Inyati in all about seven weeks. The district traversed during his absence was that watered by the Gwailo and Umvungu Rivers, the furthest point reached being the Umgwanya. The circumstances of the first few days of these wanderings may be recounted in his own words as follows, taken from his Journal:—

"*October 7th*.—Sultry, oppressive day; very cloudy. Packed waggon, and left Inyati about 4pm. We passed through bush country, with fine open level spaces, which would be excellent riding ground; some fine old baobab trees in the distance exactly like oaks, with gnarled crooked arms. These trees have dark green foliage, and here and there stand almost isolated. Close; a very disagreeable smell frequent, Hendrik says of black ants. Now and then sweet perfumes from flowering shrubs. ... As it got dark we out-spanned about 7pm, having water for our own use in our casks. A large group of men round the fire. We had come perhaps nine miles."

"*October 8th*.—Mild, cloudy, breezy morning. Crossed the dry beds of two small rivers (branches of the Lelongwe), with a kraal placed between them; the ground level so far. Men bring ostrich eggs; women bring Indian and Kafir corn and beans. Bought the upper mandible of an eagle from the neck of a man, hanging by a thin leather strap. Hendrik says these eagles kill goats. Also bought ostrich feathers and eggs, milk and corn. We had outspanned. Presently resuming the journey, we crossed the third arm of the Lelongwe, and then the reedy bed of a spruit, where we dug in the sand, and found plenty of nice mineral-tasted water, which the men and dogs drank. Reached the site of an old kraal, Intembin, about noon. Hendrik calls these people 'Maholies'.[56] They are far easier to deal with than the Matabele, take what you give them and are satisfied. They asked for red, but took blue, beads, and were delighted with red with white stripe. Stopped to rest at 1.15, and made another trek before night, finally stopping about 6pm near a rather large river, with heavy sand in its bed.

---

[56] A derogatory name given to the subordinate Rozvi people, who were dispersed and defeated by the Ndebele. DS

"*October 9th*.—Overcast, delicious day. Started at 7am, and about 9 crossed the Tchangani[57]—the largest river we have yet seen since leaving Inyati—and outspanned, continuing the journey in the afternoon for about three hours. This last trek was a very pleasant one, over falling ground. As we outspanned (about 4pm), John told me that a 'honey's (bees') nest' had been found by Hendrik. The boys went off and it was found in the hollow trunk of a large tree, into which the bees went by a hole in the side of the tree. They put fire into the hole, having kindled a small one close to the tree, and then with an axe cut open the trunk. The bees seemed on the whole pretty quiet, and I don't think their sting can be bad, as the men seemed tolerably indifferent. The cells, when taken out, proved full of grubs … One of the boys was carrying two squirrels killed by a dog; another had found roots. I tried the latter, and found them slightly bitter and at the same time sweet. They are chewed and the juice swallowed. The only leaf visible is contained in a small green shoot, apparently just coming out of the ground, but the roots are very large and long. Another boy brought a pretty duiker[58], which he had killed with an assegai."

"*October 10th*.—We seem on a sort of plateau, with lower ground in front. Beyond is high land, blue in the distance. Starting a little before 7am, we reached the Umvungu about 9, a big reedy river with water in its bed. When we arrived one of the boys was calling out, and we found he had shot a sable antelope. Many flowers are now springing up in the veldt, and the tints of the trees are very lovely, reminding one of an English spring, or, in some respects, of autumn; different shades of green and yellow. In the course of the afternoon we entered very thick bush, the thickest I have yet met with in South Africa, and more like English wood in general appearance than what we have hitherto seen, the trees budding with delicate tints of fresh green, brown, and yellow. Soon after entering the bush fresh elephant spoor was announced—the first I have yet heard of—and a few minutes later we came on a broken tree lying across the road, and more fresh elephant spoor. Emerged from the thick bush about 5.20pm, and soon afterwards outspanned at a spruit."

---

[57] Shangani. DS

[58] A small antelope. DS

The following day (October 11) the party reached the Gwailo River, which was crossed without difficulty. A half-caste Cape man, who was hunting here, named Nelson, rode up and gave a very bad report. He had shot fourteen elephants in two months, and a few ostriches. He said the Mashonas, hunting the elephants with their assegais, and shouting, had driven them away. His plan now was to go to Damaraland, *via* Lake Ngami, where he had been before and found elephants abundant.

Resuming his journey in the afternoon, Frank Oates now struck across the veldt to the south-east, and crossed the Umgwanya River the following morning, proceeding afterwards a few miles up its banks. At this point he had intended to encamp for a few days; but hearing from two natives who came to the waggon that there were still elephants in the thick bush which had been passed through the day before, he felt tempted to return there; and on the 13th, re-crossing the Umgwanya and Gwailo Rivers, in a more direct line than he had taken Coming, went back in the direction of the Umvungu. "A boa-constrictor,"[59] he here writes, "six feet six inches long, and as thick as my wrist, lay its length upon the ground, and was skilfully transfixed by one of my boys' assegais, and pinned to the ground. The lads were evidently afraid of his bite, but the men say that it is harmless. ... The Mashonas use these snakes as an article of food."

Next day the spruit which they had outspanned at on the 10th, near the thick elephant bush they were making for, was reached, and here, a short way off the waggon-track, under some remarkably picturesque kopjes, the landscape all budding with the green of spring, a camp was formed, where the party remained about a fortnight hunting. The boys made themselves some snug huts of branches and dry grass to sleep in. Here the Journal again takes up the story:—

"*October 4th.*— ... Nelson came up to the waggon when we were outspanned. He had not left, but had stopped about near the place where we had outspanned when we first came through the thick bush. He had come on a herd of many (he says forty) elephants, driven six out of the herd, and shot four, but lost two of them—one a large bull. He had killed two bulls. This occurred the day before yesterday. I walked away with him in the evening towards his waggon. We found some nests of

---

[59] Most likely an African rock python (*Python sebae*). DS

amadavats[60]—the little pink ones, I fancy. Some were in course of construction, some finished; all hanging like fruit from a tree. One I took contained two eggs, white speckled with red. Macloule[61] gave me this evening two goatsucker's[62] eggs he had found, partly sat on. The nest is very slight, and placed on the ground.[63]"

"*October 15th*.—Soon after 7am started with boys to hunt. ...Maqueban found the carcass of an elephant killed a few days ago. The two teeth—one broken, but as heavy as the other—weighed together 20 lbs., as I found afterwards. The boys rushed to the carcass, and were soon at work dismembering it. It may be one of Nelson's, but my boys think it died before Sunday (the day Nelson killed his). A great many kites flew sweeping round. It was a regular scene, such as one sees in pictures, the Kafirs at work cutting off trunk and feet and strips of flesh.

"It was a cow elephant, and vultures and other creatures had got the end of the trunk and what they could without breaking the skin. Fires were lighted and meat cooked and devoured, whilst large pieces were put aside for removal. When the filth was extracted from one of the tusks, 'Sassaybi'[64] threw back his head and held it up first to one then to the other nostril. This is supposed to be a good thing for anyone troubled with nose-bleeding on hot days. Sassaybi likewise scraped some stuff like cobbler's wax from where the tusk is inserted in the skin. He said it was to be used as a charm. ... As we travel through the bush Indian file, returning to the waggon, Echle (the chief hunter I have with me),

---

[60] A species of Indian finch, not found outside South Asia; Oates probably meant the Redbilled Firefinch (*Lagonosticta senegala*). DS

[61] The guide.

[62] Nightjar. DS

[63] Frank Oates collected, during his wanderings, a considerable variety of birds' eggs and nests, some of the latter very remarkable in their construction. Two of these are represented in the accompanying woodcut, the first of which— probably that of an Egithalus or Penduline Titmouse—is of the consistency and texture of fine blanket, and nearly white in colour. It appears to be made from white cotton, or some similar vegetable substance. The second is ingeniously composed of the finer portions of reeds, in the manner of close basket-work, and is found in great numbers along the banks of rivers, and in marshy places, affixed to the rushes.

[64] One of the boys.

meeting a small tortoise, picks it up, spits on it, and puts it to his forehead. He says this is lucky when you want to get elephants, and he says, however large the tortoise is, this is done. He is then allowed to walk off."

THE FIRST ELEPHANT.

"*October 16th.*—Shots heard near the waggon early, and Nelson arrives, having shot a fine bull eland quite near to my waggon. He says he was looking for elephant spoor when he found the eland, and drove him seven miles. He is a mighty brute, bigger than an average bullock. The hide is very thick. We had breakfast on eland steak fried in fat, and enjoyed it very much. Nelson says, when in Damaraland, he got a young elephant, but it died from neglect coming through seventy miles of the 'thirst land.' He says they are easy to keep, and so are young ostriches. The latter can be driven with the bullocks. He says there are plenty of crocodiles in the river beyond the Gwailo.

"Nelson showed me, when we were out together in the veldt the day before yesterday, some remains of Mashona huts destroyed by the Matabele. He says they are to be found all over the veldt, and bones amongst many of them. Some of the Mashonas are subject to the

Matabele. Those that refuse allegiance are mercilessly hunted down. They are all formed of independent little tribes, and when war is made against one the others don't assist them. Therefore they fall an easy prey. The impeys sent out against them for their cattle are what I heard of at Gubuleweyo. Nelson says lately in an impey a kraal was taken, the young men killed (they throw away their scanty dress and run and are killed 'like springbok'), and the old men and women burnt to death. The young women and children were made slaves of, and the cattle taken. Nelson's Matabele boys wanted him lately to drive off some cattle, saying the king might give him fifty of them, but he refused. The cattle and all the animals are kept in the same place as the Mashonas themselves live in (the same house, Nelson calls it). They are thus easily surrounded by the Matabele. The Matabele despise those who own allegiance to their chief, and call them slaves. One of the latter in Nelson's employ blew his face off with some gunpowder, doing something for his master on one occasion. 'Never mind,' said Nelson's Matabele, 'it is nothing, he is a dog' (the usual epithet). The man's father came to Nelson and asked to be paid, and was quite satisfied with a few coils of brass wire. Once, when Nelson killed a rhinoceros, a number of Mashona came for the meat and began fighting. They would cry, 'This is mine,' 'This is mine,' and two were killed. Nelson went away, feeling, he says, quite frightened at the scene. An assegai was thrust into one man's heart by another who was quarrelling with him before Nelson's eyes.

"In Damaraland, he says, the Bushmen are much better to get on with than the Matabele are here. They work for you like slaves for a little meat. They are under independent petty chiefs, and bring magnificent ostrich feathers for a small strip of limbo or other very trifling payment. From what Nelson says, it must be a capital place for the hunter, ivory being large, white, and plentiful, and easily got, and the natives most willing to assist."

"*October 17th*.—Sleepless night; dogs barking at hyenas. I was kept to the waggon yesterday with a sore heel, and to-day did not go far. Nelson came to the waggon in the afternoon. He tells me that, on the opposite side of the road, about ten miles away, is a 'fountain,' with one or two waters intervening, and plenty of game. He does not know whether the king allows any one to go into this veldt; but it is a good country for a waggon to travel in. … I went out with him a little in the evening. He says he has seen two elephants' tusks from near the Zambesi of 70 lbs. each—the largest he ever saw. He has seen an elephant with four tusks, and a Boer he speaks of shot one with eight; one of 70 lbs., the others of about 2 lbs. each.

"When Nelson was a young boy, his father, he tells me, trading near Sechele's[65], being at feud with the missionary there, who had surrounded his waggon with forty Kafirs, and incited them to seize his goods, he determined to blow them up; but, in applying the light to the inside of the waggon, where was a lot of gunpowder, he was not quite quick enough, and was himself blown up with the missionary (a German) and the Kafirs. Nelson himself lay many hours on the ground insensible, much scorched. He had been standing close to the front wheel; his father was on the front-box. Nelson must have escaped thus lightly almost by a miracle. When he came to himself, he saw the wreck, his father and the Kafirs lying dead, and was pursued and fired at by Kafirs. The bullets passed close to him, and the Kafirs pursued, but could not catch him. He has still scars on his legs, made in passing through the thorns, and one on his face, caused by the explosion. He spent three days wandering in the veldt without food, but, it being the rainy season, he had water, and on the fourth day he came to a waggon.

"There was a scene today when Nelson's two boys, who claim the ivory we got the other day, came to the waggon. Nelson told me not to give it to them, but did not want them to know he had given me this hint. The ivory, it seems, would not be his anyhow, as the king's man who is with him hunts on his own account and would claim it. My boys were resolute to keep it, and we let them fight it out by themselves, which they did very noisily, finally saying it should be referred to the king. It seems to me that, picked up in the veldt, it belongs to the finder, unless the shooter has followed it up himself. This Nelson says his men did not attempt—though he advised it—saying it would be useless."

From this time till the 27th of the month, the party remained in the same camp, making frequent excursions thence in search of game, first in one direction, then in another. Here they met with more quagga[66] and sable antelope than any other game, but there were also eland,

---

[65] Sechele was leader of the Kwena people, based around Molopole, north-west of Gaborone, near David Livingstone's mission at Kolobeng. The German missionary was probably from one of the Lutheran missions established in Botswana in the 19th century. DS

[66] Zebra (*Equus quagga*). DS

koodoo[67], and sassaybi[68], besides some of the lesser antelopes and wild pigs in abundance. "Near the spruit on which we stand," writes Frank Oates at this point, "is the most really picturesque bit of craggy and sylvan scenery I have yet seen. Our present camp indeed is far the best in that respect we have ever yet had. It is now spring, moreover; the first rains have fallen, and refreshed nature is beginning to resume her long-lost garb of green."

The following quotation from the Journal of the 18th gives a pleasant glimpse into one of their longer rambles from this camp:—

"Started about 7.30am, and walked nearly three hours, first through the thin, then through the thick, bush, striking a path during the walk which we followed to the south-west, and which brought us out under a huge spreading baobab, the largest tree I have yet seen since leaving Pietermaritzburg. They call it the 'Indunas' tree,' for here the indunas from the neighbouring kraals are wont to sit and drink beer when anything particular is on hand. The huge trunk is blackened all round with fire, but the tree seems uninjured, and spreads its huge canopy from a framework of crooked boughs, like a gigantic oak. Stretching my arms round the tree at the height at which I stand from the ground, it took me four times, all but about a foot, to encircle it—say about twenty-three feet for its girth here, but below this it is much more, as it increases towards the roots. Other trees of the same kind stand about, but they are less. A splendid view, such as recalls Wharfedale to the mind, here suddenly bursts in sight. The Umvungu River flows in the valley; at our backs is the thick bush, through which we have come; but before us stretches the green Vista of woods far away, till it becomes blue in the distance We waited here about two hours, and returned as we had come."

In this way the whole surrounding district was gradually traversed. The weather during the stay at the present camp was already beginning to be wet, and there was no improvement in this respect, but the reverse, from that date. On the 27th, moving their position, they again encamped a few miles further to the westward, where they remained till the middle of November, hunting the district and at times leaving the waggon for some days together. Elephant and giraffe were met with on this occasion, the rest of the game being mostly the same as

---

[67] Greater Kudu antelope (*Tragelaphus strepsiceros*). DS

[68] Tsessebe or topi antelope (*Damaliscus lunatus*). DS

that found near the previous encampment. The chief trophy of the chase here obtained was a fine bull elephant, its tusks weighing together 108lbs.

An eclipse of the moon occurring during this period, an opportunity was afforded of observing the effect of this phenomenon on the minds of some of the party. "Soon after sunset," writes Frank on November 3rd, "the moon rising, I think, a little before, I noticed the upper part of the moon, indeed, all but a small crescent nearest the horizon, covered with a dingy, smoky shadow. It was an eclipse. I asked John what it was. He said, 'Smoke.' The moment it was shown to Macloule he uttered a cry of conjuration, as it were, and rushing out with a brand, threw it in the direction of the moon. His explanation is that we shall hear something; all the hunters out in the veldt will now return home to hear the news. People are looking at it in Gubuleweyo, England, everywhere. It is a custom, it seems, at all the kraals, when an eclipse is seen, for the people to rush out and throw brands, shouting at the same time. When I suggested a shadow on the moon, he dismissed the suggestion summarily, and when asked to explain the appearance by any other cause, said the moon was changing colour. As the eclipse progressed, I pointed out to him that the shadow kept rising, and more and more of the moon becoming visible, but he only said, 'It looks bad now.' I looked through the telescope, as it was nearly over, to note the exact time of the shadow passing away. Echie took a hasty glance through it, and turned away quickly, saying he did not like to see it."

By the middle of November, when they left their second camp, so much rain was already falling that hunting became difficult, and a return to Gubuleweyo was decided on. Starting back, therefore, on the return journey on November 16th, they reached Inyati, travelling slowly, on the 23rd. Here Frank Oates was detained about a week, having much trouble and annoyance in paying off the boys he had engaged there for the hunt early in October, and it was the 2nd of December before he once more found himself at Hope Fountain, near Gubuleweyo, the residence of Mr. Thomson, whence he wrote home the following letter:—

"REV. J. B. THOMSON'S,
HOPE FOUNTAIN, MATABELE LAND,
December 4th, 1873.

"I find there is a good opportunity of writing a line home, as a trader is going with a waggon straight to Hope Town, and starts tomorrow. He has only been a fortnight coming here from Bamangwato, so he travels pretty quickly. You will, no doubt, before you get this, have received the last letter I sent you, in which I think I told you that my visit to the Victoria Falls had been abandoned. I was within 150 to 200 miles of them, and had made every preparation for the journey, having got the king's leave to proceed, escorted by one of his chief men, and was already packing the things for the bearers to carry (twenty was the number I required though I should have been content with fifteen), when all at once the unforeseen difficulty of getting a sufficient number of them presented itself. The king had told me there would be no difficulty, but I was then fifty miles from him, having taken my *waggon* to be left at Inyati, whence I was starting

"On my walk to the Falls. I see now clearly enough that I was deceived by the man who was given to assist me, or by the headman of Inyati, who had made no attempt to get the men for me, but lulled me with fair promises, whilst in reality doing all he could to prevent my obtaining them. The fact was my guide did not wish me to go to the Zambesi; partly, no doubt, because they would have had to hurry more than might have been agreeable, but principally from fear of the fever, of which they have a great dread. The king, however, knew what he was doing when he assured me that for two months to come there was no danger whatever, and this was far more time than enough to accomplish my much-desired object.

"I have now spent two months in the neighbourhood of Inyati, sometimes leaving the waggon for days, and sleeping in the veldt. This was always satisfactorily managed even on a pouring wet night, as the Kafirs in a few minutes build you a hut of branches, perfectly water-tight, with a bed of dry grass upon which to place your bedding. Two Englishmen, tourists, have visited the Falls this season, and I hear that one of them said they were so fine he would rather walk barefoot from Durban to see them than leave them unseen. (Mrs. Thomson, finding me writing in the dark, has just sent Mr. T. to me with a candle, which I hope will improve the style of my letter, for I fear it wants it.) The old guide, who was given me by the king, and whom I suspect of doing me out of the Zambesi, was very anxious for me to go to the king to-day, as he has to deliver me back to him in person, and never lets me go out of his sight for a moment if he can help it. This opportunity of writing home, however, is keeping me this evening.

"My old man is the cousin of the king and nephew of Mosilikatze, and the king sent him with me as a special mark of favour. If any harm had befallen me he would have been held responsible, and with most fearful zeal did he fulfil his office. He would never let me sleep without a hut, or do anything he deemed imprudent or unhealthy, carrying his care of me to such a pitch that it was often a very great bore. I am told that if I go away again into the veldt either now or years hence, I shall have to go with this same man, Macloule, or, should he not be living, with one of his sons. I would have forgiven him everything if he had taken me to the Victoria Falls.

"A puppy has been added to my establishment. It was one of a family born in the veldt, on the banks of the Gwailo River, and, with its brothers and sisters, carried over its master's shoulders in a small bark cage when we were on the move. I had several narrow escapes of being bitten by the mamma, who hated me, though I always did my utmost for the comfort of the family.

"I have still two of my original four dogs with me, one of which is a great favourite of mine, and one pony. The time is approaching when horses that have not yet had it, get the horse-sickness, which it is a great chance they get over. A good 'salted' horse, or rather pony (that is one that has had the sickness and recovered from it), is worth £50 to £100, instead of £20. The king has been telling people to ask me to sell him my pony, and he also wants a gun of mine, for which he has put aside two huge tusks of ivory, double its value. He has been inquiring very much for me, and is anxious to see me back. Tea is nearly ready, so I will now say good-bye. I am anxiously looking forward to getting letters in two or three months at latest. My letters are all to be forwarded to me and await me at Bamangwato."

The day after writing this letter Frank Oates took his waggon on to Gubuleweyo, and once more drew it up in front of Mr. Fairbairn's scherm. The recent rains had wonderfully freshened the country since the outward journey, and the last trek, made through a green meadow-like district, recalled to the traveller's mind the aspect of the country round Oxford in early summer.

The vegetation had of late been frequently remarkable for its beauty, and a number of flowering shrubs, many of them sweetly scented, had been observed from time to time. Flowers of other kinds were also becoming plentiful, and many varieties of wild fruit were met with. Some of the latter Frank Oates describes at Umvungu in his Journal:—

"There is a kind of fruit growing in trees here," he says, "which the boys get very eagerly. It is really excellent. It is the size of a large walnut[69], with a hard case cleft in four, inside which are glutinous woody

---

[69] Probably the snot-apple (*Thespesia garckeana*). DS

fibre and seeds. The seeds are thrown away, and the fibre chewed. The latter contains a large quantity of sweet glutinous matter, the part rejected looking just like wood. There is also another excellent fruit," he continues, "not uncommon, which on a small tree, and is larger than a very fine orange[70]. In shape it is spherical, and the outer case, which is hard, is easily broken, and the contents laid bare. The pulp that surrounds the seeds is the part eaten. This is brown in colour, and deliciously flavoured, reminding one a little of roasted apple. The pulp of one of these fruits forms quite a refreshing little repast. I believe they are common near Pretoria—so John tells me—and no doubt found all over the veldt. The boys always make a great rush to get them. When quite mature the outer rind is yellow, and they seem to fall to the ground as soon as they are thoroughly ripe."

The description of the first of these corresponds closely, it may be remarked, with that of a fruit named "manéko," which was met with by Livingstone near the Zambesi, in the centre of the continent. The last-named is of occurrence in Zululand, where it is called "inhlala" (famine), from its value to the natives in times of scarcity.

Besides these, other fruits were also met with in the district, including a sort of wild grape, acceptable enough on hot days, but somewhat deficient in juiciness and flavour.

No great amount of game was seen upon the journey.

KNOB-BILLED GOOSE. – *Sarkidiornis melanonotus.*

---

[70] Probably the monkey-orange (*Strychnos spinosa*). DS

CHAPTER V

Stay at Gubuleweyo—New Year's Day—The Great Dance—Cattle slaughtered—Departure of the king; the royal procession—A dispute referred to him—Lobengula's court.

FRANK OATES remained at Gubuleweyo or in its immediate neighbourhood some time—from December 5th 1873 to January 26th 1874. This was considerably longer than he had originally intended, but he was partly detained by the weather, which, besides being close and oppressive, was for a long time very wet and unfavourable for travelling, and partly that he might see the Great Dance, which took place in the early part of January. After this some trouble with his servants still further delayed him, as the case of one of them had to be taken before the king. He was able, however, meantime to make some additions to his collections of birds and other objects of natural history, though owing to the state of the weather he attempted little hunting; indeed, near the kraal, large game was invariably scarce and wild.

The incidents of the first part of his stay—until the end of December—were apparently of little interest. After that came the preparations for the Great Dance, which took place on the 8th of January. The following day dancing was again continued, though with much less ceremony, and the 10th was the day appointed for a state slaughtering of cattle—one of the annual customs gone through at this season. This over, the king took his departure next day for a neighbouring abode of royalty. Commencing with the new year, the entries in the traveller's Journal, with some particulars of the above events, stand as follows :—

"*January 1st., 1874.*—Intensely hot, as yesterday was, and as they say it will be till the rain falls. Sent bullocks to fetch wood for making a scherm, having engaged John Jacobs and two Kafirs by the day. Rode over to Thomson's to dinner (two and a half miles) and lost myself amongst the kopjes. The fine hot day and the luxuriantly green country and rapidly-growing Indian corn make it seem more like June than New Year's Day to me. Petersen, Fairbairn, and Mandy went to Thomson's in cart, and we sat down to a most excellent dinner—roast and boiled mutton, potatoes, cabbages, and turnips, plum-pudding, and mince-pies. Such dinners as this and my Christmas dinner at Petersen's are worthy of notice, considering how few and far between they are. Pleasant evening just before and after sunset; moon nearly full.

"*January 2nd.*—Fine hot day; heat, however, by no means so oppressive as it has been for the last day or two, on account of a pleasant breeze. Unpacked the front-box of my waggon. King called, and asked for his bottle of brandy and some large shot. He afterwards sent a boy for the brandy, whom I accompanied back to the king's, and having given the brandy and shot, offered him six muskets I had been hoping all this time to sell him, and without any trouble got four fine elephants' teeth for them, about 10lbs. of ivory altogether.

"*January 3rd.*—Moonlight night—full moon, I think. Looked out early; the moon was still gorgeously bright, and surrounded by a halo of light in a violet sky, studded here and there also with a star. In the east was the deep red of approaching sunrise. Morning at first slightly overcast and tolerably cool, but the day soon became very hot, though tempered somewhat by the wind. Decided to have a new sail made for the waggon. Myers working at the old framework, patching it up. Having things out of the waggon, and also out of the tent (as I was rearranging the latter), I stayed about a good deal, not trusting John. A lot of cheeky 'majachas'[71] (warriors) about. Whilst one of them was selling me honey, a lot came in, and I saw one abstract a knob-kerry of rhinoceros horn from under the waggon, and throw it out of the scherm[72]. He then ran away, seeing himself detected, but did not go far, and afterwards came and stayed outside the scherm, asking for a 'tonso' (present). However, this must have been mere bravado, as he was too much on his guard to give me a chance of thrashing him, and when I removed a bush for him to come in, only came in a foot or two, and bolted when at length I approached him. I bought guinea-fowls' eggs, some tobacco, and a dancing-stick. The second of the two sheep bought for a cotton blanket and a shirt was killed

---

[71] *amaJaha*, Ndebele, 'strongly-built people'. DS

[72] These knob-kerries, which answer the purpose of a lifepreserver, are made of various kinds of wood or of rhinoceros horn, and carved according to the fancy of the maker. They are sometimes adorned with beads (see one of those in the woodcut), but the more ordinary form is that of a short stick with a single rounded knob at the end, to give it weight. The natives can throw them a great distance with marvellous accuracy, being often able to bring down a bird on the wing with one of them.

this morning. It is wonderful what a lump of fat the tail is. A miserable little famished boy, who, they say, was picked up in the veldt and belongs to the king, came into the scherm on being invited, and had food. He speaks by nodding his head. He is a pitiable object, and coughs. ... Wind rose high at night. Mutton and guinea-fowls' eggs for supper. There are plenty of 'majachas' here now. They are everlastingly dancing. This seems to be their whole drill.

"*January 4th.*—Cool cloudy morning; a drizzling rain. There are caterpillars here of very pretty varieties. Old well-known forms both of caterpillars and moths are reproduced in this country, with a change. The king sent me a caterpillar lately—green, with green moss-like tufts; a flesh-coloured stripe on each side; on the back a row of snow-white spots, circled with blue, and white spots also along the sides. A string of people came this morning from Inchlangin for the dance. Macloule called on me his arrival; and again in the evening, when he ask me for a blanket, saying he had lost a child through going with me, and had missed the time burying it. I sent him away till tomorrow. The day has been cloudy and cool, but fair and delightful.

"*January 5th.*—Hot day, and though there was a good deal of wind I felt the heat. Gave Macloule a cotton blanket. Myers and Hendrik working at my waggon sail. Took Hans, and went to king's. Dance going on, consisting of the men of two large kraals, forming a circle, 'marking time,' and waving sticks, whilst the king, with rhinoceros-horn knob-kerry, acted as bandmaster. There was also singing. Nina[73] requested me to stand up and join, which I did. Every now and then a man rushes out into the space in the middle, shaking his shield and brandishing his assegai, enacts his fighting, and shows how many he has killed, whilst loud shouts are raised on all sides. The usual dress consists of a head-dress of black feathers, and a bunch of monkeys' tails round the loins, with white frills of ox-tails on the arms, and (in the case of veterans I suppose) a long solitary feather to top all, and a piece of fur round the head. The king had on a broad-brimmed black felt hat, a huge bunch of monkeys' skins round his middle, and carried an Elcho sword bayonet (my present) and a rhinoceros-horn knob-kerry. When the dancing and singing was over, the men defiled past the king in companies, singing a monotonous but not unmusical chorus, which they accompanied by

---

[73] A sister of the king's.

rapping their shields with their sticks, producing a dull heavy sound. Strings of girls bore huge calabashes of beer, under the weight of which some of them staggered, to the kraal. For the most part they were magnificent specimens of shapely young Kafir Women A tall handsome girl, who has been sometimes begging at my waggon, was a looker-on, and presented a fine picture of a well-developed savage woman. She seemed fully aware of her own striking appearance. A lot of old Mosilikatze's wives sat watching.

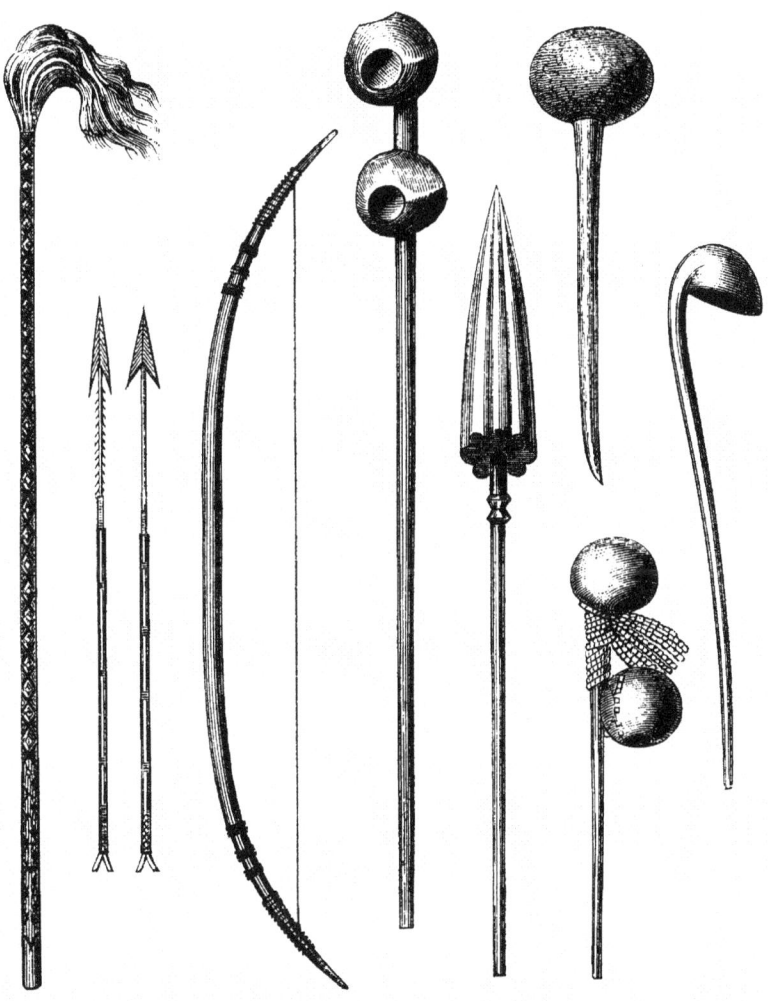

DANCING-STICK, BOW AND ARROWS, AND KNOB-KERRIES.

"There is a good deal of wind to-night, and the moon is obscured by dark gathering clouds. Tonight, after I left the king, I was standing beside a group of Kafirs cutting up the carcasses of two oxen just killed, when the king's dogs made a set at me. Afterwards the boys came to my waggon asking a tonso for calling them off. I suspect they set them on on purpose.

"*January 6th.*—Intensely hot, and though there are clouds, the rain still keeps off. Sent John with Wankee[74] to cut a tree for a disselboom, and he says the axe was taken from him on the pretext that they must not cut wood now, and that the axe would be returned. ... I asked if I could go shooting, and they say no, not till the dance is over.

"*January 7th.*—Sky overcast, but the heat is still intense. Crowds of people about, as yesterday; difficult to keep the scherm clear. Dancing going on at the kraal. Heat insufferable. The tent was a furnace, but at sundown there was a little thunder, and it was pleasant and cool. A beautiful mild looking rose-tinted sunset.

"*January 8th.*—Day of the Great Dance. Very heavy rain fell at sunrise. As rain fell, girls bathing in rain-holes. Things in tent got very wet, and it was late before I could come out and begin to dry them. The heat soon became great, but the sun kept being more or less obscured by clouds. I learnt it was the day of the Great Dance, and hurried the drying and locking up of my things, so as to be ready to go and see it. Some majachas came out, and had a row, and bruised one another near waggon.

"As soon as I had finished packing I joined the Thomsons, whose waggon had drawn up in front of Myers's store, where the dancing was to be. Meantime, Thomson says, they had been going through ceremonies at the kraal, where dancing was still going on, but very shortly they expected the king and people out. However, Thomson and I went to the kraal to see, and were well repaid. In the midst of a large circle formed by warriors, four wives of the king, dressed all alike, and modestly covered, were dancing, or rather slowly pacing. Each had a checked print over her shoulders, and a black skirt reaching low down. With them was a future wife, partially clad in gaily-coloured calicos, but without skirt. The wives,

---

[74] The title (Zanze or Hwange) of the leader of the Nanzwa people, who live around the Hwange district of north-west Zimbabwe. DS

Thomson says, are very nice women. As I went with him through the crowd, I could not help seeing what respect is shown him, and how all make way for him.

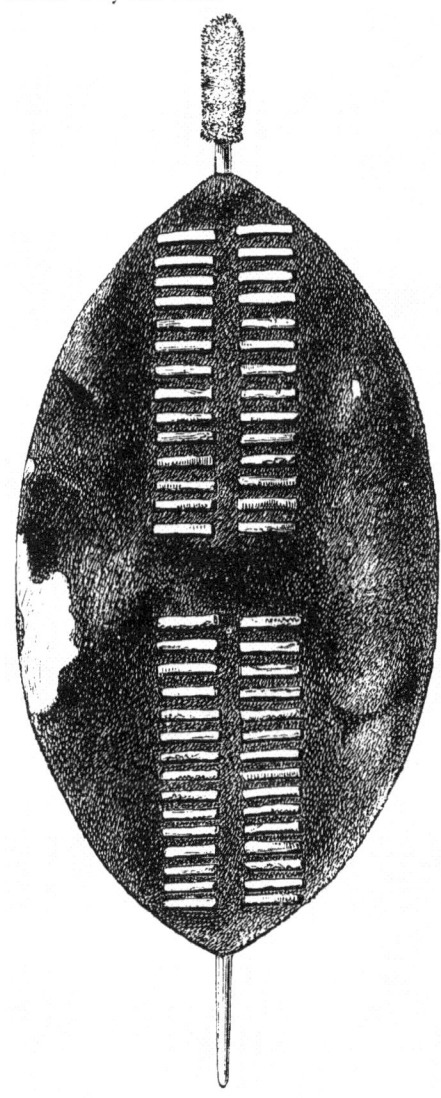

OX-HIDE SHIELD.

"Suddenly the royal sister appeared, and presented a most singular, not to say magnificent, appearance. It was something like the appearance of the *prima* at the opera, or the leading spirit in some gorgeous pantomime She is very stout, and tremendously *en bon point*, and her skin is of a coppery hue. She wore no dress, and the only covering above her waist was a number of gilded chains, some encircling her, some pendent. Round her arms were massive brazen bracelets. A blue and white freemason' apron appeared in front, and looked strangely anomalous there, though really not unbecoming. From her waist also there hung down behind a number of brilliantly-coloured woollen neck-wraps, red being the predominant colour. Under the apron was a sort of short black skirt, covering the thighs, made of wrought ox-hide. Her legs and feet were bare, but round her ankles were the circlets of bells, worn by the women to make a noise when they dance. Her head-dress was decidedly pretty—a small bouquet of artificial flowers in front, and amongst the hair, standing in all directions, feathers of bee-eaters' tails. A small circular ornament, fashioned out of red clay, was on back of her head. She put herself in posture for the dance, but did not move very much or energetically whilst keeping time; she suffered too much from adiposity. She held one of the large oval black and white ox-hide shields, surmounted by a jackal's tail, such as are carried by the warriors. The wives held long slender wands upright in their hands. The men, when they dance, usually carry a carved stick, with which motions are made, whilst it is generally held upright. The girls carry very pretty brooms, which they likewise raise and move about to time; but the girls' dances were yet to come.

"The dress of the soldiers is very striking, and suggestive of savage warfare. Over the shoulders, and continued into a sort of hood, which either surmounts the back of the head, or hangs loose behind the neck, is a large fabric of jet-black ostrich feathers. Around the forehead is a circlet of tawny fur, and a single long steel-coloured crane's feather rises above, giving a most artistic finish to the picture. Around the loins are a collection of monkey and cat skins, dangling in long strips, together with a number of tails, some of the latter nearly large enough for those of leopards, which hang in thick bunches nearly to the ground. Around each arm is a graceful, wavy tuft of white ox-tail hair, and some- times the same around the legs. Very little limbo is worn unless a strip or two—usually of blue selampore[75] or white calico, well worn and defaced—around the waist. The shield and assegais complete the picture[76]. If all were uniform in appearance the effect would be much heightened; unfortunately the dress is not *de rigueur*. Some omit the fur round the forehead; some both fur and feather; and some of those in command have shabby shirts or hats on, contrasting badly with fine warrior costume of the majority. The only military evolution gone through is marching past kraals, or what we should call companies, the men singing, dancing, and making some most unearthly and awe-inspiring noises the while. One sound is produced gutturally, and resembles the low growl of a wild animal. Another is made by striking the shields—a sound resembling distant thunder. Then they have a way of whistling, not unlike the cat-calls of a London theatre. During their dances a warrior rushes out into the middle of the circle from time to time, and goes through the pantomime of his late exploits, brandishing spear and shield, and rushing wildly about. He denotes, by repeated thrusts, the number of people he has slain, whilst the surrounding warriors shout loudly.

---

[75] Indian calico. DS

[76] The woodcut on the succeeding page illustrates a variety of different assegais. The heads of these weapons are wrought by the natives themselves, and fastened to the shafts by strips of raw hide, which shrink in the drying, and become as hard as a band of iron. The length of the shaft is usually from three to four feet.

"Standing about are many pretty girls in most fantastic head-dresses, worn only on special occasions, and highly prized. Predominant is the pink bead, appropriated by the royal family. A small group of waggon-drivers, either those who have come up here with white men, or who belong to the doctor's party, whose waggons accompany the king in all his movements, are dressed to the height of fashion—as near as they can manage it—in European dress, for which the stores of the place have been ransacked, and high prices paid, no matter at what sacrifice. One has a chimney-pot. These fellows are usually the greatest scamps in the country—idle, vain, insolent, and vicious. The king is dressed much like his warriors, and looks himself. He is a fine-looking and has an agreeable expression and a ready smile. He is one of the darkest-complexioned people I have seen belonging to this nation.

"Now Thomson tells me we must make haste and return to the waggon, as the soldiers are beginning to march out, and they are all going outside, accompanied by the king and his court. We return, and the troops march out and take up position in a huge, dense circle outside the kraal. There may be three or even five thousand of them, and perhaps ten thousand people in all."[77]

"*January 9th.*—Hot day; short heavy in the afternoon. Dancing at the kraal—second day (or was Wednesday also a day? If so, this is the third). Different parties dancing; majachas and girls separately, though in some cases girls are introduced into the majachas' dance. King had waggon taken out by Kafirs. Selous[78] looked at my guns. Rain came on, and he sat in my tent. He tells me how he was once lost between Bamangwato and Tati for four days. He had had a cup of coffee, and gone out hunting. That night he slept in the veldt; it was July, and the nights were very cold. He had only a shirt and trousers on, and had no matches. He used his three cartridges in trying to make a fire. The second and third days he still wandered. I think it was the end of the second day that he lost his horse. The evening of the fourth day he came to Palatswe water, and got milk of a Kafir. He walked back next day to his waggon at Tchangani pool—he thinks about twenty miles. It was on the evening of

---

[77] Here the day's entry ends abruptly, with only a few brief notes intended for the writer's future guidance, and unavailable for another's use.

[78] This gentleman, Mr. F. C. Selous, had already been out some time hunting in South Africa, and was subsequently again met with by Frank Oates near the Victoria Falls. [The noted hunter and explorer Frederick Selous. DS]

the third day he reached a hill, by moonlight, whence he saw other hills he knew. Started before daybreak, and that night got the milk. He thinks he could have gone another day without food or water. He had nothing whatever, between the coffee, at starting, and the milk. He carried his gun, perspired profusely, and suffered much from cold at nights. He experienced a difficulty in swallowing.

"A letter from Mandy, at Inyati, to-day, states that he saw a crocodile there the other day, which got hold of his dog, and pursued himself in his bathing hole. It was ten or twelve feet long, he says.

"Dancing in little parties going on all day; the girls very lively in their dance. Bought a goat for about three quarters of a pound of beads.

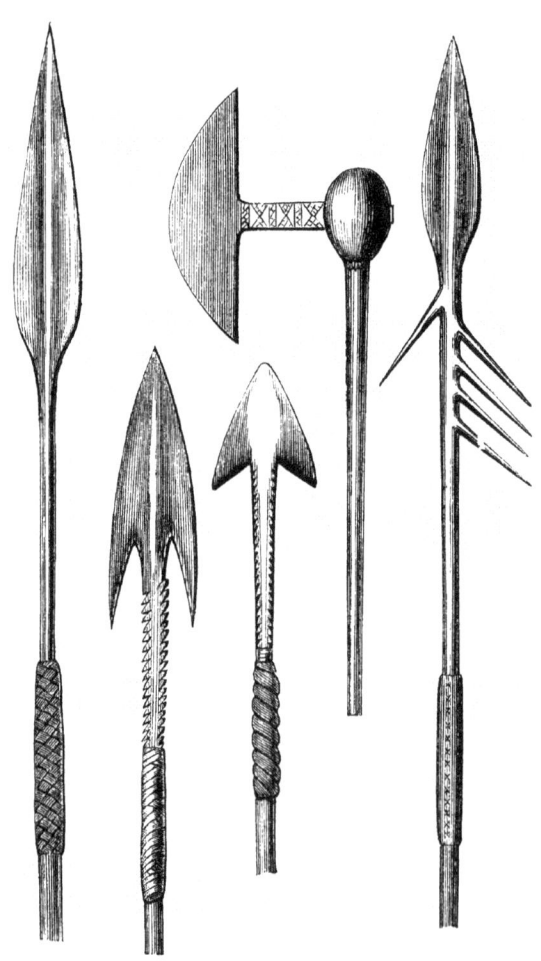

ASSEGAI-HEADS AND BATTLE-AXE.

"*January 10th.*—Very cloudy day, inclined to rain. Went up to kraal, where slaughtering was going on. I had heard nothing of it, but the number of bullocks slaughtered this year must have been next to nothing compared with former years. I saw a dozen or twenty down, or being assegaied. The bullocks are driven together, one out of the number being intended for slaughter. The opportunity is watched for to hurl the assegai, which sometimes remains in the ox, who runs some distance before he falls, bleeding at the nostrils, and soon dies. They are stabbed in the region of the heart and lungs. The first thrust is often not successful, as it is not easy to hit the victim in the right place when he is in a state of excitement. I went to see the king, who was looking very sulky. There is no dancing to-day. It appears the king is very angry at the fighting of yesterday."

"*January 11th.*—Heavy rain very early; a little bright sunshine about breakfast-time, when I partially dried the things that had got wet in the tent, causing me considerable discomfort. It soon came on to rain again, however, and rained more or less during the day. I was to have taken my things out of Myers's store and packed the waggon, but the rain prevented me. In the morning I heard the king was inspanning to go to some neighbouring abode of royalty, and hurried to take him his horse After handing it over to him, and being told to give it in charge of Petersen, I asked him if he would buy a saddle and bridle, to which he replied, these were always supposed to go with the horse, the saddle being part of its back. However, I hope he won't insist on this any more, and, indeed, I may away without seeing him again, unless I do so voluntarily. Piet, who interpreted for me, told that the king is very angry about the disturbance and will probably kill a number of the people, and for this they think he is going away in such a hurry, There were twelve black, or nearly black, bullocks in the royal waggon, and, when it started, the throne was carried—as it always has to be done—on a boy's head. It is a straight-backed, substantial, and extremely plain, green chair, with red daubs on it. Over the back and seat is stretched a piece of lion- skin. The dogs rushed off with the waggon, the second waggon started, in the back of which I could see a lot of meat and two young lambs or kids trying to keep their pins amongst the miscellaneous cargo inside; the majachas started, and the royal procession was on its way. Busy a good deal in Myers's store. Unpacked and packed boxes there, and watched the rain. Terrible soaking wet evening and night. I managed, however, to keep dry in bed."

From this time for some days the weather continued so persistently and miserably wet, that it seemed out of all question to think of commencing the return journey to Tati, which the traveller was now preparing to undertake. The heat, at the same time, was also so intense that any exertion was laborious, and even the occupation of writing was a task. About the 18th, however, there was some improvement, and two days after this he was ready for a start, when the dispute with one of his servants above referred to necessitated his seeking a fresh interview with Lobengula, whom he followed to his present quarters, but a few miles off, on the evening of the 20th. This dispute arose from Frank Oates's dismissal of the Kafir driver Dick, who had come up with him from Natal; the latter maintaining his right to retain the services of the young lad Jacob, whom he had originally brought with him for engagement in Pietermaritzburg, and who still accompanied the party. The two appeared to bear no relationship to each other, and Frank Oates would have been glad to keep Jacob in his service, but the latter seemed afraid to come, and it was agreed to refer the question to the king. The Journal of this time continues:—

"*January 20th.*—Fine, bright, windy morning; a few clouds in the sky. Finished what was left to be done to the waggon, and was going to trek when Jacob came and claimed his wages, and I decided to go away to the king's to-night, and thence start on my journey. A Kafir woman has also claimed Jacob as her son. Though Jacob asked for his wages and said he did not wish to leave Dick, he half admitted directly that it was only his fear of Dick that made him say so, and that he really wished to go with me. After the waggon was loaded, I waited some time for Jacob's return, he having gone with his would-be mother to the king's. He did not come back, and I inspanned for the king's. After about ten minutes' delay in getting off—bullocks and bad trek-gear—started fairly about half-past five, and in about an hour and forty got to where the king is, meeting Jacob with the woman going to Gubuleweyo. Jacob turned back with me. The king has said the woman is not to claim him. It seems she gave Jacob some locusts and milk when he was hungry, for he and Dick have fared badly of late. She then professed to see a likeness in him to her lost child, taken in the war, and he did not deny it, and afterwards she insisted on keeping him. Jacob still says he wants to go with me, but is afraid of Dick, and also wishes for his wages, as Dick urges him to get them, though he knows Dick will appropriate them. He will let it be arranged before the king, he says. The sun set as I trekked, and the peculiar aloe-like trees of this country had a fine effect against the glowing sky. I should say this trek is four and a half or five miles pretty direct. The last two days have been fine drying days, but still there are some very soft places in the road. Supped with Fairbairn on some excellent beef, and had a long chat with him. Cool, starlight night, with heavy dew."

"*January 22nd.*—Fine hot day, but with slight clouds, and at night a heavy shower. Fairbairn had a row in trading with the king, who had chaffed him a good deal last night. A large quantity of ivory had come in (Fairbairn was here by the king's express desire, to trade), and a small tooth had been put down before him. He had made his offer for it, which did not satisfy the king. Fairbairn said, 'It is a small tooth.' 'Did you ever shoot as large a one?' asked the king. This is considered a poser. Then a hot argument ensued between Fairbairn and the king, through John, the king maintaining that Fairbairn would show unequivocal signs of fear at the sight of an elephant. Fairbairn said white men were not afraid of them; whereupon the king cited, H—, a big man, who had not even shot a little calf; W—'Where are the elephants *he* shot?' Many white men had said the same as Fairbairn, and where were the elephants they had killed? Then Fairbairn referred to Selous, a small man; he not been afraid, he said. 'Would he tell if he had shown signs of fear, or were you there to see?' asked the king. Then the king told Fairbairn that he was getting rich and did not want his trade. Fairbairn got angry, and the result was that this morning he had a row. The king sent some large decayed teeth, which Fairbairn bought, and then some other teeth, which he could not buy, and which were sent to Gubuleweyo and sold; but in the meantime the king had offered Fairbairn two small teeth for a double-barrelled gun, less than cost price, and Fairbairn had left the king in disgust.

"Went to the king's kraal with John, and greeted the king, who was lying in his waggon, but as, after greeting us in return, he took no further notice of us and remained lying, I went away and had a nap in my waggon. Fairbairn afterwards had tiffin with me, and then we went together to the king, but he was still in his waggon—if not asleep, lying invisible; put out, I think, about Fairbairn. We waited long outside the kraal, and at length, near sundown, an induna came in white man's clothing, and with a shield, wearing feathers on his head hanging under his hat, and accompanied by warriors. He, to call the king, began shouting out compliments in a loud voice, amongst which the words 'Mosilikatze' and 'Incose'[79] (king), were frequently repeated, and a request made that

---

[79] *iNkosi*, Ndebele, 'king'. DS

the king would treat him kindly. This referred to beer and beef, which of course he would get. At last he finished, and went away unnoticed by the king, who, however, soon came out, and Fairbairn, John, and I, went to him, Dick and Jacob following. It was so late that we did little.

"Had supper on Australian meat in Fairbairn's waggon. Rain came on, and I heard showers during he night. When we left the king, he chaffed John, and said he looked weak, as if he was hungry. Last night John had asked for meat, and he said he had no beef and his sheep were poor. He seems really not to be killing oxen at present. Fairbairn has told Nina that we are eating tinned fish. Fish is held in utter abomination by these people, and Nina said her brother ought not to let us eat it. Fairbairn says they used, when they wanted meat, to rig a dummy fishing-rod, and march off with it, taking care to pass in sight of the king, and the moment he suspected fishing, he would send them a large piece of meat.

"One sees all shades of colour in these people. Makalakas are much darker as a rule than the Matabele, who are usually coppery red or sometimes yellow. The king, however, is black, and, I believe, about as black as any of his race, and far more so than most. He deserves his epithet of 'black king'. The dogs are a great source of fear at present. They are constantly attacking people, and lately half, if not altogether, killed an induna. Fairbairn says the king showed him his own trousers torn the other day, as proof that even their master was not exempt."

"*January 23rd.*—Wretched rainy and gusty morning. Nina in Fairbairn's waggon, as she was also a good deal yesterday. She is very fond of him, as of other white men; and is said to wish to marry a certain white trader here, who has left for a time—hoping, I believe, that she may be married when he returns. She can't marry till the king takes his wife from whom the future king is to be born. His present wives have nothing to do with it.

"John Lee's waggon arrived to day, to my great pleasure. I had just returned from visiting the king, whom John and I had found standing at the entrance of his kraal in a Mackintosh coat. Dick and Jacob joined us, and the case of Jacob was discussed, Dick also urging the hardship of his own dismissal, in which the king seems partly to agree, and says it would be better not to leave him in *his* country, but where we can try the case with our own laws. At length the king went to his hut, saying this case would take a long time, and it was not a day to discuss it. Certainly the weather was against a law-suit being carried on in the open air. In the evening I went again to the king. Lee was sitting on the front-box of his waggon, and went over my case with him, and thus I got a decision quickly. The king said his decision had been that I was to take Dick *and* Jacob, but I had refused to do this, so now I must pay the wages of the boy, as he considered Jacob, having been brought by Dick, was under his protection. I sent for them, and paid the money to the king, who promised to keep it for Jacob as far as he could, though he said if they left country he must then give it up. Supper again with Fairbairn."

"*January 24th.*—More promising morning, though cloudy and showery. Fairbairn, Lee, and I, to the king. Fairbairn does a good trade with him after the row. Nina and her friends were eating a large dish of excellent vegetable marrows. The smoke got into my eyes, and Banyai kindly motioned me across the hut. John Lee killed a lung-sick heifer of the king's, and opened her chest with a saw, taking out the liquid which accumulates in the cavity of the lungs during the sickness. With this I helped him to drench some young cattle of the king's. Each has about a small beakerful. Lee says he never lost one that he drenched in this way."

"*January 25th.*—Lovely morning. Rose and dressed leisurely. The heat soon became intense, and of that moist character that seems to make it far worse to bear. Felt quite prostrated by it. The wife of Lee's boy, who tried to leave him, and is now undergoing punishment after being tried before the king, came crying to my waggon. Lee drove her away. It appears that the boy had to pay Lee £6, which the girl owed the latter, before he could have her, both being in Lee's service, as well as the father-n-law, mother, and sister of the boy. The boy told Lee he had paid the money to the king. This was a lie, so Lee demanded the money of the king in the presence of the boy. Thus the offence was shown to be against the king, and Lee told the king it was for him to punish it. two indunas present seized the boy, and he was half throttled, and much knocked about. They would have killed him there and then, had it been Lee's wish. The king said, 'Is he to be thrown out?' which means put to death. Lee, however, said he should be satisfied by the boy being tied up, which was done. ... Went with Lee to the king's afterwards. More drenching was going on. I saw the boy tied up; he could neither sit nor stand, but squatted on the ground, his arms nearly on the full stretch, fastened on either side to one of the poles that support the large wooden on which meat is piled. When the sun set Lee was told, if he did not give the word to have the boy taken away, he would rot where he was. The king and the indunas then chaffed the poor wretch as, Lee having consented, he was cut down. He was told that he had been kicking Mosilikatze's bones.

"The scene, with the king sitting on his front-box, would make a picture: the setting sun; the dark green trees beyond the kraal, and the green walls of the newly-erected kraal; the yellow beehive-like huts; the yellowish trodden grass in the space; the herds of goats and sheep, with lambs and kids, and pack of dogs, crowding round the king's waggon; the group of natives, some all but naked, some adorned with feathers, some with a single article of European dress, as a hat, crouching on their haunches, forming the court of the black king; tusks of ivory lying about. To complete the picture, a white trader or two should be introduced, not above crouching before his sable majesty, who sits there in his broad-brimmed black felt hat, pipe in mouth (a small briar-root, worth perhaps 2d. at home), cotton shirt not over clean, unbraced baggy trousers, and large clumsy shoes, a benignant smile generally on his black face."

The day after this the king took his departure for another place, John Lee left for Mr. Thomson's, and Frank Oates started back to Tati.

MUSICAL INSTRUMENT.

CHAPTER VI

*Return to Tati—Changed aspect of the country—Constant delays—
The Mashonas—At Manyami's again—John Lee's—Letter home—
The Inkwesi—Wild fruit—A hornbill's nest—The Ramaqueban
Rivers—Graves of Englishmen—White Ants—Bushman remains—
The Tati reached.*

FRANK OATES'S plan on leaving Gubuleweyo was to return slowly, by way of Tati, to Bamangwato to prepare himself with a fresh outfit of goods and other necessaries for a renewed attempt to reach the Zambesi early in the year; unless on his arrival there he should find letters which required his return to England. As it was yet too soon to think of making at once for the Zambesi, he took his time upon the road to Tati, not arriving there till near the end of February. He stopped to hunt some time upon the Ramaqueban, and, the whole journey, progress was inevitably slow, owing to the heavy state of the country from the recent rains. The waggon was constantly sticking, and delays were endless. The route taken was the same as that by which he had come to Gubuleweyo, but the country was now rendered so much more attractive with the advancing season, that some extracts may be given from the Journal.

Leaving the neighbourhood of Gubuleweyo, as already mentioned, on January 26th, he reached Kumala River the following day, and on the 28th again pushed forward towards the Shashani, where he arrived after many stoppages two days later, John Lee's farm being reached early on the morning of the 1st of February. For three days before his arrival at John Lee's, the Journal reads as follows, the first extract finding him at a point in the road still a few miles from the Shashani, where his waggon had sunk deep the night before, necessitating a halt :—

"*January 29th*.—During the night some rain fell; the morning was cloudy, but fine. Got the waggon clear with some difficulty, and started about noon, but it stuck again after going a few yards, the dissel-boom breaking, which was shortened and used again, causing a long delay. ... At length we started fairly about 5.40pm. The sun was getting low, and, as we went through some really beautiful scenery, he set, and the sunset scene was a lovely one. I can now fancy that South Africa may have much fine scenery, and I wish I could see the Zambesi. In the foreground was undulating and broken ground, covered with long grass, showing in some places a silvery white colour, in others a yellow, and in others a green one. Beyond, the deep green of the trees—not uniform in height and growth, but reminding one in their graceful diversity of hedgerow trees or those of copses at home—rose distinct against the deep violet kopjes on the horizon and the sunset sky. The upper part of the sky was blue, with large lilac clouds; lower down, the blue was streaked with pale yellow, and this again, as it approached the kopjes, became golden streaked with lilac. We trekked on well through the changing light, for it never became dark, and, ere the sunset hues had faded from the sky, the moon was shedding a clear light over the romantic scene. Fireflies were flitting, and I felt the morning trek, when we entered Pretoria, come back forcibly to my mind. That was then to me a wonderful change, from high veldt to bush veldt, and the time of seeing it—in the weird light of early morning—added to the charm. The road now, as then, was very rough and steep, over stones, up hill and down; and at about 8pm we crossed a steep-banked river. The water and the bank on which we landed was so steep, that the oxen, the moment before they scrambled up, were up to their breasts in water, but we did it in gallant style.

"On we went, and at last were rising through what in Rocky Mountain phraseology would be called a 'park.' The word is an appropriate one, and I know no other that would describe this lovely spot, reminding me of similar scenes in the Rocky Mountains. The ground was open and park-like, with a fine sward and a few isolated trees, whilst all around—forming a complete amphitheatre—rose rugged kopjes in the distance. The moon shed a bright light on the whole. Suddenly, smash went the dissel-boom, away went the oxen with it, down went John most ludicrously on to the ground from the front-board, and the waggon came to a standstill. The great awkward tree, stuck in by Wankee[80] and John when we first came to grief, had at last become useless, and now we set about making ourselves comfortable for the night, intending to cut a fresh dissel-boom in the morning. It was about 8.20 when this ludicrous breakdown happened, and it is long that I have so thoroughly enjoyed a laugh as I did then at John's expense. I was not sorry that we were stopping here, and, as I drank in the scene with delight, those parks in

---

[80]A native temporarily engaged at Gubuleweyo.

the mountains of the Far West were present to my mind, and I felt happy, scarcely knowing why. The part of the country we have passed through is called the 'neck.' To-night I heard the strange melancholy baying of wild dogs—an animal I have never seen."

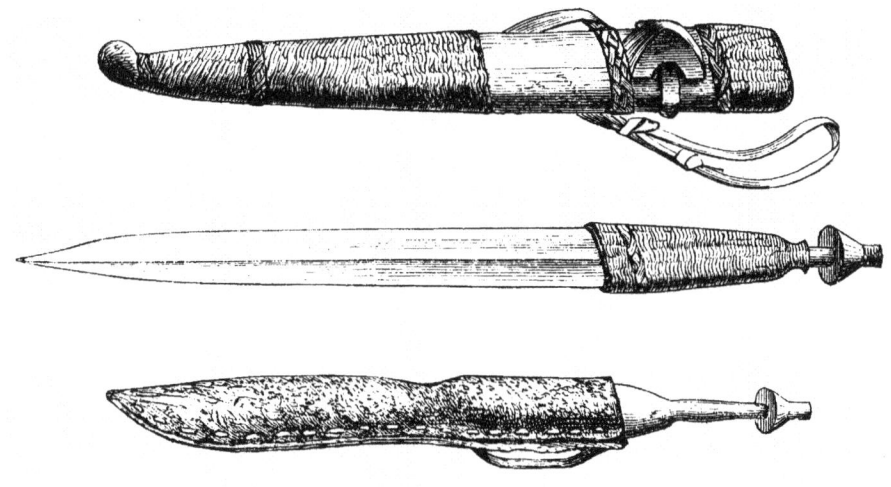

NATIVE HUNTING-KNIVES.

"*January 30th.*—My pleasure in the place where we are outspanned was put an end to this morning by a crowd of noisy forward Matabele from a kraal a little distance off amongst the kopjes on our right. My men had sent early, and beer and large quantities of milk were brought. There were a few slaves here too, quite different in appearance and bearing from their conquerors. They are quiet and humble in demeanour, and profusely ornamented, where they can afford it, with brass wire[81] in rings round the wrists, of what I have been told is Portuguese or native workmanship, though I think it may be brought up by our own traders. Blue cut beads, too, and skins are much worn. These original inhabitants, Mashonas I think, are far more in keeping with the scene, to my mind, than their supplanters.

---

[81] Brass wire is considerably used by the natives of South Africa for purposes of ornamentation. Above are represented two hunting-knives, the upper one of which has the sheath and handle (which are of wood) handsomely adorned with fine twisted brass wire. The sheath of the lower knife is of raw hide strongly sewn together.

"Wankee cut a dissel-boom, and we inspanned about 2.15pm First we went uphill, and then began to descend through a tolerably open grass country, with trees about as far apart as one sees them in an orchard. The country we passed through is extremely pretty—grass long, trees graceful and varied, broken crags, with kopjes all round. Through it we descended to the Shashani, which is in a valley, and we must have crossed it say about 3pm. We then soon crossed a spruit, and after this in a heavy part of the road, where the ruts had been worn into holes, we stuck. This would be about 3.40pm. We made vain efforts to get out, let the oxen feed a little, and again tried, and tried in vain. The front oxen, and indeed all the oxen, were very stupid, but I blame the driver, and, though it was a fine moonlight night, he would try no more till next morning."

"*January 31st.*—Fine hot day. Stupidity again in Wankee. He first tried to pull the waggon back and then forward, and finally raised it and put stones under it, as ought to have been done last night, for it was taken out at once when this was tried. Two girls from the kraal we passed yesterday came to the waggon *en route* for Manyami's. They were overtaken by us on the road afterwards, and went some distance in the waggon, and again came to the waggon at Manyami's. Two little looking-glasses delighted them beyond measure, and each little gift caused an exclamation of delight and gratitude, 'O Bossa!' They were perfectly unsophisticated; one I thought pretty. They sang, evidently studying the most fascinating smiles whilst looking into the mirrors. After we moved I had the oxen unyoked to feed for a short time, and we started fairly at noon. The country was again extremely pretty and well wooded, the road winding like a labyrinth amongst the picturesque kopjes. We crossed several spruits, some of them awkward ones, and at one had a good deal of trouble, but it had a good bottom, and we pulled through. We reached Manyami's and outspanned on high ground under an abruptly-rising kopje about 3pm.

"Here old Manyami came to see me, and greeted me with a small pot of beer, begging a 'limbo' for his wife. I gave him a cup of coffee in return, and about the value of the beer in limbo, as I am not disposed to be over generous. I bought some calabash pumpkins, which I found afterwards were like excellent vegetable marrows when boiled; also a water-melon, the second I have bought within the last day or two. They are in excellent condition now, and very refreshing. I also bought some milk, which my boys like.

"Vincent came up on his way to Mungwato with a waggon and sixteen oxen, returning from Gubuleweyo, where he had been with a load, His waggon went on, and he remained behind to help me. I find him an excellent driver and a very energetic fellow, and I believe he would be very glad to go with me, as he is tired of trading under Hogg. However, he must go on now.

"The sun was getting low as we inspanned. We soon came to a very bad place—a huge pit in fact—where the road had been, to avoid which we had to go through a very soft piece of ground into which the waggon sank deep, and I thought it was a case of a regular stick, but Vincent got me out of this well, and showed his great superiority as a driver. We got over some bad places after this, but at length got into a heavy rut, the wheels on the off side of the waggon being deep in it, whilst those on the other side were high on firm ground. It looked like a serious case, and the sun set on our efforts. The dissel-boom was pulled out twice, but at length so firmly locked with chains, and the wheels raised so effectually with stones placed under them, that, when Vincent left his work, which he had been going at like the fine energetic fellow he is, and we sat down for a moment to drink a cup of coffee, the waggon looked like getting off. This it did without difficulty, and we started again about 10pm. We had one more stick afterwards in a deep rut, but Vincent levelled the ground in a few minutes, and we were off again, and finally crossed Mangwe drift without a mishap. This was the greatest feat of all. The river was full of water, the men were nearly up to their armpits (one crossed clinging to 'Blackberg's' tail), but we went through it without any delay or trouble, and I was indeed thankful that our dissel-boom was chained. After this we trekked a short distance along a good road to John Lee's. Here were Dawson's[82] two waggons sent up by Cruickshank, and Vincent's waggon sent by Hogg. Skinner's[83] waggon was some little way off. Skinner and Dawson were waiting for the river to go down. We outspanned about 1.30am, and had supper."

---

[82] James Dawson, a Scots trader and agent of James Cruickshank. Dawson traded at Bulawayo until August 1893. After the defeat of the Ndebele, he was one of the party which pursued Lobengula across the Shangani River, and discovered and buried the bodies of Allan Wilson's Shangani Patrol; marrying, in 1898, Wilson's fiancée. Dawson committed suicide in Scotland in 1921. DS

[83] Probably Peter Skinner, a Scots trader based at Shoshong, who died in 1875. DS

At this point Frank Oates remained a few days, hoping for some improvement in the weather. Soon after his arrival he wrote home as follows :—

"MR. JOHN LEE'S, MANGWE,
"MATABELE COUNTRY.
"*February 1st, 1874.*

"I take the opportunity of a waggon going to Bamangwato, to send a few lines to let you know how I am getting on. I wrote last to you from Mr. Thomson's at Hope Fountain. Since then I have been detained at Gubuleweyo, the King's Town, first by bad weather, and then, as the time of the grand dance of the year was approaching, I waited to see it. The people come from all the neighbouring kraals, and dance and feast for two or three days. It is the feast of the first-fruits of the season, and Mr. Thomson advised me to stay for it. After this, fearful rain again delayed me, and then I had some trouble with my men, and dismissed two, and had to have the case of a third tried before the king. At last, last Monday, I got under weigh once more, with a new waterproof tent on my waggon. The journey here is about three days under ordinary circumstances, but it took me six, in the present heavy state of the country and badness of the river drifts. I had many sticks in the mud and breakages of my dissel-boom. Last night I arrived here, and to-day is Sunday. The man to whom I am going to give this letter drove my waggon for the last eleven miles. He overtook me on the road, and let his own empty waggon go on. We were about six hours in accomplishing the distance, including delays, but, thanks to his timely help, I pulled through. The last river we had to cross, the Mangwe, was so swollen that the water was up to the men's chests, and looked as if it was coming into the waggon. The men who were not in the waggon had to catch hold of the oxen's tails or struggle through the stream as well as they could. It would have been very unpleasant, especially with bad helpless drivers, to have broken my dissel-boom in the middle of the river, and I felt very glad when we safely landed on the bank.

"From here I intend travelling leisurely to Mungwato, where I hope to find letters. When I get there I shall decide whether or not to make another attempt on the Victoria Falls. By leaving Mungwato about April, I should have the fine season before me, and could probably reach the Falls and return to Mungwato in the space of three months The worst of this country, however, is that movements here are so slow and dependent on the caprice of natives, and one is too much cut off from the world. Yet I believe the Zambesi would repay one for much sacrifice of time and patience. It is impossible, I am now convinced, to get on with Kafirs and Hottentots without severity. Kindness is thrown away upon them, and makes them worse than they are. I believe I shall have to give the latter method up altogether, and resort to castigation, which is an alternative I don't like. They are, almost to a man, dishonest, lazy, and impudent.

"The scenery about here *is* pretty I admit, especially at this time of year. Some of my moonlight treks between the King's and this place were very delightful, and wakened a little enthusiasm and thoughts of former days, such as the usual dull uniformity of South African scenery fails to elicit. The ground is broken up into rugged crags, piled one upon another in such a manner that you can't help wondering how the mischief they ever got there. The veldt is covered with long grass, like English mowing grass. The trees are, for the most part, like English woodland trees, but less in size; in some places forming a thick bush, in others scattered over the greensward like English timber. Occasionally a remarkable tree occurs of unfamiliar aspect, but this is quite the exception. The kopjes are numerous; some, merely small piles of huge stones, with trees springing from the interstices; others, hills of respectable size, built up of crags, and sometimes shutting in the horizon on every side. Here and there a stream runs through its deep stony bed in a deep valley, and then comes the tug of war, and the moonlight scenery is forgotten, whilst one's lungs are exerted yelling to the oxen, calling each by his uncouth name.

"My dogs always ride with me in my bed. One of them is a most faithful friend and agreeable companion to me. I should miss them very much. I had to sell my pony to the king, to keep in his good books, but was sorry to do it, although he may die now any time of horse-sickness. If he lives he is a valuable animal, and henceforth 'salted.' Birds are few here, and, for the most part, not striking in appearance. The same applies to flowers.

"Old John Lee's voice is droning away about some oxen, and the family circle surrounds me, as I write this letter. Lee wants to borrow my waggon for two months to send for some meal, and to do his best to make me comfortable here in the meantime, but I have made a mental vow not to let myself be talked into the arrangement. ... I shall be very glad to hear recent news of how all are at home.

"*P.S.*— ... I am adding this P.S. in the waggon, but I miss John Lee's drone, which I find helps me write. He discoursed on locusts to-night. As he says, Kafirs eat them, horses, sheep, and all sorts of game eat them, lions eat them, wolves eat them, birds eat them—they *must* be very nice; only white men and vultures don't eat them. I believe but for locusts an immense number of people would have died of famine last year at Mungwato."

It was the 6th of February when Frank Oates left Lee's, and the 9th when he reached the Inkwesi River. The country round Lee's farm is of a somewhat striking character, and, though much healthier than most of the surrounding district, is not wholly free from the annoyances elsewhere occasioned by the summer rains. "The scenery here," writes Frank Oates, "with the swollen current of the river and huge magnificent boulders, is as fine in its way as any one would wish to see. The gardens, however, which have suffered terribly from drought, are now suffering equally from the wet. They require both irrigation for the dry, and drainage for the rainy, season." The way in which Lee lived with his family round him, and the sort of relationship existing between them, afforded an odd example of a Dutchman's life in the interior. "It reminds one," says the traveller, "of feudal times: old Lee, the lord; his brother, a wretched serf; his father-in-law, not much better; all his poor relations living about in little huts round his big house."

Amongst the waggons stationed at John Lee's during Frank Oates's stay there was that of Smith, the Dutchman, whom he had formerly met on his way up country, near the Impakwe River. Smith was now starting on a hunting trip towards the Tati, and the two again agreed to travel together. Before leaving Frank Oates engaged John Lee's brother, Karl, to accompany him as driver to Bamangwato.

The country was still heavy, though somewhat improved by the last few days of comparatively dry weather. A few miles before reaching the Inkwesi, the road lay through bush veldt and corn-fields, with kopjes interspersed at intervals. "The corn-fields are close to the road," writes Frank Oates, "and a large fence renders the road so narrow that it is a difficult matter to drive a waggon. Some of my own loose oxen crossed a corn-field, and of course a row was made. The Hottentot, Klaas, from Lee's, had to give a coat, and some lead and powder, because when he stuck his oxen trampled the corn whilst in the yoke, the road being altogether hemmed in by the corn-fields. Karl says he will get the extortionate payment refunded when John Lee knows. This is the second crop of Indian corn, the former one having been destroyed by locusts. We passed the Hottentot during this trek; he had had to kill one of his best oxen, his driver having broken the ox's leg by throwing a stone. Here we come," continues the writer, "to the last kraal, about two miles from the Inkwesi, amongst the kopjes. There is a fine sugar-loaf-shaped kopje, craggy and tree-covered to the top, and very steep. I wish I had time to try the ascent; there must be a glorious view from it. The colours on the stones from lichens are most beautiful, yellow predominating. The Kafirs were most impudent and troublesome. The headman, a young fellow in European clothes, is a good-looking and well-behaved fellow. He sat on my front-box; our object is to get boys from him. There were five men killed by the king, at Lee's, Karl says, for refusing to come to live here; they said it was only fit for monkeys. Near here was old Makobi's kraal, where all were massacred for deceiving the king, after owning allegiance to him. A large quantity of milk was brought to us for sale. Heavy showers came on, but the night was fine, clear, and starlight. Where we passed Klaas, an elephant had passed during the night. They followed his spoor, but lost it. Smith shot a cow-elephant near here a year or two ago, and they say a surly toothless bull-elephant lives about here now. The kopje looked very pretty at night when all was quiet, and its dark sugar-loaf form loomed up close to us against the starry sky."

Next day (February 9th), on reaching the Inkwesi, Frank Oates chanced to be alone, Smith having gone on in advance, in company with the Hottentot above referred to. "After Karl had been to the local kraal about boys," writes the traveller that day, "we inspanned at 10.30am, and trekked about an hour, when we came to the drift of the Inkwesi. The induna rode on my front-box. Some of the road was rough; scenery pretty. Had to chop down part of a tree against which we were running. We found Smith had crossed, and I sent in boys to try the depth, and, though it was deep, I resolved to push forward, for fear of rain and a swollen current. In some places it was over a man's middle. We stuck in the river; had many attempts to get out, but without success. Two small oxen got half drowned, and we outspanned them and inspanned two large ones. The boy who was leading the front oxen let go the strap he held them by, and we had a great deal of trouble. At last we off-loaded a large part of our cargo, sending it over on the boys' backs. I worked hard; so did Karl. I then undressed and left the waggon before they tried to get it on again. Old Smith now came up to us, in the unadorned garb of nature, and mounted the front-box. (He thrashed a young nigger for laughing at his appearance.) They got the waggon out this time, but some of had to swim. Very little water got inside, and we loaded up again, and at sundown inspanned to go a few yards to where Smith and Klaas encamped. At night we all had supper together, Smith contributing some excellent 'stamped corn'. This is a capital dish. The corn is first crushed, then boiled, and, when this is over, salt and butter or fat stirred up with it. It is something like stiff rice-pudding."

AFRICAN GREY HORNBILL.—*Tockus nasutus.*

Advancing together the following morning, the three stopped for a day or two's hunting a few further on, beyond the river. Here buffalo and blue wildebeest were met with, and the spoor of ostriches was seen. From a fine rocky plateau in the neighbourhood a good survey of the surrounding district was obtained. "Looking to the south-west," writes the traveller, " we saw the conical range of the Tati hills, between which and ourselves lay a fine green bush-covered plain, through which flow the Impakwe and Ramaqueban Rivers. This plain extends far to the west and north, but to the north-east is again broken by kopjes in the direction of the Mangwe, whilst the fine craggy hills of the Inkwesi rise nearer in the same direction." Some delicious fruits, not unlike greengages, known by the natives as "marula,"[84] were picked up about here on the march. Between skin and the large stone in the centre of each was a sweet liquid with scarcely any pulp. "We found," adds the writer, "a number of berries, of which we ate a good lot. These grow on low bushes, which have a sweet-scented yellow flower, a smell like that of sallow bloom. The fruit is reddish-brown, about the size of a haw; dry, sweet, containing a stone. It is called 'Kafir plum'."[85]

---

[84] Marula (*Sclerocarya birrea*). DS

[85] Wild plum (*Harpephyllum caffrum*). DS

Here too a hornbill's nest was found. "The boys," says Frank Oates, "brought me a young hornbill, and I was taken to the nest. A hollow tree, with a hole in it, high up, was where the bird had come from. They poked out and pulled the wing-feathers off the old hen when I was not looking. I kept both birds. Karl says the old hen never leaves the young, the cock feeding them all, and that she gets quite bare of feathers. The number of young is two. The natives, he says, are very fond of them to eat, roasted."

The party next moved forward (February 12th) to the Impakwe, a further distance of about six miles. "Here," writes the traveller, "is some distinct stonework forming a circular wall, inside which are remains of bricks coated with a substance as if smelting had been done here. No mortar has been used, and the work is rough and I should say of no great antiquity, the stones being small and loose and easily displaced, so that I think they would not stand any great length of time. They are cut in an oblong form and properly placed for building. Karl says it was made for smelting copper, and used by the people whom Mosilikatze found here. That it is any older I should much doubt. Shot here," he concludes, "a beautiful sun-bird, whose beauty awoke my slumbering love of ornithology." Birds had been scarce of late, but became much more plentiful at the Ramaqueban, which was reached the following morning.

Encamping on this river, they still remained a few days longer in the neighbourhood before finally separating, usually taking from here different directions during the day in search of game, and meeting again at night. The game in the district, however, for the most part proved scarce and wild, a circumstance afterwards accounted for by the fact that other parties had been and still were hunting the neighbourhood at the same time. There was, nevertheless, abundant evidence of its being a good game country; and, as it was, giraffe, koodoo, waterbuck, and sable antelope were met besides wild pig, quagga, and sassaybi. The spoor of elephant and rhinoceros was also seen, none however, very recent.

The Ramaqueban—at this season a fine broad stream, with long grass and a large undergrowth of rank weeds upon its banks—was crossed in many of their rambles, and near it on one occasion were seen the graves of two Englishmen. "Started at nine," writes Frank Oates on February 16th, "crossed the Ramaqueban, and passed the graves of two Englishmen, who died here, one of fever, one killed by an elephant. The latter had come from England to shoot, and was killed by the tusks of the first elephant he saw. The fever is very bad on this river; the vegetation is extremely rank, and water lies very deep over much of the veldt. The graves," he concludes, "had been surrounded by stakes to keep off the wolves, but the river, overflowing its banks, had nearly washed them away; still the heaps of stones covering the bodies and a few stakes remain."

GIGANTIC ANT-HILL.

The same evening, wandering far into the bush, Frank Oates slept out with some of his boys who had accompanied him. "We stopped at 5pm," he says, "and huts were made. It was a hot night and the big fires made it worse. The white ants[86] too kept tumbling over me all night,

---

[86]"These 'white ants' (termites)," writes W. Oates, "are the curse of all African settlers and travellers, devouring everything except iron or tin, whilst in time even houses succumb to their ravages. They form, however, an article of food in many places amongst the natives, by whom they are much esteemed on account of their slightly acid flavour. The enormous structures they erect are frequently carried up the trunk of a high tree, or may sometimes be seen standing alone at a height of 18 feet, as in the accompanying sketch, which was taken between Tati and Shoshong. The Dutch Boers and others make use of these anthills for cooking purposes, hollowing out the lower portion of the heap, and filling the hollow thus formed with wood, which is lighted, and, when consumed, renders the receptacle an admirable oven, retaining its heat for a great length of time."

and knocking down leaves from the roof. We were perhaps sixteen miles from the waggon."

Still, however, though in a less tried district, there seemed but little game, and what was seen was wild. Returning to the camp next day, "I stopped in the afternoon," he writes, "when the boys found a nest of small bees, full of delicious honey, on which and coffee I dined sumptuously."

And now discouraged by the wildness and scarcity of the game, the Dutchman soon after—about the 20th—took his departure, returning to John Lee's, the Hottentot having left two days previously for the Shashe River, whither he been summoned to join another Dutch hunter, Piet Jacobs[87], in search of elephant.

A little before the latter's departure Frank had chanced to hear from him that, at a spot not far from their encampment, some miles up the river, a number of Bushmen had been murdered the previous year, and he resolved, if possible, to visit the place, that he might obtain some of their remains. In this search his informant had undertaken to accompany him, and had even sent to Tati for a reliable guide to the spot, when suddenly, at the last moment, he changed his mind, and excused himself from going upon the plea of illness. The circumstances of his defection and some other incidents of the day are thus related in the traveller's Journal :—

"*February 18th.*—Fine day; the first day without rain for an age. Last night Klaas (the Hottentot) told me he was going on to Tati today, being too unwell to accompany me in my excursion in quest of the bones, but would leave me his Bushmen—the one he had sent for from Tati, who knew the place, and the one he has had with him here. The former was out hunting, when his fourteen companions—men, women, and children—were killed at their hunting kraal by the Matabele. He found them all dead on his return. It seems that they were a party of Mungwato Bushmen, and some of them had taken meat belonging to some Bushmen from Manyami's. The latter complained to the king, who said the Mungwato Bushmen were to be killed. This was last winter. This

---

[87] A legendary explorer, born around 1800. Jacobs was an ivory hunter, and one of the first to systematically exploit the wildlife in the Ndebele kingdom, killing between 400 and 500 bull elephants in his lifetime. Jacobs helped to bury Frank Oates in February 1875. DS

morning Klaas went away, leaving the two boys. I now found he was *going away to hunt*. Jacobs had sent for him to hunt for elephants, said to be on the Shashe. Presently the two Bushmen took their guns and skins and walked off. I immediately felt the strongest suspicion, and called Lee's attention to them. He questioned them, and they told him they were going to hunt. I felt very uneasy, and wanted him to stop them, but he seemed to think it was all right. However, they did not return at night. We think Klaas had arranged all this. ... One of Smith's boys, a Matabele, was one of the party who killed the Bushmen, but he says he thinks he could not find the place, the leaves being now on the trees. He could find it, he says, going from his own kraal, but not from here. He evidently, however, does not want, or care, to go. It is somewhere, a day or a day and a half's walk off, up the Ramaqueban."

The two Bushmen, as Frank Oates had anticipated, failing after this to reappear, the search for the remains had now for the present to be abandoned, but later in the year, as will presently be seen, he succeeded in obtaining possession of them.

The Bushmen of this country—such was Karl Lee's account of them—appear to be scattered over the whole district north of Mungwato, keeping principally near the waggon-road, to get hunting jobs and bits of meat.

WOODEN VESSEL.

They are without chiefs, and have no fixed place of abode, and no crops, building themselves rough temporary huts when they want to stop anywhere for a time. They are capable of carrying immense loads, and sometimes help the Matabele with their corn, receiving a little of the grain in payment when they return into the veldt. They have no guns, only assegais and dogs, and many of them have wounds of buffalo upon their persons. They snare buck, and occasionally get big game with their assegais.

Still lingering a day or two longer on the Ramaqueban after the departure of his companions Frank Oates completed the journey to the Tati on the 23rd, whence he did not start for Bamangwato till the 4th of April.

Chapter VII

Hunting trip on the Semokwe—A native musician—Gigantic baobabs—Return to Tati—Journey to Shoshong—The Bamangwato and Matabele nations—Fighting amongst the natives—Start back for Tati—Misadventures and delays—Fresh arrangements.

ON reaching Tati, Frank Oates found that a hunting party was just about to start thence for the Semokwe, and being asked to join them, he arranged to do so before going on to Bamangwato. The following is an extract from his Journal of this date (February 23rd), after his arrival at the settlement:—

"Tati," he writes, "presented on our arrival a very pretty and lively appearance. I like it better than any place I know of, to stand at. Here are no crowds of rude people to come round the waggon. All is green, and numerous little well-built houses dot the ground; of course I mean well-built for the interior of South Africa, but it is rough work enough nevertheless. There are the three waggons of the Gardens[88], two English brothers hunting in the country, and the waggon of Mr. Thomson, on his way with his wife and children to a missionary meeting at Kuruman. There is Nelson's waggon, who is going away for a time, and possibly will visit England. He leaves to-morrow according to his present plan, with Mr. Thomson, they carrying the mail. Then there is Klaas's waggon, and Jacobs's[89] waggon; the latter living here with his wife and daughters until the regular hunting season. He makes short excursions from here, and is now about to set off for the Semokwe for a three weeks' hunt after elephant. A troop of they say at least 200 came close to Tati lately, but, probably hearing the engine, turned. One account sets them down at a still larger number. In the letter I found awaiting me here from Willie, written when he came out of the hunting veldt, he tells me he has been to the Semokwe, where he has had good sport. Seventeen elephants, he tells me, had just been killed on that river; this would be by

---

[88] Francis and John Garden. DS

[89] Piet Jacobs, the Dutch hunter, referred to in the previous Chapter.

Fejune[90]. Captain Garden and his brother are accompanying Jacobs on his projected hunt, and I am going to join them too. Klaas and Henry Wall are also going, and a lot of Bushmen. Jacobs shot a fine lion close to Tati lately; brought him to bay with dogs early in morning, and shot him from horseback. They trapped another; the third, a lioness, escaped. They had been taking Jacobs's bullocks. … A lot of people came up to my waggon when we outspanned, and Mr. Thomson invited me to supper. In the evening we all met at Brown's. Brown has given me a piece of bread. I enjoy it without butter or anything else with it; it is a wonderful treat."

YELLOW-BILLED HORNBILL.—*Tockus flavirostris.*

---

[90] Jan Willem Viljoen, an ivory hunter and sometime mineral agent for the Transvaal government. DS

The following day the large party here alluded to started on their hunt. Before leaving, Frank Oates wrote to his brother William, now in England, as follows:—

"TATI, *February 24th, 1874.*

"It is quite a pleasure to get a letter from you—I mean the one you left for me here. I shall get no more now for five or six weeks, when I expect to be in Mungwato. I am sorry that wretched old croaker, Palmer[91], put you in a funk about me. He says it would be a good thing for people travelling to have 'portable coffins'. I am thankful to say my health is excellent. I did not, as doubtless you know by this time, get to the Zambesi. I believe the king was at the bottom of it (not of the Zambesi; but excuse grammar). I took my waggon fifty miles on the way, as far as Inyati, and then put all out for fifteen carriers to take. It was a fortnight's walk through 'the fly' to the Falls. After waiting nearly a week, it transpired that no boys were forthcoming as promised. Partly, I think, they were afraid of fever, and partly of the natives, with whom they are at war; partly also they wanted to get back in time to cultivate their gardens. However, I believe I could have got them myself easily, had I not trusted to the man given me by the king.

"I then sent back to Lobengula, asking him for hunting veldt. I had given him your shot gun, and his sister some furniture print of gorgeous pattern. He gave me a fine veldt between the Gwailo and Umvungu Rivers, where I was six weeks. I then returned to the royal residence, and asked the king to let me go back to the same place. He was very crusty, and asked if I wanted to die. I told him would take my chance, for I did not think there was the least danger *then*. It is when the rains cease and the rank vegetation rots beneath the sun that it is so bad, and that is not till March in most parts, I believe, though earlier on the Zambesi. However, he said, if I wanted to die, why could I not die somewhere else, and not in his country, and made so many difficulties I had to give it up. I then had so many delays—bad weather, and one thing or another—that I waited till the big dance was over, which is quite a thing to see when one is here.

"After this I had difficulties with my men, and had to part with Hendrik, Dick, and Jacob, all of whom you will remember. About Dick's dismissal I had to wait a week or more, as the case had to be tried before the king, and Jacob was finally handed over to the tender mercies of

---

[91] A trader of that name at Tati. [Grey Palmer's gloominess was justified; a year later his 23-year-old bride died two weeks after her arrival in Bulawayo. DS]

Dick. Hendrik I dismissed for refusing to cut some bushes, to make a fence round my waggon to keep the niggers out. This he considered 'slavish work,' and preferred dismissal to demeaning himself. Then the king would insist on buying my little horse, still well when I left in January, and got the saddle and bridle for nothing.

"Since then I have been coming slowly from the King's. I have been hunting, and have Lee's brother to drive for me now, and take me to Mungwato. Here I have fallen in with Captain Garden and his brother, and am joining them and some others for about three weeks' hunting in the veldt. I am spinning out the time, so that if I find all things favourable on reaching Mungwato, I can start in April or May for the Zambesi. ... I have seen Vincent, the driver, who is death on Solomon[92]. He said he wanted to kill him, but did not like to do it without your leave, which he asked, but you said it would be rather inconvenient to you just then to have him put out of the way."

On the 24th, as already stated, the hunters left the Tati, and crossing the Ramaqueban and Inkwesi Rivers, struck thence eastwards and crossed the Sakasusi or Dry River on the 26th, a crowd of Bushmen, with their wives and children, accompanying the waggons. The following day they reached the Semokwe, a fine river surrounded by a sea of green bush stretching in all directions, and here[93] they formed their camp. "In the evening," writes Frank Oates in his Journal after their arrival at this point, "a boy, who comes from the Zambesi, and knows the Falls, which he calls 'Metse-a-Tunya' (water-sounding), came and sang, playing on the string of a bow to which a gourd was attached. He sang the 'Song of the Elephants Feeding', now and then pausing and imitating the looking round for danger, then recommencing the feeding, or imitating the running of the elephants. The words were very distinct, with no clicking. The following occurred over and over again, the song sounding very monotonous, but not at all harsh or unpleasant:—

" 'Wanga marank,
Swot ma ben a marank,
Watem ba marank,
Obeza marank,

---

[92] The latter was W. Oates' Kafir driver, who, it may be remembered, had turned out a consummate rascal.

Wamba marank.'

One of the boys from Mungwato, whose language this man knows a little, explains that he speaks of the game feeding by the river—'all the game.' The minstrel was delighted with some tobacco. He is a fine, well-made, powerful-looking, and nice-featured young fellow, with a pleasant childish expression."

Next day a large troop of buffalo was encountered near the river, out of which were obtained a cow and three-year-old bull, which supplied the camp with meat. "Went after supper," writes Frank Oates that evening, "to see the Bushmen and their wives dance. They do this when full of meat, making a great noise. The women stand in line, shuffling their feet and clapping their hands, whilst the men come and perform antics in front of them—one now and then stepping out from the ranks and approaching near to the women with dancing and gestures. Now and then one excited will rush away half mad into the veldt, and return again when tired. They must work very hard in this dancing."

On March 2nd, leaving the waggons by the river, the party started for a few days' hunting in the bush, taking with them a couple of pack-oxen. After following the river for some distance nearly south, they entered some very pretty country, characteristic of the best South African scenery—rugged kopjes and thick bush, the kopjes rising round on every side, and stretching far into the distance. Here, crossing the river, they encamped their first night, advancing the following morning in an easterly direction several miles. In the course of this afternoon (March 3rd), some trees of unusual size were noticed by some of the party whilst riding in pursuit of eland. "The first which arrested my attention," writes Frank Oates, who was one of this number, "was so striking that I let the others go on following the spoor, and reined in my horse. The tree was perfectly gigantic in girth, thickening as it got higher, though of no great height. It was swollen and bloated in a most extraordinary manner, and is of the same kind as the 'Indunas' tree'—a baobab. Though still flourishing, it is a mere shell, and, looking in at a hole in the side, I saw that it was open to the sky at the top. Inside was a good-sized chamber, strewed with minute bones of rats or some small mammalia. No doubt generations of owls have long had their abode here; one flew out on our approach. We saw another tree afterwards, probably as large, but I did not ride up to it."

SALT PAN, BAMANGWATO.

After this the same general direction was again pursued till evening, when temporary huts were constructed for the night, which, however, unfortunately proved a wholly ineffectual shelter from rain which fell early the following morning, thoroughly saturating everything inside. The day itself was fine and hot, but was again succeeded by heavy rain at night, which induced the party on March to retrace their steps to the waggons, recrossing Semokwe in their march, which was now swollen with the recent heavy rains. One of the Bushmen was carried off his legs in crossing the river but, seizing hold of another of the party, regained his footing, and reached the opposite bank in safety. The big rifle he was carrying escaped with a severe wetting. After this the party moved slow towards the Tati, halting a short time on the banks of the Sakasusi, and elsewhere upon the way; and reaching the settlement on March 17th. The game met with during their absence had been much the same as that Frank Oates had found in his former journeyings further to the north, and included besides buffalo, quagga, pallah, and sassaybi, all which were obtained early in the hunt—rhinoceros, wildebeest, and koodoo.

Still remaining at Tati a few days after their return there, Frank Oates, as already mentioned, started thence for Bamangwato on April 4th, accompanied by a hunter and two traders, also on their way south. By the middle of March the weather seemed to have become quite settled, and the days were almost universally fine and hot, with only an occasional slight shower or a little drizzling rain. This absence of wet had greatly changed the aspect of the country, and that in a short time, for, the day after leaving Tati for Bamangwato and crossing the Shashe River, the veldt presented to the travellers a dry, parched appearance, very different from anything which had now for a long time been witnessed. The grass was yellow, and many of the trees already bare. A week's trekking brought the party to Bamangwato[94], which was reached on April 11th, after an uneventful journey.

Here Frank Oates found letters awaiting him—the first he had received from England since leaving Pietermaritzburg nearly twelve months before—and, all seeming favourable, at once determined on prosecuting his journey to the Zambesi. There appeared now every reason to anticipate a prosperous and successful expedition, and he began at once to make this preparations for it, laying in fresh supplies at the stores, and otherwise completing his equipment.

Very little worthy of note occurred during the time he was detained at Bamangwato. One evening, however, a great noise and shouting at the kraal, kept up till late, announced the return from the veldt of a number of boys who had been out for circumcision. The following day, according to custom, the same boys went forth again, and Frank saw them starting. "Party, say of two hundred boys, went out," he writes, "into the veld. They are those who returned yesterday from circumcision, and I am told will have to go to the veldt every day for a week and look after the cattle. They presented a striking and uniform appearance. Each had a knob-kerry and a wand, and round the middle a bit of skin. All these and their entire bodies were rubbed with red ochre, their heads shaved except the crown, on which the hair was quite short, crisp, and bead-like. All the crown and the part around it was brilliantly metallic, of a dark steel blue, produced by some preparation of a kind of lead got here."

---

[94] The accompanying woodcut, from a drawing taken a little south of Shoshong (Bamangwato), represents one of the salt lakes of this district as seen in winter. The water in these lakes is then all dried up, and their beds, composed of salt and sand, present a dazzling white appearance.

CHURCH AND MISSION STATION, SHOSHONG, BAMANGWATO.

The evening after this occurrence (April 24th, the traveller's preparations were completed, and a fresh start made up country, but before proceeding further with the narrative, it will be proper here to give quotations from some of the letters written during his present stay at Bamangwato. Five days after his arrival he writes to one of his brothers:—

"BAMANGWATO, *April 16th, 1874.*
"At last I have your and the Mater's letters dated September 22d, and containing the first news I have had from home since I left Pietermaritzburg. When I arrived here and found no letters I did not know what to think. Mr. Mackenzie, the missionary, and his assistant, Mr. Hepburn, were both absent, having gone—as well as Mr. Thomson, the Matabele missionary—to a meeting at Kuruman. I had asked Mackenzie to keep letters for me at his own house, and requested Hathorn to forward all letters to him from Maritzburg; so when I arrived here and found none I could not make it out. To-day, however, a note arrived, the monthly mail coming in. This note was from Hepburn, telling me that a letter and newspapers were at his house for me, and directing me to apply to a converted native who is studying for the church, and

who, with others like him, forms a college adjoining the missionary houses. I was not long in going up, and found the things as he had said, amongst his books. ...

"I left Tati for this place on the 4th of April, and reached here in a week. I had to come here for supplies. It is about 150 miles; but the journey is no trifle. I generally trekked during the night, and slept comfortably, the ground being soft sand for the most part, and the waggon going slowly and without jolts. We usually made two treks of perhaps three hours each, say from 3 to 6, and from 8 to 11pm, and set off again about 2am and trekked till sunrise, which was about 6am, making about four hours. Call our rate of miles an hour in heavy ground, this gives twenty miles a day, roughly, and this is good trekking, and could not be kept up for long. Now, however, there is still plenty of grass and water, though winter is setting in and the rains nearly over. Two waggons accompanied me, with two traders and a hunter in them. The latter is quite a young fellow, who left England three years ago. He was educated at Rugby. One of the two traders was Fairbairn, who supplied me with goods at the town of the Matabele king; and the other, a man named Dawson.

"On my birthday I thought of you all, and old times—and had a good wash[95]. ... I hope not to be more than a week or so here in all, before returning to Tati, *en route* for the Falls. Selous, the hunting youth above mentioned, set off to-day. His partner George Wood[96], a Yorkshireman, is waiting for him at Tati. They are both professional ivory hunters, and have a good deal of roughing it to do. Selous was once lost for four days and three nights in the veldt. The morning of the first day, when he left the waggons, he had nothing but a cup of coffee, and had neither a drop of water nor a morsel of food of any description till the evening of the fourth day, when he found his way back, and got some milk of a native. He thinks he could have held out another day.

---

[95] A rare luxury at the present time, only to be indulged in on great or special occasions, owing to the increasing scarcity of water with the cessation of the rains. "I am miserable,' he writes one day about this time, "for want of water to wash myself in, ever so superficially."

[96] Wood specialised in hunting on foot, and was able to penetrate to areas infested by tsetse fly where mounted hunters were unable to travel. It had its risks: after travelling through the Barotse Valley in 1882, Wood, his wife and child died of malaria in 1882 in Pandamatenga. DS

"The brothers Garden are going to the Zambesi the same way. There is another way of reaching the Falls from here, shorter than the Tati road, but at certain seasons deficient in water. It is to the left of the Tati road. I should have preferred it, but wanted to leave some things at Tati. and was not sure of finding water, going by it. It appears, however, it would have been all right had I decided on that route. They tell me here two English tourists, one of them called Bond, have just left here, trekking slowly to the Falls. This year and last the Falls have been in great request apparently, as Garland and Dawnay visited them last year, and now the Gardens, Bond, and myself, are all bound there, this. Selous too is very anxious to see them, and will probably manage it. We are still in lots of time, in fact the great fear now is of going there too soon, but I shall go slowly and remain where it is healthy till it is the same at the Zambesi.

"The boys, as one's Kafir satellites are called whatever their age, are far more liable to fever of course than their 'bosses.' Lying out with only a skin or blanket and a fire, to keep the cold away at the unhealthy season, is not likely to prevent an attack of fever. Three or four of my boys have had it. I have given them quinine, and there is only one of them ill now. This fellow I call 'Quilp.' He is perhaps eighteen, and a perfect dwarf. The race he belongs to, the Bushmen of this country, are usually tall. These Bushmen are a curious race, who probably had their homes in the veldt long before the Mungwato and Matabele people came here and conquered it, and before the races they conquered came. The Mungwato people are an utterly different nation from the Matabele. The latter have two other nations, the Makalaka and Mashona, living in bondage under them, who are far more ingenious and versed in the arts than their conquerors, having mined and worked metals and woven stuffs for ages. They are not all conquered yet; but the Matabele king is constantly sending out parties of warriors, who steal their cattle, kill the old people, and carry the children into slavery. The little slaves grow up in the families of the Matabele, and when they are old enough to marry, become free and are incorporated into the nation, in which way Lobengula increases his people and his power. The slaves call those of their conquerors to whom they are allotted, their 'fathers,' and they have to work for them, though more like adopted children than anything else. Many of the conquered people, however, are not made part of the nation, but suffered to live on with a Matabele headman placed over them. It is usually slave boys that one gets as servants. They have to look after the cattle and make themselves generally useful, carrying one's arms, blankets, or anything else required, when one goes for a day or two into the veldt. I have now six boys, all young, which I always prefer, besides my driver[97], a stupid creature, who requires constant blowing up and the use of unpleasantly strong remarks. When these fail altogether, I shall have to try the argument of knocking him down, which may be slightly beneficial. This is supposed to attach a boy to you. The worst of it is none of my boys are much afraid of me.

"I think I shall be very well supplied for my coming trip. I shall have meal, coffee, and brandy, which I have got here. Sugar is not present, but may possibly turn up before I leave. However, that doesn't matter much. Coffee is of the first importance, then comes tobacco. To be without these two is a thing I have never yet come to. Meal too is a nice thing to have, though not indispensable, as you can buy Kafir corn, which, when cooked, keeps you going. Brandy, likewise, I am very glad to have got.

"There are, besides the parties I have enumerated, a lot of Boer hunters going to the Zambesi with their wives and families. Those who go by Tati will leave it about the middle of May, I think, and I suppose the Falls can be reached and seen, and you can be returning in August if you wish to leave so soon. I look forward to the time when I shall be *en route* for home. When I got Willie's letter, and saw the place where our waggons had stood together, I could not help feeling a sort of yearning for home, and today when I got your and the Mater's letters, it seemed as if it would be so jolly to be with you all again soon, but then I comfort myself with thinking that it will only make a few months' difference, going to the Zambesi, and I did not like the idea of leaving the country without accomplishing my object. I hope all will continue to go on well at home.

"There has been some fighting going on here of late amongst the natives. It took place just before I arrived. You may be aware that Kama left here, and old Sekomi, his father, remained behind with Kamani, Kama's younger brother. Kama, however, it is supposed, will return and rout Kamani[98]. Sekomi is looked upon as nobody. Kamani is a gentlemanly well-dressed darkie enough, and the other day he and his men gave

---

[97]This refers to John, the man whom Frank Oates had engaged as interpreter at Gubuleweyo some months before, and whom he had since retained in the capacity of general servant. He had recently acted as driver in the place of Karl Lee, who had returned from Tati to his brother's farm, instead of coming forward, as intended, to Bamangwato.

[98] Kgamani. DS

Matchin[99] a warm reception. Matchin is his uncle, or something of the sort, and once for a short time supplanted Sekomi. He thought the dispute of the brothers a favourable opportunity for retaking Mungwato, but failed. His people had to climb the steep mountain which flanks the town, turning to fire as they fled, whilst Kamani's men shot at them from the plain. A great deal of ammunition was expended, but comparatively few natives slain. There were a dozen or so lying about on the slope of the mountain when I arrived, but the hyenas and crows had had a 'high old time,' and little was left of them but the skulls. A lot of huts were destroyed during the fight; and one of the traders here seized the opportunity to burn down the empty huts all round the store where he lives, and it certainly improves his view.

"It seems next to impossible to convert natives here to Christianity, though a good many them profess it. The worst of it is that when they get so far converted as to wear 'continuations', they become incorrigible thieves and drunkards. I always infinitely prefer the raw unconverted heathen for my own use, and everyone else that 1 know does the same. I like extremely the three missionaries that I know, and believe them to be most excellent conscientious men. They believe the chief result of their labours is yet to come, and I hope they may be right."

By the 24th of April, as already mentioned, all was ready for a start, and, leaving Bamangwato after sundown, a trek of two hours was accomplished that night. The following morning a like distance had been traversed, when the waggon was suddenly brought to a standstill by one of the wheels giving way. It was fortunate, as it happened, they had not got further from the reach of help, and the broken wheel was at once taken back to Bamangwato. It was a tedious business, however, getting it repaired—so slow are people's movements in this country—but at last it was ready, and, some fresh oxen being purchased to strengthen the span, the journey resumed early on the morning of May 5th. Before starting a couple of waggons arrived from Lake Ngami with two traders, both looking dreadfully ill from the effects of fever; indeed they seemed to have had a very narrow escape. They had buried one mail, and reported the death of another at the Lake—Henry Gray, the trader who, the year before, had accompanied Frank and William Oates a good part of the way up country when they first left Pietermaritzburg.

---

[99] Matsheng. The chieftaincy of the bamaNgwato was intermittently in dispute between Sekgoma and his half-brother, Matsheng. DS

Before resuming his journey Frank Oates wrote home a few lines to his brother William, as follows:—

"BAMANGWATO, *May 4th*, 1874.

"I wrote to Charley a few days ago, telling him I was just setting off for the Zambesi. As bad luck would have it, one of my hind wheels came to grief in jolting over that vile piece of road you must remember, about ten miles from here, and there I was, laid on my back. However, I put the wheel on a sledge of branches, and brought it with six oxen to be mended here, and once again am off. I am going to ride to the waggon to-night by moonlight, and hope to be at the Makalapsi River before the sun is very high. …

"We have reckoned up about thirty waggons going Zambesi way this year; some are hunters, some traders, and some tourists. I expect most of them will stand at the same place, beyond Daka, and one must walk from there to the Falls. I suppose twelve white men at least will be at the Falls this year, so I shall not be alone, and one will be in the way of help in case of emergency arising, which is not likely. I am sparing no pains to get a good outfit. I have now twenty-six oxen, and am determined to be as well provided in every way as possible for the journey."

After writing the above Frank Oates rode out, as he intended, to his waggon, and by 3am on the 5th of May was once more upon the road. Again all went favourably for something like three hours after starting, and a further distance of five or six miles had been accomplished when, to the traveller's unspeakable vexation, a fresh catastrophe of a like kind occurred, this time the tire of the same wheel breaking, and necessitating another halt. He now rode back into Bamangwato to see what could be done, the upshot of which was that he there bought two new waggons, and yet more oxen, so as to divide his load and lessen the risk of future accidents of this vexatious kind. He also secured the services of a Dutchman named Van Roozen, and his son, the former of whom would act as driver to one of the waggons, and make himself generally useful.

Whilst still completing these arrangements he added a short supplementary letter to the last, from which the following are extracts:—

"*May 9th*, 1874.

"Since writing the letter of May 4th, which will reach you at the same time this does, I have broken down again. After finishing my letter to you I rode out to the waggon, inspanned, and trekked. I had gone perhaps five or six miles, when the wheel came to grief again, the tire breaking, and I had to return here. It has ended in my buying two new waggons, and selling the old one. ... The great difference in my plans, however, is, that I have found a Dutchman and his little boy, who have agreed to accompany me. The former wanted to go hunting with some one, and I engaged him to go with me as driver and general overseer, but have stipulated that he shall only hunt when and where I think fit, as, for instance, when I leave the waggon standing to visit the Zambesi. Of course if he gets any ivory or feathers he gives me half, as is always done in these cases, and there may be enough to pay his wages as driver. His boy is a handy little fellow, and can take charge of a waggon."

It was the 13th of May, when again, for the third time, Frank Oates started north, but the further tracing of his fortunes must be left to the succeeding chapter. Before, however, concluding the present period of his wanderings, the following brief extract may be given from another of his letters, written about this time, with reference to his dogs. He says:—

"I have the nicest dog now I ever had. He is a pointer, and a most sensible creature. Dogs are indispensable here, if only to guard the waggon. My pointers are both well; I had four originally, but sold two here when I went further into the interior. One poor thing is dead, and the other far from flourishing. It was August when I left them, having a difficulty in feeding so many dogs; and now when I return in April, poor 'Flirt' knows me, and won't let me out of her sight for a moment. She had known me three months, but had formed a very strong attachment to me. She follows me like a shadow. They accuse her of stealing soap, and she has a *penchant* for departed negroes. The fact is she is not overfed. I wish that I had kept her, I have besides two puppies. One is five, the other three months old, and I have had them from their tenderest infancy."

The pointer referred to at the commencement of this paragraph was the traveller's favourite, 'Rail', the attached and devoted companion of all his wanderings, his friend in solitude, and faithful to him even after death.

"ROCK" AND "RAIL."

Chapter VIII

Again at Tati—Fresh causes of delay—Lions on the Motloutsi—Threatened by natives—Forthcoming prospects.

By the 21st of May Frank Oates was again back at Tati from Bamangwato, this time completing the journey without further mishap. Little worthy of note occurred upon the road. The weather was now settled; the rains had ceased, and the days were usually bright and fine. The general aspect of the country was bare and brown, though, where water was met with, there was still for the most part a corresponding freshness in the landscape, as was the case at 'Tchakani Vlei', a beautiful pond, surrounded by wood and covered with water-lilies, which was reached the second day of the journey. Again at the Palatswe River, further on, was water and abundance of fresh grass, the latter supplying excellent pasture for the oxen. But some days forced marches were required, to get from one watering-place to another, these in the winter season being few in number. This scarcity of water sufficiently accounted for the general absence of game upon the route, only a few small antelope occasionally showing themselves the whole time. In crossing the Motloutsi two lion were observed quite close to the waggons, and Frank Oates gave them chase, but, as related in a letter referring to the events of this period, was thrown off the scent by the wiles of the Dutchman Van Roozen[100], who sought to avoid an encounter. The signs of animal life were rather more numerous on the Shashe River, where some fine water-holes were found in the sand, into one of which a crocodile had crawled, leaving the track of his tail behind him at the water's edge. Here pallah and other game spoor was abundant, and three or four large monkeys were observed crossing the river-bed. Birds too were numerous, including herons, kingfishers, and bustards. In the course of the journey one or two snakes were met with, one of which was of a fine silvery hue upon the back, and salmon-coloured beneath. Another, quite black, and of a very deadly kind, evinced a remarkable facility for swelling out its head to an enormous size when alarmed or angry. This snake had a habit, it was said,

---

[100] Van Rooyen, a hunter, probably from Zeerust in the Transvaal. DS

of hanging down from the trees like one of their branches and attacking such creatures as might pass beneath[101].

On approaching Tati the traveller was struck with the fine autumnal tints of the trees, and observed ahead of him the picturesque range of hills towards the Ramaqueban. At Tati itself the grass was parched and yellow, and everything had already assumed its autumnal or winter garb. Here he was met on his arrival by Mr. Fairbairn from Gubuleweyo, from whom he learnt with pleasure that the king had sent leave for him to go to the Zambesi, a fresh permission having been required. The other travellers for the Zambesi, mentioned above in one of Frank Oates's letters, had most of them already started northwards, but for one reason or another he was himself yet detained some days longer at the settlement.

WATTLED STARLING.—*Dilophus carunculatus.*

---

[101] This may be Oates's Vine Snake (*Thelotornis capensis oatesii*), collected by and named after Oates, which inflates its neck when threatened. DS

The only incident of much novelty which occurred during this time was an angry scene with some Kafirs at the mine, arising out of a second attempt he had made, when last at Tati, to get possession of the Bushman remains he had failed to secure when hunting on the Ramaqueban in February. The story of his encounter with these men and other circumstances of the time are related by him at some length in the following letter home :—

"TATI, *May 29th*, 1874.

"I have been here just a week to-day *en route* for the Zambesi. I have been delayed, in the first instance, by the illness of Brown, who is managing Sir John Swinburne's mine here in the absence of Nelson, who has gone to the colony; and since, by having something done to my waggon wheels. I have been able to be of a little use to Brown, and did not like to leave him as he was, but he is now better It does not much matter losing a few days, as I always thought the 1st of June would be early enough to leave here, in order to reach the Zambesi as soon as the healthy season there has fairly set in. I may now wait two or three days longer, as there seems a possibility of my getting my waggon wheels shortened. I shall be glad if I can get this done, as wood in this country shrinks so much that the tire often becomes loose, and then a blacksmith is wanted to shorten the tire unless the wheel is wedged.

"I am fortunate in having secured the services of the Dutchman and his little boy, whose engagement I informed you of in my letter from Bamangwato. These people are very useful to have about a waggon. There are a thousand shifts, which any one who understands the subject can have recourse to. A Kafir is scarcely ever the slightest good, even if he has been working about waggons all his life. I have now, moreover, far more comfort in the waggon I appropriate to my own use, as it is no longer crammed to overflowing, half my cargo being stowed away in my second waggon, which the Boer occupies. My oxen too are, on the whole, in a very satisfactory state, and I have all the necessary stores. I don't suppose I need be more than a month in reaching the place where my waggons must stand, and then it is two or three days on foot to the Victoria Falls; but of course I shall go slower than this, and may not be back here till November, or even later. I feel now as if all was going well.

"I was eight days in coming here from the place where I last broke down, and had few incidents on the road. Van Roozen, the Dutchman, however, got a fright one morning from a couple of lions, and showed himself to be rather a coward. We were entering the dry bed of the Motloutsi River about two hours before sunrise, and I was asleep in the waggon. It appears that Van Roozen had gone across the river in front of the waggons to ascertain the nature of the opposite bank, which he had just climbed when the roar of a lion resounded in his ears, and he asserts that he was chased by a couple of them, and 'ran like a horse.' The latter part of his statement, no doubt, is perfectly correct, and also it was true that there had been two lions within a yard or two of him at one time, as we saw by the spoor at sunrise. I found the remains of a pallah they had killed in the bed of the river, and the spoor of the lions going away into the bush, and set off to follow it with the dogs and the Dutchman. The latter was in a great fright. I should have thought nothing of it if he had candidly admitted as much, but he thought to put me off by making believe to follow the spoor, and then conveniently losing it. The Kafirs too are most terribly afraid of lions, and will always lose the spoor; indeed it is almost useless to attempt to follow it with them, but I had thought better things of a Dutchman calling himself a 'hunter.' The fact is, for one man to go alone, or only accompanied by Kafirs, may be dangerous, but for two white men with double-barrelled rifles the danger is very slight; as, in the remote contingency of an attack, one could help the other, but really Dutchmen are only a degree better than Kafirs. Still they are wonderfully useful about a Waggon, and my having this one with me takes a great deal of bother off my hands, and may save me no end of trouble and delay. My grand mistake was not taking a good man with me from Natal in the first instance at £8 or £10 a month.

"I have had a row with some rascally Kafirs here in this wise. Last year a party of unfortunate Bushmen—men, women, and children—were killed by a party of Matabele. The Bushmen were supposed to have been hunting where they had no right, or committing some other offence—probably an imaginary one. Hearing of this, I thought if I could find the place I could take a sack and fill it with bones, and I instituted inquiries accordingly as to the locality, offering a blanket to any Kafir who would take me to the spot. A Dutchman, who lives here, when he is not away with his wife and daughters in his waggon on a hunting expedition, offered to act as my guide, and it was settled that I should give him £5 for doing so. He, however, changed his mind about going, but told me he had got one of the Matabele who killed the Bushmen to go with me in his stead. This fellow was working here at the mine, but when he was brought to me he also refused to go, evidently thinking I had some ulterior object in wanting to go to the place—perhaps to get him punished. These people, too, are very superstitious about going to places where others have been killed.

"This occurred when I was last here, but on my return I was waited on by another coloured gentleman, who said he too had helped to kill the Bushmen (and a ferocious beast he looked)—What business was it of *mine* to visit the bones? All this, of course, arose from the Dutchman having made it known that I wanted the bones. The ferocious-looking Kafir further went on to say that he should complain of my conduct to the king, the only way to avoid which catastrophe being to give him something out of my waggon, to bribe his silence. Moreover, he hinted that if I did not comply, he should not stick at helping himself and went through a pantomime with his knob-kerry (a stick with a round knob at one end, with which Kafirs knock their enemies on the head), illustrating what he would do to *me*. All this was bounce, though no doubt he would have liked to do it had he dared, and he thought to frighten me. My pusillanimous Dutchman at once begged me to give the fellow something. This I stoutly refused, not only as a disgraceful proceeding on my part, but as an act of bad policy. I knew better than to show him I was afraid of him, and I knew the king was not likely to go against me, even if the worst came to the worst. There were two other Kafirs with this one, also from the mine, to back him up. Finding the Dutchman disposed to be friendly with them, the spokesman asked him for a cigar, seeing us smoking, and the Dutchman wanted me to comply, as a preliminary to talking the matter over. All I said, however, to the Kafir was a word or two of his own language, meaning 'Go away, you scoundrel.'

"It was Sunday, and at this moment a white man who works at the mine came up, and I told him the case. He knew the Kafirs, and at once ordered them off, giving one of them a good slap on the side of the head, which upset him. Then they all jumped to their feet and brandished their knob-kerries. I threw off my coat, and my ally and I stood ready and waited for the first blow to be struck, whilst Van Roozen stood afar off. This attitude decided the Kafirs not to risk a fight, and they said they would go with me to Brown and talk the matter over. We went accordingly, and Brown told them if they wanted to do so to take the case before the king, and they soon subsided and slunk away. I might have had the greatest possible annoyance if it had not been for the plucky conduct of Dobie from the mine.

"Fairbairn's waggon was stopped when he came here by some Matabele, and he gave them some goods, but vowed he would complain to the king and get them into trouble. I suppose these three Kafirs thought they too could get something. The king, I believe, would kill them if he knew. There are, of course, no prisons; and when any of his subjects go too far they get put to death, and thrown out to the hyenas.

He is an excellent friend to the white men here, and his people live in fear and trembling of their lives. Since I was at the royal residence, I am told he has killed some dozen of the leading men of the country for making suggestions to him. 'I must show them,' said he, 'who is king—and he showed them.

Winter has now fairly set in; it is extremely cold at night, and not hot even during the day—at least not hot for Africa. The rivers are dry and the bush withered, and all is yellow and autumnal looking, and will remain so till the rains fall in October, and the fresh vegetation springs up. Then the trees will soon be all green, and many of them blossoming, and there will be many wild flowers. Now things are bleak and barren looking enough.

"Before I leave here I shall write a few lines more. ... I hope every one is well, and shall live in hope, for what else can I do? I can't expect to get any more letters till my return from the Zambesi. It may be some little time before you hear from me again, as I don't know that any waggons will return till November, though there are no end of them gone to the Zambesi. Should any precede me back I can send a letter by them. If, however, you don't hear, you must take for granted all is going well with me. Humanly speaking, there seems no reason for uneasiness."

On the 8th of June, his waggon at last ready, Frank Oates added a few lines to this letter, announcing his intended departure on the following day, and on the 9th he started for the Zambesi. There seemed now no reasonable probability of anything occurring to interfere with the successful issue of his journey, yet in reality, as things turned out, this was only the first of three separate attempts he made to reach the Zambesi from this point the present season. By the shorter route now to be adopted—for he was not going by Gubuleweyo—he would proceed pretty direct northwards, passing through the country of the Makalakas, who are subject to the Matabele and hold the key to the Zambesi country by this approach, Before crossing the boundaries of these people, it is necessary for travellers to have first obtained mission from the king to proceed, and such a permission Frank Oates distinctly had; yet, in spite all remonstrances on his part, the Makalakas refused to let him pass, thinking, perhaps, to reap some profit from his discomfiture, or, it may be, that Lobengula would in reality be no worse pleased if he were stopped. Indeed the traveller did not himself entirely exonerate the king from blame, but suspected at one time he was playing a double game—on the one hand giving him leave to proceed to the Zambesi, whilst on the other purposely neglecting to send the needful instructions to his subjects to let him pass. The king was anxious to encourage a certain number of traders in his country, but may have looked with suspicion on one whose objects were less intelligible to him.

At all events, be this as it may, it is perfectly certain that these Makalakas threw every possible obstacle in the way of his advance—and not once only, but each time he reached their boundaries—whilst several traders, going and coming, were permitted to proceed upon their journey, and the final fatal issue of his expedition to the Zambesi was practically the result of the behaviour of these people. It is true that other circumstances, irrespective of proceedings, combined to hinder and delay him, again throwing his journey into the unhealthy season of the year; but these alone would not have been of the same vital consequence, and the period of his misfortunes dates from the time when the Makalakas—the king's permission already plainly granted—first turned him back, as related in the succeeding chapter, and forced him to seek a fresh interview with Lobengula. In such a country, with but a brief healthy season, delays like this were little short of fatal.

But it is time to follow him in the first of these ill-starred journeys.

NATIVE BUILDING, SHASHE RIVER.

Chapter IX

Fresh start for the Zambesi—The Ramaqueban again—A lion Singular building—Wild fruit—First kraal of the Makalakas— Stopped by the induna—Return to Tati—To Gubuleweyo back—Fresh leave obtained— Altered arrangements for journey.

ON first leaving the Tati, on June 9th, the old ground, as though he had been making for Gubuleweyo, retraced as far as the Ramaqueban River, where, on June 10th, the traveller halted a short time to hunt. Giraffe, quagga, and blue wildebeest were now abundant in this district, and ostriches were also met with. Van Roozen too, the day before they left, succeeded in shooting a lion which had threatened to attack his horse—a great feat for this intrepid sportsman. An account of this adventure, along with some other matter, is given in the traveller's Journal of this date, as follows:—

"*June 12th.*—Mild, cloudy day, after a very mild night. ... Just before sundown Van Roozen returned from hunting, having shot a lion. It seems he had been following a sable antelope bull, and was about two or three miles from the waggon, down the Ramaqueban, when a lion approached his horse quite close. He yelled, and turned his horse. The lion retreated, but soon stopped and seemed inclined to renew the attack. He dismounted and shot the lion at, he says, about 30 yards. He then saw another lion creeping towards him—both 'mannetjes' (males)—and he (Van Roozen) made off. After his return he and I rode back together to the dead lion, which we found, and proceeded to skin. He was a yellow-maned one; Van Roozen says the black-maned one is quite distinct. In this the mane was short, the teeth very large and discoloured, but perfect, and the lion apparently in his prime, though he must have been hungry, as he was in poor condition. Van Roozen was alone when it happened, and he probably wanted to get the horse.

"Van Roozen tells me of an Englishman, named Brown, who was killed by a lion on the Crocodile River. One day this man and his son had found and taken three cubs, and the old lion came up to them. The son wanted to fire, but the father forbade him, and threw one cub down, which the old one took away, and they took the others to the waggon.

The day following the old man took his gun, and said he was going after ostriches. He had one young Kafir boy with him. It seems he had gone to the place where the lions were, and had met the old one, which he fired at, but did not kill upon the spot, though I believe it was found dead afterwards. It had torn the flesh off one of his arms and both his legs, but he had taken his gun, gone to a hole where buffalo wallow, used his pannikin to wash his hands and face, and gone on to the waggon-road (the son followed the blood spoor). He had put his gun in a tree, and hung up his powder-flask, and gone on the road a hundred yards when he had dropped and died."

The day after Van Roozen's encounter with the lion, Frank Oates, whilst out hunting, again visited the carcass, and, kindling a fire, cooked some of meat. On this the boys who were with him, and both his pointers, had a feast, and he tasted it himself, which he found to be coarse in and not unlike quagga meat.

Resuming his journey to the Zambesi same afternoon, he now broke fresh ground, for a day or two in a northerly direction close to the Ramaqueban, a really magnificent river when viewed from the ground above, its broad sandy bed stretching far away into the distance through the veldt. The dry beds of a number of spruits, all rising quite near the river, and suddenly becoming large before falling into it, were crossed as he proceeded. It is no wonder that rivers, thus fed by so many tributaries along their entire course, fill with such amazing rapidity directly the rains fall, and swell into large streams almost at their source. Next turning towards the north west, he presently struck across back towards the Tati River, and joined the more direct road from the settlement to the Zambesi, which here for some distance kept up the river's bank, the country assuming that broken rugged appearance—here with rough craggy kopjes, there with small open park-like glades—which makes at irregular intervals so pleasing a change in this otherwise little-varying landscape, and compensates where it occurs, for much that is uninteresting.

The Tati, itself one of those rivers which become large so near their source, was again itself shortly left behind, the waggons trekking forward in a direction nearly north. On June 17th, a few miles further on, another river was crossed, and the following entry made in the traveller's Journal:—

"*June* 17th.—Fine morning, after a mild starry night; warm day. Inspanned at 6.20am. I rode across the veldt to the right; grass very wet.

Saw a small buck and three sassaybi, but they got my scent. Going in a direction generally north, I struck a deep sandy river, with plenty of water-holes in it, and banks steep and rocky in places; crossed it, and kept down it till I found the waggons, which had crossed it and outspanned perhaps a mile and a half further down. Just before reaching the waggons (8.20am), I came to a most singular building, built on a little isolated kopje in the midst of the level tree-studded veldt, but with other kopjes near. There has been an excellently-built wall running round the sides of the kopje, and a regular entrance into it. The boys say it was built in old times by the ancestors of the present race of Makalakas, and was the king's residence. No white man, they say, helped to build it. It is not seen from the waggon road.

"The river, which we outspanned at, and which (as before stated) contains plenty of water, flows away towards the south-west, as shown by the reeds in its now dry sandy bed[102].

"Started again at 1.20pm and went about eight miles; first through 'mopani veldt', with fine trees in it, and a little before outspanning passed through a range of low kopjes. This 'mopani' is usually very heavy land, so called from the mopani trees[103] (not unlike alders) which grow upon it. Of the fruit-trees referred to, one was my old glutinous friend of the Gwailo hunting veldt—plentiful, but not yet ripe. It is very woody, but when chewed exudes a fine glutinous gum. Another has a small fruit like a little rosy-cheeked apple, containing seeds, and something of the crab nature, but not at all acid. Another, which I should say was also of the apple kind, and like the last in taste and texture, was

---

[102] This river, represented in most of the recent maps as taking its rise but a few miles from here, and flowing away directly to the westward towards the salt lakes, is in reality—so the traveller afterward learnt from at least three distinct witnesses—a part of the Shashe River, the same river which is crossed on the Bamangwato and Tati road, a few miles before reaching Tati, coming north One of these witnesses, Mr. Dobie of the mine, had, moreover, struck the river, he said, about thirty miles northward of the drift on which the waggons were now outspanned, and had found it a big river even there, where, according to the maps, it is not even in existence. The slate formation in which the gold is found runs, it seems, to a narrow point as far as this river-drift, and there ceases altogether.

[103] Mopani or mopane (*Colophospermum mopane*). DS

as large as a plum and of the same colour, and grew on a thick low bushy large-leaved tree[104].

"In the evening, where we were outspanned, I found a large colony of birds[105] established in three large nests (half-built, I think) in the branch of a tall tree. This is the noisy familiar bird I first met with at Tati."

Proceeding forward on the following morning, still through the veldt of large mopani trees, and passing amongst numerous fine rocky kopjes—rising up on every side in bold craggy heaps from the level veldt, tree-covered like the latter wherever trees could find root—Frank Oates next crossed two or three small spruits, now dry, of which the largest was about five yards wide. At this there was a delay of about half an hour, caused by one of the waggons sticking in its sandy bed, and when he had crossed it he outspanned upon its bank. And here, as he rested—the Tati now well behind him, and his imagination full of hope in the future and interest in the present—it is likely enough he may have congratulated himself on the successful progress of his journey, but scarcely probable he should have reflected on the possibility that here, not many hundred yards from this very spot, he might but a few months hence, when returning from the Falls, find his last lonely resting-place; yet so he did.

Again, after a brief rest, renewing the journey about mid-day, he still advanced a short distance further in the same direction before coming to another halt; and here the Journal once more takes up the story :—

"*June 18th.*— ... Inspanned again about noon, and crossed another spruit with a sharp turn in it. Soon saw cornfields, then the bright green of tobacco-fields and a kraal[106], and outspanned at 1pm. I was pleased with the appearance of this little kraal, surrounded by its green fields of tobacco, and emerging suddenly to view from amidst the mopani trees; but I little thought of the disappointment in store for me here. Though we had trekked so short a time, and made our previous trek so short as to be scarcely worth mentioning, I almost decided to outspan here before I

---

[104] Probably wild plum (*Harpephyllum caffrum*). DS

[105] The Red-billed Black Weaver-bird (*Textor erythrorhynchus*).

[106] This kraal, the first outpost of the Makalakas, is described as "Wankee's" in the traveller's later Journals, and is so marked upon the map.

found that it was absolutely necessary I must. The people told us that there was a message from the king, which the induna would convey to me, but he was away at another kraal and must be sent for. Sent a boy with the oxen to water, which is some distance off, employing a man from the kraal as guide. Meantime I made it known that I wanted goats and corn, and ere long was hard at work dispensing beads, handkerchiefs, and snuff-boxes. The main run was on the large lavender beads, next came the small lavender ones, and a few wanted blue cut ones. Mealies were brought in large quantities, but sold principally in small basketfuls. There was plenty of Kafir corn too, but not so much as of the Indian corn. Tobacco also was brought, and the sweet kind of beans that are like nuts' kernels.

"The women crowded round to sell. They were many of them recently smeared on their heads with something black like pitch, babies and all. Many of the girls have the hair matted thickly together in lumps. One hanging over the forehead, the end of the lock having brass rings fastened to it, droops down to the nose, and one to each ear. The hair is all drawn out in matted locks. A profusion of brass rings are worn on the arms, and heavy bead necklaces round the neck. Many of them are pretty. There are distinctly perceptible the dark and the light skinned; some nearly black, some copper-coloured The men are much given to wearing carved charms and other ornaments and curiosities A lion's claw or a vulture's beak are favourites amongst the latter division. They wear skins—karosses with the hair worn inside. John says there are both Masahras (Bushmen) and Makalakas here. I was surprised to hear from him that there are many Bushmen living in kraals and not wandering in the bush, as I had an idea they were exclusively a gipsy race, but it appears by no means so universally. The induna is an old Makalaka, who does not talk the Matabele language, but as it was not till the day after our arrival that I saw him, I will leave him for the present.

"Presently an individual arrived in white clothes, who spoke a little Dutch. Without ceremony he jumped up on my waggon-box, and I concluded he was the induna from his free style. I begged him to excuse me, as I was very busy buying corn, after he had asked John a question or two, as, 'Was I going to the Zambesi?' I never thought I was to be stopped, and went on buying corn, and he seemed glad to let me do so, till at last he came to his final interview—for much of the time he had been with Van Roozen. He then told me that the king had sent to stop all waggons from coming on, on account of the sickness, but the induna himself would be here the following morning. My feelings this evening were ones of intense disappointment, but still I hoped something from my interview with the induna the next day."

"*June 19th.*—Very cloudy day, night; inclined to rain. The induna and a large crowd here early. I took down the substance of the induna's words. They were thoroughly confirmatory of my worst fears. He said though they here would not stop me by main force, the kraals ahead would do so. *They* spoke as my friends. If I persisted in going on, they would send to inform the king, who would despatch a party of Matabele to seize my waggons and take possession of my goods. I thought best to take down the substance of what the induna said to me, in order to report it to the king. Umganulo, an induna, he stated, brought the following news from the king four days ago, and went back immediately—All white men going to the Zambesi to be stopped, and their boys killed if they attempt going on with them; waggons to be taken to the king if orders are disobeyed. The king too has stopped people going by all other roads to the Zambesi, and messengers also passed here the day before yesterday, going on to the Zambesi, to tell all white men who are already there not to return till the rains fall, as they may bring sickness. The king has also said that no one may go across the veldt to him from here, but all must go by way of Tati."

"*June 21st.*—Rather cloudy, but fine. Got up about 5am. … Girls here very early with corn; also some goats brought for sale, of which I bought two for a cotton blanket, also a little more corn, some leather bags, and a calabash. A tall lad, formerly a driver for Palmer, and a most free and easy individual, having relapsed into the national dress, offered his services to me as a hunter, if I should return this way. I ask John his character. John says he once took a knob-kerry to Mr. Palmer, when the latter wanted to thrash him. But he was not to blame for that, says John; a notion of John's which I had let him see did not meet my approval.

"Some of the girls who came to-day were very profusely ornamented with beads. The thick matted hair, plastered together with black wax-like cement, is disposed of (as I noted before) in three principal locks; one falling over the forehead between the eyes, and one in front of each ear, mounted with brass rings. The ears are pierced with small rings. Round the neck hang chains of beads, tastefully arranged and blended. A leather kaross, or dressed skin, is worn as a robe, and this is hung with long strings of beads. Long strings of beads too hang round the hips, and in front are long strips of leather. Round the waist are numerous brass rings and bead rings also. The girls are by no means shy.

"To-day poor Mozanga told me of some trouble he was in, and I thought he complained of a beating, but it seemed he had heard of the death of the induna of the kraal where I engaged him, a young man, who they say died in the Zambesi hunting veldt. He must have gone there at a very unhealthy time. Mozanga wept bitterly; he is a very kindhearted boy.

"I went with Umfanimboozi to shoot some birds, whilst the oxen, which had got loose, were being fetched, and went through some tobacco 'gardens'. The pink blossoms and green leaves are very pretty..."

This same afternoon (June 21st) the traveller reluctantly commenced his journey back to Tati, resolved to revisit the king, and ascertain from his own lips the real truth of the induna's statement. The fine clear nights, during a part of which he now made a point of trekking, were brilliant as he returned with glittering stars and constellations, the Southern Cross at this time conspicuous amongst the latter a little after sunset. Four days after starting he was back at the Tati settlement, and on the 30th of June started on horseback to the King's Town, with eight boys to take his baggage.

On reaching the King's, Lobengula tried to laugh the matter off, and this time, as an assurance of good faith, appointed one of his own people, a son of the headman, Manyami, to see him safe through the country of the Makalakas. Frank Oates was again back at Tati on the 15th of July, and here, before starting once more for the Zambesi, he made some fresh plans and arrangements for the journey. What these arrangements were may best be learned from the ensuing letter, written at this time from Tati, and containing, besides, some particulars of his recent journey to Gubuleweyo. This letter is as follows:—

"TATI, *July 21st, 1874.*

"I am, you see, at Tati once more. ... I left here for the Zambesi on the 9th of June, and on the 18th—travelling very slowly, as I had lots of time before me—reached the first Makalaka kraal—on the Zambesi road. Here I was stopped, being told that the king had sent a special order to turn all waggons back which might come that way. They also said that all waggons coming from the Zambesi were to be turned back, and not allowed to leave until the rains fell, which begin about October. It was in vain I pleaded that I had special leave from the king. They said their orders were peremptory—all waggons to be turned back, and if the people with them refused to obey, the waggons were to be seized, and all the boys who persisted in accompanying them killed. This of course frightened my Kafirs, and all I could do was to turn back, and go to the king in person.

"On the 25th of June I was once more at Tati, and decided to ride to the King's Town, but a fresh difficulty arose in getting boys to go with me, as my own boys say the white men are the cause of all this trouble, for they bring the sickness, and they are afraid the king will kill them for accompanying white men. At last, however, this difficulty was surmounted, and I set off on the 30th of June with my two horses, and eight boys carrying my baggage. Gordon[107], a Mungwato trader, arrived at Tati *en route* for the King's whilst I was making my preparations, but says there were no letters there for me when he left. He could not go on even to the King's without special leave, as the king has heard of 'red-water', the Natal cattle disease, and is in a great fright about it. Indeed, if it got amongst his cattle, his nation would suffer terribly. It seems, too, from recent reports, that it is contagious, though we never used to think so.

"Dorehill's waggon[108] and the waggons of another trader had been stopped on their way to the King's Town at the Inkwesi River, where the first Matabele kraal is, and were there when I came up.' I got on very well up to the time of my reaching these waggons, and stayed a couple of days at them with Dorehill, who was awaiting further news from the King's. On leaving the waggons I met the messenger he had sent to the king returning with a message from the latter to Dorehill that he was to ride on and see him. I went on, but had great difficulty in keeping my boys from turning back. However, I explained to them that if they kept with me there was no likelihood of their being hurt, as no white man's servants ever were interfered with, whereas, if they turned back, they might be killed. They would of course have liked me to turn back with them; but seeing I was determined to go on, thought it was their best chance to remain in my company. I of course knew there was not much fear of anything being done to them as long as they were with me, as the king holds everything belonging to white men sacred, and his people dare not commit any violence on Kafirs protected by a white man. The fact is my boys were principally Makalakas, who are slaves to the Matabele, and whose lives are considered worthless.

"One night I was very angry with them, for I had been riding on in advance, and kept on riding after sundown, as the country for miles

---

[107] George Gordon, a Scot from Elgin who traded in Shoshong. DS

[108] Mr. Dorehill had been met by Frank Oates previously at Bamangwato, and subsequently accompanied him part of the way on is final journey to the Zambesi. [George Dorehill arrived in South Africa in 1871, and worked as a trader in Bulawayo and Shoshong for several years. DS]

round was on fire, and I wanted to get past the fire before we encamped for the night. I lay down with my head on a log, to await their arrival, and fell asleep. By and by I woke up, and found it was colder than agreeable, and at once guessed that they had stopped behind. I had to ride back a good way before I came to their fire, when I pitched into them. They had been afraid to come on after sundown, as the Matabele don't allow their subjects to travel by night, though of course a white man can do what he likes.

"The next day Dorehill overtook me. He had set off the day after me, but without food or blankets, and was very glad to share mine. The day we rode on to Gubuleweyo, the King's The king seemed surprised to see me, but did not speak to me the first day I saw him, except to greet me, and send me to his sister to drink beer. The next day, when I told him what had occurred, he seemed rather amused than otherwise, and told me the Makalakas had been trying to frighten me, and that he had never sent them any order to stop waggons. I believe, however, he is the one to blame, and had probably neglected to send word to the Makalakas to let me pass. I had written to him from Tati for leave to go to the Zambesi, and he had given it, but could never have sent word to the Makalakas, who are his subjects, and very much given to stopping waggons that have not a special permit from him. He now gave me a Matabele boy, at my request, to accompany me.

"The little horse I sold him for £23 when last at his town had got over the sickness, as I fully expected he would, and was 'salted,' and must be now worth from £80 to £100. I should never have parted with him, had not Mr. Thomson advised me so, in order to ensure his goodwill in case I wanted to go to the Zambesi. It seems, however, he did not do for me what he might have done, and it has been suggested to me that this was because I refused to sell him my gun also! I think I told you that I gave him a gun when first I saw him, but he wanted very much another I had, offering me £60 or £70 worth of ivory for it, but I persisted in refusing to let him have it, and then it was he asked for the horse, and would not let the subject drop till he got the animal, and got him at his own price. I am afraid he is very little better than the generality of Kafirs, and certainly I have experienced anything but generous treatment at his hands—indeed scarcely fair play. Yet there is no doubt that he is very much afraid of anything befalling white men in his country, either from sickness or any other cause, and now, when he told me to go to the Zambesi, he added, 'Unless I was afraid of the sickness.' This idea of sickness, and the new fear of a contagious cattle disease, brought by white men, are causing a good deal of trouble. Dorehill, however, got leave to take his waggon on, and intends to go the Zambesi when he leaves the King's. I rode back with Dorehill as far as his waggon, and there met Mr. Thomson and his wife once more, returning to the Matabele after being absent at a missionary meeting at Kuruman[109].

"On reaching Tati I had some more trouble, which has ended in my making fresh arrangements altogether. John, my Kafir driver, refused point-blank to go with me to the Zambesi, and though I could have compelled him to do so, I thought it best to be rid of such an unwilling servant. Brown's waggons are starting for Potchefstroom and by them this letter is to be taken, which I hope will reach you by the end of September. John's only chance of leaving is to get away with these waggons, and of course if I say the word Brown will not let him go near them, and he cannot possibly go alone. However, I told John I should not stop him because I did not think him worth keeping, and he will leave with the waggons to-morrow. Then the Dutchman in two instances had acted very badly whilst I was travelling with him, and when I was obliged to return to Tati I secretly intended to get rid of him, though I did not tell him so.

"It was the 15th of July when I got back here from the King's, and the very same day a trader arrived from the Zambesi, coming to get a fresh stock of goods. He had had to drive his own waggon, having lost his driver and other boys through being at the Zambesi in the unhealthy season. Indeed, he went there at what is supposed to be an extremely unhealthy time. I think it was February when he left here, and April and May are, I believe, the very worst months on the Zambesi. I left, as I have told you, early in June, intending to be back again before the end of the year, which everyone says is the proper thing to do. Both Garland and Dawnay succeeded seeing the Falls last year by doing so, and this year there are others who have probably seen them this time. Now it is not too late to go there this season still, though the time one can spend there is shortened by not leaving earlier, for it takes about a month to reach the place where the waggons stand, and allowing another month for visiting the Falls, and a month for returning here, there is no doubt the Falls could be comfortably visited during a three months' absence from Tati,

---

[109] This was the last occasion on which Frank Oates encountered Mr. Thomson, who, some time after the events here narrated—in 1877—returned to England, to convey thence, under the auspices of the London Missionary Society, a party of missionaries to Lake Tanganyika. He accomplished the journey successfully, but unhappily was attacked by sunstroke soon after his arrival, and died from its effects in September 1878.

and there would be nothing remarkable in doing it all in two months with good oxen and good servants. So I can still go there, and be back again as soon as I ever intended to be.

"I am now coming to my new arrangement, which I think is in many respects a very promising one, for a final attempt to reach the Falls. The trader I speak of ('Stoffel Kennedy,' or some such name[110]), has actually been at the Falls. He was there with Garland last year, and knows the country well. He knows where the poison-plant is, and where the tsetse-fly. He knows the people of the country, and all its ins and outs. He is I think partly of Dutch or German origin, but is to all intents and purposes an Englishman, and is very much liked. He offered to postpone his own trading trip, and turn back at once with me to the Zambesi, guaranteeing to take me to the Falls if I would make it worth his while. He would then, he said, take me there and bring me back, not going as my servant, but undertaking the whole management of the expedition for me. Now I knew I should have one waggon and span of oxen to sell when I came from the Zambesi, and he was willing to take these now at a fair price, deducting the sum which he wanted as a reward for his services. It was a little time before I could make up my mind, but it seemed such a chance for me as I might not soon have again. As for the Dutchman, I had even gone so far at one time as to vow that, rather than set off again with him, I would give up the trip; and though I modified this resolve afterwards, yet I knew he was not so likely to get me to the Falls as this man who knows all the difficulties. Then I thought, after all the time I have spent in order to get to the Zambesi, and being still bent on going there, the best thing would be to embrace this opportunity. I should not even have had the Kafir, John, in the other case, but only the Dutchman and his son, who cannot speak the language, and with the former of whom I had had a most unpleasant row more than once.

"It ended in my entrusting my fortunes to the new man. Brown, I may add, thinks I have done well, and I have every confidence in his judgment. He is a man of whom I have the very highest opinion, and,

---

[110] Actually Christoffel Schinderhutte, a German hunter and trader who had visited the Victoria Falls in 1873. Five months after Oates' death, he became drunk on Cape brandy in Shoshong before departing with a consignment of goods for Pandamatenga. In the throes of *delirium tremens* he shot some of his own oxen; knocked a servant under the wheels of the waggon, where he was crushed to death, and then shot his guide before running into the bush. His shoes and part of his beard were found later, and it was concluded that he had died of exhaustion or been killed by animals or friends of the dead servants. DS

indeed, the more I know of him, the more I like and admire him. Personally, I have experienced the greatest kindness from him at all times, and know how to appreciate it.

"Stoffel is going to take his own waggon and the ten oxen he bought of me, leaving the new waggon here. ... Brown has just refused £110 for a little 'horse'—of course you know 'horse' means ' pony' every time I use it—which he bought for £80. A good horse is worth anything to one here, and I cannot wonder at the price given for 'salted' horses. Suppose, for instance, I had had to go to the King's on foot, and got foot-sore, where should I have been? The question is one not easily answered; but I suppose at any rate I should not have got on as well as I did. The absurdity is, that for a small insignificant-looking pony you have to pay the same price as for a good English hunter. A day or two ago we had some races here. We could only muster four horses, but by varying the riders and riding races over again, we managed to get five races, in all of which I rode, and got the reputation of being a good jockey, as out of the five I rode in I won four."

Favourable as the above arrangements seemed for a renewed attempt to reach the Falls, the traveller's hopes, as will soon be seen, were again doomed to disappointment; and this in a most un-looked-for manner.

KLIPSPRINGER.—*Oreotragus saltatrix*.
(Height about 20 inches.)

CHAPTER X

Third start for the Zambesi—Again stopped by natives—Fresh leave from the king—The journey resumed—Frank Oates's companion obliged to leave him—He goes forward alone—Breakdown of his waggon—Annoyances from the natives—Help from Tati—Return there—Letters home—Future plans.

LEAVING Tati on the evening of the 25th of July, on his third attempt to reach the Zambesi, Frank Oates halted for the night a few miles beyond the settlement, completing the distance to the Ramaqueban the following morning. Here, whilst waiting a couple of days in search of game and for other purposes he was again unexpectedly stopped by natives, professedly armed with authority from Lobengula to stop all waggons from advancing northwards. The story of this encounter, with its immediate consequences, is thus related in the Journal:—

"*July 27th.*—Fine and oppressively hot, after a cold night. The days are now very hot, though the nights continue cold and frosty. I was going to ride over to the Inkwesi to-day, with a letter from Brown to Greit[111], and to see if Greit could let me have one of his drivers. However, before I set off, a Matabele came down the Zambesi road, bearing a shield, and accompanied by a Makalala bearing another. A second Makalaka appeared later, but the moment the Matabele arrived, he came up to the waggons, and began interrogating us. On hearing that we were going to the Zambesi, he began to leap and dance about like a madman, brandishing a battle-axe. I thought it a case of temporary insanity, brought on by smoking 'dacha'[112], but it appeared from his statement he had been sent from the king to the Makalakas, with a fresh order to stop waggons, and was now going on to Tati, to tell white men the same tale.

"I had difficulty in keeping the dogs from attacking him, and once he brought his battle-axe within a few inches of Stoffel's skull. He

---

[111] Augustus Greite, a German who arrived in Matabeleland in 1869; he later retired with his family to Marico District in the Transvaal. DS

[112] A kind of hemp, much used for smoking by the natives. [Dagga (*Cannabis sativa*). DS]

became quiet, however, when Makabo (Manyami's son)[113] told him the facts of the case, and said I could go on, but my boys, who were subjects of the king, would be killed, and if I went on I had better pay them off here. I therefore decided on sending to the king—first, to ask for further security for my boys, second, for leave to take Stoffel with me; and decided to send off Manyami's son with two others, with a letter to the king and another to Thomson.

"At night there was a tremendous conflagration close to us. It was a splendid sight, but made me a little nervous. However, it was principally on the other side of the road, and died before it came quite close. The effect of the burning trees and long line of fire was very fine. One tree in particular, showing all its twigs red-hot or in flames, reminded me of some part of a display of fireworks."

The following morning Makabo was duly despatched with two boys—Umfanimboozi and Umfan—to the King's, and Frank Oates remained hunting on the Ramaqueban, till their return a few days afterwards, with a favourable answer to his message. On the 10th of August he was once more moving northwards the same way as he had gone before, halting again on the 11th for a couple of days' hunting higher up the river, at a point where game seemed more than usually abundant. This was the place where the road branches off from the Ramaqueban across the veldt again towards the Tati.

"I now feel," he writes at this point, on August 13th, "to be realizing almost for the first time some of my old visions of South African sport. To-day, soon after starting, I ascended a kopje near the waggons, and saw a large herd of quagga. Counting roughly, I made out a hundred. It was a beautiful sight. All around was the sea of bush with here and there bare patches, and here and there kopjes—some of the latter far distant. The winding spruits, too, lay as in a map. The quaggas were quietly moving on, or standing and playing, or brushing away the flies. It was a scene such as I used to fancy must be common, and which probably was so when the accounts I have read were written, and may occur often still in more remote districts.

The day previous the traveller had shot koodoo, hartebeest, and pallah, and seen an immense herd of quagga and blue wildebeest, numbering not far from a hundred of each sort. Amongst the lesser antelopes, the graceful klipspringer, found only in the hills, was met with in this district.

---

[113] The man appointed by the king.

Resuming his journey to the north-west on the 15th, and travelling through mopani veldt, he again struck the Tati River in the afternoon at the same point where the pleasing character of the scenery had been first observed by him when he was here months before. A spring or 'fountain' of fresh water welled up at the foot of a picturesque kopje, and a mile or two up the river was abundance of water in the river-bed.

"The river here," writes the traveller at the latter point, "flows to the south through a deep sandy bed, kopjes hemming it in on either side. The scenery is remarkably pretty for South Africa, and the long reach of river flowing away to the southward is an object to attract the eye. The water actually runs in the bed here, though there is far more sand than water, and big stones than either. Stoffel says there used to be plenty of elephants here. This was the place where they passed through the kopjes on their way south, and last year he and Garland saw fresh spoor here. Out with rifle down river; pretty little grassy parks amongst the kopjes, and on the kopjes themselves very thick bush. The river where we have struck it—the 'poort' as Stoffel calls it—would be a pretty subject for a sketch."

Again pushing forward the following and two next succeeding days, still by the same route already traversed, Frank Oates once more reached— on August 18th—the first kraal of the Makalakas, the former scene of so much trouble and vexation to him. A few days previously it had chanced that Stoffel had slightly hurt his finger, and here, as it began to give him pain, they waited a week before proceeding further from all reach of help, to see what course the injury would take. Supplies of corn had here to be obtained, and the interval of waiting was occupied, partly in striking bargains with the natives, and partly in rearranging the contents of the waggons, to receive the grain; neither of them the most agreeable of occupations, as the following extract from the Journal shows:—

"*August 20th.*—Windy day; rather cloudy. The wind rose very much towards night. ... I am now lying in my waggon, glad to rest, wearied out principally with worry, and the dissatisfaction of finding time so miserably wasted as to-day has been; packing, unpacking, stooping, watching lest things are stolen, and having one's patience tried in buying of the natives, putting up with their disagreeable presence and impudence, to say nothing of the annoyances one is subjected to by one's own servants. I had to knock the disgusting servant of Makabo off the dissel-boom before he would go. He was bothering me for a snuff-box, and would not go away for civil speaking. I am not patient or industrious enough for waggon life. To-day has been one of nothing but unpleasantness to me."

At length, on the 23rd, it became evident that Stoffel must return and seek advice from Mr. Thomson, the missionary, who had some skill in surgery. This change of plan involved a corresponding change in all the arrangements of the journey, and such of Frank Oates's goods as had hitherto been carried in the trader's waggon had now to be taken in his own, already sufficiently loaded when they left the settlement. On the 24th Stoffel took his departure southwards, and two days later Frank Oates went on alone towards the Zambesi. It was a lovely moonlight night when he resumed the journey, the waggon running heavy through thick mopani veldt. The prospect of success in his present enterprise seemed nearing its fulfilment, yet in reality he was but on the eve of a fresh misfortune. "We passed a kraal," he writes in his Journal, "on the left side of the road, perhaps two miles from where we started, and had gone perhaps one mile more when, in crossing a small 'sloot'[114], one of the wheels gave way and came down, broken to pieces. So much," he concludes, "for the new waggon, and for my hopes and expectations!"

The day after this catastrophe, which appeared in its results fatal to all hope of his reaching the Zambesi that season, late as it had now become, he arranged to send his driver—a Kafir named Klaas, whom he had engaged from a Mr. Horn upon the Ramaqueban—and three boys, with the broken wheel to Tati, and also with a note to Mr. Brown, asking for assistance. The annoyances during their absence of about a fortnight, from the natives of the neighbouring kraals are described at length in some of his letters, largely quoted from below. It is therefore sufficient here to say that he was wilfully subjected by them to every possible inconvenience, was in constant peril of being robbed, and at one time even appeared to be in some danger of his life. The whole of this time he could not leave his waggon, lest he should return to find it plundered, and even his own boys were not to be depended on.

At last, on the 8th of September, the needful help arrived, and he was released from his state of bondage. He had just had a most threatening visit from a noisy crowd of natives, when the messengers he had sent returned from Tati with all that he had asked for. After relating in his Journal the incidents of this unpleasant interview, he thus concludes the story:—

---

[114] *i.e.* stream, or ditch

"They left me," he says, " the noisy crew; and still, though I felt relieved, a gloom hovered over my feelings, and I lay down to rest. It was then with delight indeed that Maclinwon's announcement, 'incolo'[115] (waggon), broke on my ears, and that, rushing out, I beheld Klaas driving a waggon to my scherm. True enough, Brown had managed to procure an old waggon to help me out, sending me also a wheel of the Scotch cart and four oxen, to ensure my having sufficient. There was a long letter from him, and four newspapers sent for me from England, with news of letters from home awaiting me at Tati."

This was indeed a welcome release to the traveller from his present troubles; but, with such information as he now possessed regarding the period and duration of the healthy season for visiting the Zambesi he felt that by this time it was too late for him to attempt to reach the river, and that, for the present at all events, he must abandon the idea of getting there.

On the 10th of September, therefore, he once more unwillingly started back on the return journey to Tati, where he arrived on the 18th, to find, with delight, a large packet of letters awaiting him from England. After the harass and annoyance of his recent experiences, he was glad to rest here for a while, and was comfortably quartered the chief part of his stay in the house usually occupied by Piet Jacobs, the Dutchman, who was now absent in the hunting veldt. This house was cool and airy, with a thatched roof extending far on every side, so as to form a verandah.

The following entries in his Journal, soon after his arrival, relating mostly to natural history subjects, may here be read with interest. He writes:—

"*September 20th.*—Rather windy, but pleasant day, after a cold night. I liked my new quarters. ... Tonight, as last night, sat at Brown's talking. We discuss some questions in natural history. ...

"Wild dogs have been discussed. Dobie has seen them in packs, he says, variegated in colour, with white patches here and there, differently placed in different animals. Brown has seen them, and says they are like what he imagines a European wolf to be—and I think he has a good idea what the latter is like. Johnson says that, when coming here, he saw a hare run against the waggon wheel when they were outspanned at the Shashe, and kill herself; and by the light of the fire he saw distinctly, standing twenty or thirty yards off, a wild dog. He says it was a

---

[115] *iNqola*, Ndebele, 'waggon'. DS

good deal like a European wolf—an animal he knows—with a fine coat and bushy tail, upright ears, I think, and a long nose. Brown says they often run pallah into the station here, when the natives, hearing the cry of the pallah, rush out from the different white men's establishments to assegai it and the dogs are usually found to have torn at the place where such creatures generally commence their attacks, and even dragged out a portion of the entrails. They must hunt the pallah, he says, for hours with dogged perseverance and fairly weary him out. I know myself what a fleet creature the pallah is, and have no doubt for miles he would far outstrip a pack of dogs.

"Brown says a fine dog in a wild state once hung about here for some time, stealing meat at night, and playing with the tame dogs. He was very cunning, and was off at the slightest indication of danger. If he was heard outside the house and the least noise made inside, he was off. Many shots were fired at him, and he escaped for a long time, but at length was shot when on one of his visits. He lived in the veldt, and always rushed into the bush, just like a hyena, which he resembled closely in his habits. This was no doubt some white man's dog that had run wild and acquired the habits of a wild animal to a certain extent."

"*September 23rd.*—Pleasant breeze. Did not do much, or feel up to much. Another chat at Brown's in the evening. Brown tells me that once four young guinea-fowls were brought him, which became extremely tame. One only, a hen, survived. She became wonderfully tame, and would follow the Tati people about. When a Tati waggon was sent for wood, or for any other purpose, she would go and return with it, not following strange waggons. She would follow Nelson when he rode to the 'Blue Jacket'[116], wait for him, and return home with him. Latterly she got into the habit of going with the oxen when they went into the veldt, would start with them, remain all day, and return at night with them, marching in front. She would even join wild guinea-fowl, if she came across them in the veldt, and would leave them as soon as she found she was getting too far from the waggon or person she was with at the time. She is supposed to have been killed at last by a nigger by mistake. Brown had had her eight or ten months."

With these extracts the present period of the traveller's wanderings, so far as his Journal is concerned, may be allowed to

---

[116] A mine near Tati.

terminate. The weather, which had up to this time continued cool at night, began towards the end of September to be intensely hot and oppressive, though still liable to considerable variation; so much so indeed that one day about the middle of October the extreme cold brought the swallows into the houses for shelter and protection.

The Zambesi now abandoned, Frank Oates, on the 8th of October, sent two boys with a message to the king, asking for leave to hunt a few weeks on the Shashani, which was readily accorded him; but he did not start immediately—his waggon required some repairs, and he was not feeling well. Whilst thus waiting a while longer, to recruit his health and complete his preparations, two gentlemen—Messrs. Bond and Robertson[117]—arrived on their return from the Zambesi, having gone there early in the year. They had shot elephants near the river, and the former had made some pretty sketches of the Falls. Other parties also now came in from the Zambesi.

At length, on the 3rd of November, Frank Oates once more set off into the veldt—not to the Shashani, however, as he had intended, but again in a northerly direction, for reasons shortly to be stated. Before starting on this occasion, he wrote home some letters of considerable length, reviewing his experiences of the past three months, since the date of his last departure from Tati on the 25th of July, which may here be given almost as they stand, entire. The first of these, written to his mother, is as follows:—

"TATI, *October 1st. 1874*.

"When you see the above date, you will perhaps think that I have returned from the Zambesi; but the fates seem to have conspired against my reaching that river. After last writing home I left here on the 25th of July in company with Stoffel, the trader I told you of, and with every prospect of a most successful trip. The series of mishaps which led to my final (for this season at any rate) return here on the 18th of September, I will presently relate. I say, 'this season at any rate,' but I think I shall now give up the Zambesi altogether, consoling myself with the adage—'Tis not in mortals to *command* success'. I read somewhere of someone replying to this—'But they can *deserve* it'; and a third party, who I think showed his wisdom, suggested, as an amendment, that they could '*do without* it.' I think, to a certain extent, I deserved it for my persistent efforts to attain it, and may hope to march out with the honours of war, and 'do without it.'

---

[117] Bond and Robertson returned to South Africa in late 1875. DS

"I can scarcely express the pleasure it gave me to receive, on returning here, a large packet of letters bearing dates from the 4th of August 1873, to the 25th of April 1874; some to Willie and some to myself, and some which Willie had written to me on his way home. I suppose he had read, and sent on for my perusal, those of the letters which are addressed to him. The letters seem to form a connected series, and I doubt whether any have failed to reach me. After hastily looking over a few of them I proceeded to arrange them according to date, and then to read them through in order. I scarcely hoped that there would be no bad news. ... Skelton's death must be a terrible blow to his family, who, when I saw them last, were looking forward to a visit from him. It seems only the other day he was at Oxford distinguishing himself in the athletic sports, in which he was generally a successful competitor. I believe every one liked him, and that he was worthy of their high opinion[118].

"To-day waggons have arrived from Bamangwato and, to my great joy, another letter was fished up for me from the bag. Hathorn writes from 'Maritzburg on the 4th of August, enclosing a letter from Willie, dated June 2nd, and a line from Charley, dated June 4th. It is very delightful to be brought in Contact with you all once more after so long an interruption to communication. I don't believe anything can make one appreciate home and friends like a long absence from them. Indeed, things we think nothing of at home are often dwelt upon in memory when one is in the midst of the wilderness. The packet of letters which I have referred to as awaiting me when I came here, arrived at Tati before the end of August, and the latest written of them bears date April 25th; so that, in both instances, about four months have elapsed between the time the letters were posted in England and that of their delivery here. It is the fact of one's moving about that makes the communication with home so desultory.[119]

"To-day the rains may be said to have begun, but there will probably not be much rain for some time yet. However, this morning was dark and gloomy enough, though there are now signs of an improvement

---

[118] This refers to the late Mr. Henry Skelton, formerly of Wadham College, Oxford, who died in Borneo, in the service of the late Rajah Brooke, soon after his appointment as Resident of Sarawak.

[119] The time occupied in the transmission of letters has, since the above was written, been much curtailed, owing to the establishment, through missionary enterprise, of direct postal communication between Bamangwato and the Cape.

in the weather. I have been here a fortnight, and am waiting till certain necessary repairs are made in my waggon, my idea being to spend a few weeks in this neighbourhood before finally leaving for Maritzburg. ... In the meantime I mean to give you a little account of my doings since my last letter to you, encouraged by Charley's assurance that my descriptions of the country and the account of my wanderings are read with some little interest, though I fear I can only thank the friendliness of my critics for anything interesting being found in them. As, however, I receive the flattering assurance that they do afford a little amusement I will proceed without further apology. A mail is leaving here very shortly, as traders are now here on their way to Mungwato, and will take letters. By the way, I am writing with some of the desiccated ink I brought with me. I had a grand brew of it yesterday, and it is an undoubted success. My table is formed by a packing-case, and my chair is a box of gunpowder—but I am not smoking. I am inhabiting a deserted house made by one of the former gold-diggers here, and appropriated by a Dutch family, who, however, are from home. The *paterfamilias* has gone to hunt for ivory in the Zambesi direction, and taken his 'vrouw'[120], family, and furniture with him in his waggon."

The narrative, here broken off, was again resumed, some days later:—

"*October 20th.*

"I again take up my pen to continue the letter I began on the 1st of this month, and which I hoped would have been a long way south of Bamangwato by this time. The delay has been occasioned by the drought, rendering the journey full of risk for the oxen. I promised you a short *résumé* of my doings and sufferings since I last wrote to you. By sufferings, I don't of course mean bodily ones, but what I have suffered from rascally Kafirs, and which are only entitled to be called annoyances.

"After last writing to you, I left here on the 25th of July in company with the trader I told you of. Some delay ensued when we were one day from here, occasioned by reports of the road being stopped by the king. I had with me the man given me by his Majesty to see me safely through the Makalakas on my way to the Zambesi, and a precious rascal he was. Some people came up to the waggons with demonstrations, one of them rushing about and flourishing a battle-axe. I adopted my usual course, in such cases, of lighting a pipe and sitting on the front-box of my waggon, watching the performance, varying my tactics by turning my back

---

[120] *Vrouw*, Dutch, 'wife'.

on him. He professed to have authority from the king to stop all waggons going to the Zambesi, and lugged in poor old Mosilikatze's name, as is usual in grand orations, and made my boys shake in their shoes, metaphorically speaking, by informing them that the order was that any of the king's subjects accompanying white men to the Zambesi were to be killed.

"The son of Manyami, the man given me expressly to shut up this sort of bounce, suggested that this might be some new order from the king. I therefore lost no time in sending him off with a letter to headquarters, requesting full instructions, Manyami's son had not seen the king at all about the affair, but I had simply taken him, as the king told me, from his father's kraal on my way from Gubuleweyo to Tati. Old Manyami is the man who used to stop all waggons coming into the country till the king had given leave for them to proceed, and he stopped me when I first came myself, as I dare say I told you at the time. This is done, however, at a different kraal now—the first one passed by any waggons going from here to Gubuleweyo, about forty miles north-east of Tati. In the meantime I remained on the Ramaqueban, my ally riding over to Tati once or twice.

"Whilst I was here a trader of the name Horn[121] passed, and had to wait when he was miles on the road to ask leave to proceed, as all waggons from Natal are now stopped for fear of the disease, and Horn had to explain who he where he came from. Horn, I think, is the man who opened the Zambesi trade, but is at present trading with the Matabele. A lion killed one of his oxen on the Inkwesi one night whilst he was here, and a dozen of them took fright and ran away. I assisted in looking for them, and followed up the spoor next day till late in the afternoon, and must have been close to the oxen, but there was a Scotch mist, and it was a wretched evening, so, leaving three Kafirs to follow and sleep on the spoor, I returned to the waggons. Next day the Kafirs returned without the oxen, and thus much time was lost. The day after this Horn's partner followed the spoor to the water, but from the water followed up, by mistake, some fresh buffalo spoor, and slept on it, to come the following morning on to a herd of buffalo, which rather astonished him. At last Stoffel set off with him, about four or five days after the oxen had strayed, and they succeeded in recovering them.

---

[121] William Horn began trading with the Ndebele in 1868, and returned to the Zambesi from Natal in 1874. The following year he opened a store in Bulawayo, but died at Hope Fountain in October 1875. DS

"Whilst Stoffel was away the dogs began to bark late one night, and a man appeared at the fire in a miserable plight. He was a rebellious induna, or headman, whom the king had ordered to be killed. There are a certain number of indunas, who have certain districts given them to rule over under the king, and if they presume too much on their authority they are put to death without much trial. Some of them would be insufferable in their conduct to white men if the king did not keep them in order. This particular man, I believe, the king had given fair warning to, and told him to take a horse and fly the country, but instead of taking one he took two, and he was brought before the king, who thought it best to make an end of the matter. They took him outside the town, and hacked him with their axes, leaving him for dead. What must have been intended for the *coup de grâce* was a cut in the back of the head, which had chipped a large piece of the skull, and must have been meant to cut the spinal cord where it joins the brain. It had, however, been made a little higher than this, but had left such a wound as I should have thought no-one could have survived. It is wonderful, however, how hard Kafirs are. When I held the lanthorn to investigate the wound I started back in amazement to see a hole at the base of the skull, perhaps two inches long and an inch and a half wide, I will not venture to say how deep, but the depth too must have been an affair of inches. Of course this hole penetrated into the substance of brain, and probably for some distance. I dare a mouse could have sat in it.

"His voice was weak, but he evidently enjoyed his supper and the warmth of the fire. My boys said he was a 'wolf'—the term applied to outlaws—and that he ought to be killed or driven away. He told me that it was five days since he had been set upon; and that, after he had been left for dead he got up and ran away on coming to himself. He wanted to go under my protection to the Zambesi, an honour, however, which I declined, but I gave him a blanket and some things to buy food with and told him he must go next morning, and advised him to make for Mungwato. He asked for a pipe and for a drink of brandy, which reminded me of Old King Cole; and if he had been given to amusing himself by listening to the violin, I have no doubt he would have asked for a tune, as he seemed disposed to take things very philosophically. I poured some arnica and water into the hole, and lifted up his head a perfect stream of it ran down his back. He said if he was not killed he should see me at Mungwato when I returned. I believe he did reach Mungwato alive, but I don't know whether he remained there.[122]

"A perfectly favourable communication having been received from the king, I was all ready to continue my journey towards the Zambesi, which I fondly hoped to see in a few weeks. On the 10th of August I was again *en route*, and on the 18th I reached the first Makalaka kraal, travelling slowly. This was the same point I reached before, when I started with the Boer and his boy. Here we decided to stay, to lay in our store of corn—enough to keep our Kafirs when game could not be got, our dogs, and, above all, our horses. At the place where the waggons stand where they are left by people going to the Zambesi, the journey having to be completed on foot, no corn is to be bought, nor any on the road, as there are no corn-growing people between these Makalakas and the Zambesi. Therefore enough must be taken at this point to last till one is amongst the Makalakas again on one's way back.

"Here my companion was laid up with a bad finger. He had run the head of a needle into it whilst sewing, and not feeling much at the time had taken very little notice of it till it began to give him pain, and then he suffered terribly. The end of the finger appeared dead, and I was so much afraid of mortification setting in that I advised him to lose no time in trying to reach Thomson, the missionary, in order that he might have the first joint of the finger amputated if necessary. I should have gone back with him, but he begged me not to do so, assuring me that I should be of no use to him, which indeed seemed likely to be the case. I therefore determined to push on.

"Unfortunately my waggon was quite sufficiently loaded at starting, as I had never contemplated having to travel with only one waggon, in which case I should have left everything I could spare at Tati. As it was, I not only had to add to my own load the things belonging to me which were in Stoffel's waggon, but to take besides a large supply of corn and meal, which we had arranged at starting should be taken in his waggon also. The result was, my waggon was overloaded; and I had not gone more than two or three miles when one of the hind wheels broke, and the weight coming down on it, it was flattened under the waggon, with every spoke smashed. I felt instinctively that it was a hopeless case; and, as I stood looking at it, came to the conclusion that my Zambesi trip

---

[122]In June the following year, this man was seen by Mr. Gilchrist—whose journey into the interior is related in the concluding chapter of this narrative—living near Rustenberg, in the Transvaal, apparently in perfect health.

was at an end. Now that the season was so late, I was sure no help could arrive in time for me to proceed to the Zambesi, and therefore I saw the best thing was to take the mishap philosophically. It was one of the waggons I had bought in Bamangwato, the wood of which proved rotten. My only wish after this was to get back to Tati as quickly as possible.

"The man that the king had given me to see me safe through the Makalakas now refused to stay any longer, though I did not tell him I should not attempt to proceed. I therefore paid him as the king had directed me, giving him more, in fact, than the latter had said. He was extremely insolent, and demanded double what I gave him. However, I knew he must submit, as the king had sent him with me, and he dared not go against his orders. He left me in dudgeon, and I was glad to be rid of him. I had a very slight attack of fever at the time, and his noise and insolence were very annoying.

"After this I sent off my driver with a span of oxen, to take the broken wheel on a sledge of boughs to Tati. and wrote to Brown asking him to send me a waggon, if possible, to bring me out, and a spare wheel also for my own waggon; or, if not, to get the wheel I sent him mended for me. The oxen that I still had left had to go many miles for water every day. The mare and the goats had nothing but filthy drink from holes dug in the ground. For own use I got water from the pits, where the people dig for it, for I was in the midst of the Makalakas. I myself was a prisoner in my own kraal, for I dared not leave the waggon. I had with me three my Matabele slave-boys and one Bushman. We got on pretty well for a few days, but soon the people began to drive my boys from the water, which they claimed the right to, having made the pits. This was the water for my own use, and it appeared also that the water at which their own goats drank was denied to mine, and they and my mare were driven away from it. I sent for the induna, an old Makalaka, with whom I had hitherto refused to speak in consequence of his having stopped me the first time I tried to go through. I gave him a present of ammunition on condition of his allowing my boys to get water; and, after promising to see that all was right, asked for more presents, which I refused, and the boys were driven away just as much as been before. All I could do was to buy water for my own use of the women, who brought it every morning, and to hope that the animals managed to get a little now and then. I had also had a disagreement with the people about some goats which I had bought for a gun. The day after I bought them the gun had been brought back and the goats demanded, which I refused to give up, threatening to shoot anyone who touched them. However, as soon as they went out to feed, the goats were seized. as I fully expected they would be, but the gun had been left. After this I refused to trade any more, and drove the people away except those who brought water.

"Now, whether it was Manyami's son, or whether it was the Makalakas, or whether it was a mere chance, a party of Matabele heard that my waggon was broken, and determined to make capital out of my misfortunes. It was the 7th of September. The weather was extremely sultry, and I lay nearly all my time in the waggon, reading. This evening, however, a heavy shower of rain, with lightning, cooled the air—the first rain of the season. I had been a short walk, keeping near the waggon, and looking for a pheasant or partridge. Immediately after my return I was disgusted beyond measure to see a party of Matabele, some twenty in number, filing past with shields and assegais, and sitting in front of the waggon, after which the oration began. However, the sun set and the rain descended opportunely, and they left, saying they would return in the morning. They told my boys that I must pay for the road to the Zambesi, and that if I did not do so, they would break into my waggon and help themselves. My boys, having seen no disposition on my part to give way, were in a great fright, and said if I did not give the Matabele what they wanted they would run away and leave me. In my situation this would have been worse than anything, so I resolved to conciliate my persecutors, and next day gave hem what they wanted, amounting in value to a mere trifle, £5 perhaps, and not a quarter of what I had made up my mind to give them rather than have a row. I should have felt much more humiliated had I first refused and finally had to give way, but it was bad enough as it was. I afterwards informed the king of the whole affair, and perhaps a number of similar complaints may at last bring punishment on the offenders, who are known. I believe it was my firm demeanour of the night before that stood me in such good stead next day, as, when I voluntarily conversed with them, and asked them what they wanted, they thought it best to be civil, and said I must bring out something and they would see if it was enough. After some consultation they accepted what I gave for the induna of their kraal, and then asked for presents for themselves. I therefore added something; and when they saw I had given all I meant they went away, leaving me much relieved in mind.

"Soon afterwards, to my great joy, I heard the boys say that a waggon was coming; and, sure enough, my driver appeared, bringing a waggon borrowed for me by Brown, and an extra wheel for my own waggon. Brown sent me a note informing me he had letters for me from home, and sending an instalment of four papers, two others remaining for me in his hands with the letters. I divided the load between the two waggons, and breathed again freely when I was fairly past the Makalaka kraals on my way back. I felt like a prisoner who had regained his freedom. Before reaching Tati, however, I had another little adventure, which I must yet add to this already overgrown letter.

"I had one day left the waggon on horseback with a number of my Kafirs to shoot, as we were rather hard up for food, and had been galloping after some eland. It was late in the afternoon, and when I pulled up I saw nothing of my boys, and turned the horse's head in the direction I had come from, expecting to meet them. However, they had lagged, and I began to think I might not be going quite in the right direction. The mare strengthened this fancy, and kept working round, and wanted, I thought, to take a short cut to the waggon. I trusted implicitly to her, and let her have her head, thinking I would leave the Kafirs to go back by themselves. She, however, went in the same direction I had been galloping in just before, which puzzled me. Still she kept on in a straight, undeviating course, as I could see by the sun, and I thought if it were wrong I could easily return as I had come, when I had let her go on her own way long enough. So I gave her a fair chance and on she went. The sun set, and she still kept on as before, the stars now showing me the direction. I began to suspect something wrong, but decided to see what she really would do, as I knew I must sleep in the veldt. At last we came to a broad river without water in it, and, without pausing to look for any, she crossed it, and kept on as before. I thought it must be the Ramaqueban, which is near where I started from, and therefore, after going on some time longer, I turned her and went back to the river, hoping to find water by scraping a hole in the sand, in which I failed. I then tied the mare to a tree, and, making a big fire, had a good night. Next day I was moving at sunrise, and kept down the river, still thinking it the Ramaqueban, when, to my surprise, I suddenly came on the drift where the waggon-road crosses it, and found it to be the Impakwe, the next river that you cross beyond the Ramaqueban in going to the King's. It was now nine or ten o'clock in the morning, and getting very hot. My waggon was thirty miles away, and the mare and myself tired and hungry. I let her feed and drink, for there was plenty of good water. By the time I had gone ten miles towards the waggon she wanted another rest, being much too small for my weight. I therefore gave her a good rest on reaching the Ramaqueban, and it was late in the afternoon when I started off again. By good fortune I met some Boers returning from hunting in the Zambesi direction, and came in for some meat which a Kafir was cooking in the ashes. I never enjoyed anything more. I got back to the waggon late that night, and soon afterwards reached Tati, where I have been ever since. Incidents are rather scarce, and I have therefore made the most of the foregoing insignificant ones.

VERREAUX'S WHYDAH BIRD.—*Vidua Verreauxi.*
SHAFT-TAILED WHYDAH BIRD.—*Vidua regia.*

"I have now a new driver, my old one having refused to go with me after my first repulse by the Makalakas. My present man is a huge creature, civil enough, but too fond of brandy. He one evening made a raid when I was absent, and broke open some of my boxes, not leaving a single bottle of brandy in my possession, but how many bottles I had I have no idea. He shared the spoils with his friends, and they were at it all night. Next day I cross-examined him closely, and got a confession out of him. I then fined him £5, and reduced his wages from £4 a month to £3. He got off cheap, as it is common in such cases to tie the offender up and whip him. The whole race of waggon-drivers, with scarcely an exception, are worthless wretches—dissipated, lazy, impudent, and dishonest. It really seems that civilization has no other effect upon Kafirs than to make them worse than they naturally are.

"I must now wind up this terrible letter. I know it is far too long, but it is too late now to obviate that defect."

Another of Frank Oates's letters, written home to one of his brothers about this time, adds yet some further particulars of his late experiences. He says:—

"TATI, *October 16th, 1874.*

"The mail is in, and with it a letter from you, appreciated as usual, which I need not say is not a little. It is dated July 3d. I am sorry you seem to doubt my getting your letters. In my letter to the Mater I mention the hoard of letters, containing a complete and connected history of home affairs, which met my delighted eyes when I returned here from my third attempt to reach the Zambesi, of which I have given her an account. The road between here and Bamangwato is all but closed from the drought now, as it is the end of the dry season. The waggons that brought this mail in were delayed, and suffered considerably. Several of the oxen died, and one waggon is still in the veldt at the Gokwe River, where there is a little water, and which is the half-way house between Mungwato and here. In distance it is more than half way, but it is always a stopping-place, on either side of which stretches a parched-up country. On the first day of this month I began a letter to the Mater, expecting it would be taken on in a day or two. However, the waggons that were to take it did not set off, preferring to wait for rain, so the letter has been lying unfinished. Now, however: another arrives from you, and sets me off into the writing vein. Moreover, I am expecting very shortly to start into the veldt for a month or two, which means two months, of course, before I fairly set off home. I have in the meantime been collecting birds here[123],

---

[123]The woodcut opposite illustrates two of the whydah-finches which the traveller collected during his present stay at Tati. The general colour of the upper bird is black, with a collar of ruddy brown, fading into buff beneath; that of the lower one black and pale yellow, the bill and legs coral-red. In the winter season these birds lose their long tail feathers, and their plumage becomes a mottled brown; a great contrast to their striking summer dress. There are many varieties of these finches, one species of which *(Chera progne)* a native of the Transvaal, suffers serious inconvenience from these adornments in a high wind.

and reflecting on the vanity of human ambition. It may surprise you that I don't hurry home, now that the Zambesi affair is over. It is certainly not that I don't long to see all the familiar faces once more, and feast my eyes with English scenery. ...

"The weather is now fairly broken, and it has begun to rain again this evening, with gusts of wind, which flutter my papers from time to time. It has been dreadfully hot the last few days. After the heavy rain at the beginning of the month we have been having a spell of really warm weather, the thermometer often reaching several degrees above 100 in the shade. I have been busy having my waggon patched up and made weather-tight. It was finished to-day, and to-day the old Boer returned to his happy home and found me in possession. I said I would pack up at once, to enable him to establish himself in his house this evening, but I found I could not be ready, so he and his family are encamped outside, inhabiting their waggons. However, I held out hopes to him of vacating the place to-morrow, which seemed to satisfy him. In fact the Boers are just as at home at their waggons as in a house. They have little primitive camp-stools, on which they sit round the fire, and the women go about their household duties, and the children play about, and they seem quite at home. Of course when it rains they sit in the waggons like rats in holes—as I have already done myself, and shall now begin to do again. You have no idea how much a home a waggon becomes. I have my books and all my *et ceteras* within reach; and, though it is a little cramping, the pleasure of stretching the limbs when you do get out repays you to a certain extent.

"I expect in a day or two a reply from the king, giving me permission to hunt in his veldt. I only wish to go a short distance from here, to the Ramaqueban, and Shashani, and thereabouts—a tract of country that I know pretty well, and for which I have a real affection, so often have I roamed through its wilds. Rivers that I know well I look upon as friends. I wish, indeed, I could be set down now where I was last year, when I was sent by the king into his favourite veldt on failing to reach the Zambesi, but it is too far, and I should have to traverse the thickly-populated part of the country to reach it. The loathing with which I regard this people is in itself sufficient to deter me. The king himself is well enough, and rules the Kafirs with a rod of iron, but the Kafirs, as a nation, I abominate, and not without good reason. The

---

The long tail feathers are much used by the natives for ornaments and head-dresses.

amount of pride you must pocket when sojourning amongst these scantily-dressed gentlemen is something not to be forgotten. I don't know whether their condescensions or aggressions are the more difficult to bear with patience. Without patience it is hopeless to think of getting on at all. A long string of them filed past my abode lately, and making for Brown's store requested to be fed. This of course Brown complied with, as the land here is only held on sufferance, and these Matabele were supposed to be out on particular business — to murder a lot of poor Bushmen, as we were told afterwards. The latter are constantly being killed, and their life is one long struggle for existence. A gun almost useless to them, as the brutal conquerors of the country are pretty sure to bag it, and ten to one knock the owner of it on the head into the bargain.

"The Bushmen are the real wild men of the country, living in temporary huts, and subsisting entirely on what the veldt produces. They are wonderful runners, and possess certain mysterious instincts, raising them in that respect nearly to the level of some of the noblest animals. The Matabele on the other hand, think themselves the lords of creation, and speak of the slaves (Makalakas) as 'dogs'; and the Bushmen are only looked upon as game. I have one remarkably small creature of the Bushman race with me, who is working for a gun. He always takes to his heels and hides when he sees any Matabele, unless he is with his master and at the waggon. A kraal of these people was lately driven from the Shashe, and is now encamped close to the settlement here. I rode through their camp the other day, and felt that I was amongst the true children of the forest, resembling more the North American Indians than the usual Kafir races of this country. Their huts are made of poles, converging together at the top, these laid over with branches, and finally rudely thatched with long grass. I should say there were between fifty and a hundred of them in the camp."

To this letter, here cut short, he adds the following, four days later:—

"*October 20th*.

"Last night my two Kafirs, whom I had sent to the king, to ask leave for me to hunt a little on the Shashani, returned with a favourable answer. I gave the king a shotgun on first entering his country, much to his satisfaction, and I believe it is now his favourite gun out of the armoury he possesses. I had two cases of 200 cartridges each, and gave him one with the gun, and shall now leave the other, together with the rest of his present, with Brown, to be forwarded to him when a waggon goes up. It is everything here to have the king on one's side, as without it one would have a miserable chance of getting on. Even the king does not care to have too many white men in his country, but likes a few, to enable him to trade. He has a great objection to the Boers, who come only to hunt for skins, thus wasting all the meat, but he knows with me it is a different case, and he does not care where I go, as long as I keep him in good humour by giving him presents. He never objects to people who are in the country hunting for meat. However, he is down on you if he sees any ostrich egg-shells lying on the breakfast-table, and asks how you expect to get feathers if you eat the eggs. He also very sensible in his denunciation of killing cow and young elephants, the ivory of which is scarcely worth taking. The Boers, wherever they go, shoot everything, big or little, on the principle that all's fish that comes to the net.

"We have just had a heavy shower, and there was one last night; in fact the rainy season is setting in. Rain is very much wanted, and all the livestock requires fresh grass."

Amongst the letters, twice alluded to above, which Frank Oates had found awaiting him at Tati, was one from his brother William, who was just about to start at the time he wrote (in the June previous) on a three months' yachting trip to Spitzbergen; after his return from which he contemplated again coming out to Natal, early in the following year, there to rejoin his brother on his way back from the Zambesi, and accompany him—it he cared to go—on a short hunting expedition in Zululand, or, going north as far as Zanzibar, strike inland with him thence instead. To this proposal Frank Oates replied as follows:—

"TATI, *October 27th, 1874.*

"I have been delighted to get your letters to find there is a chance of our uniting our forces once more. When you wrote of coming out to me I was both pleased and sorry—sorry, because I thought it would be best for me to return home when I reached the coast, and yet, if you had actually met me there, I could not have resisted the temptation of setting off again with you.

"I have often wished I had you with me, and remember, when I got to Mungwato last April, to outfit, as I drove up to Gray's store, I thought if I could have a wish it would be to see your waggon coming in from the opposite direction. I did not even know that you were yourself thinking the same thing about the same time. The same idea occurred to me the last time my waggon broke down on the Zambesi road, and I was left to the mercy of the natives of that part of the country. I thought, if your waggon suddenly appeared, how I could turn the tables on my persecutors, and how we could go on together to the Zambesi. Of course, I felt certain such a thing would not occur, but somehow it got into my head. ...

"You will be glad to hear that I endorse your theory that trying to trade, when on a sporting tour or exploring, is an utter failure, and that, had we brought up light waggons, we should have been wiser—knowing all I know now. I have been allied with Dutch Boers since parting from you, and the more I see *of* them, the more I see *through* them. I have still some of my old Maritzburg bullocks left, a rare good sort, but from time to time upon the journey have bought and broken young ones. I have now a good span of four and a couple of supernumeraries, and have likewise bought a heifer, to give me milk. She is of the peculiar small breed, less than Alderneys, bred by the Mashonas. My dogs are invaluable to me. 'Rail' and 'Rock' require the greatest care, and get it.

"I shall wonder how you get on amongst the Spitzbergen game. If as successful as you must have been here, you can claim to count amongst the Nimrods. I don't know what to say to your letter of June 2d. Of course, if you should come out as you propose, it will be very pleasant to meet, and we might spend a month or two together in the Zulu country before I leave Africa, or, returning *via* Zanzibar, spend a month or two there, as you suggest. I should not care to be very much longer than this, and if, after all, you should not come now, we must do something else again together in the course of time."

The whole of these letters, above were despatched to England about the end of October. To one of them a postscript was added on the 28th, to the effect that the trader, Stoffel Kennedy, whose finger, it appears, had had to be amputated on returning from the veldt, had just arrived at Tati, and that he and Dorehill, the young trader of that name, already mentioned in these pages, were intending to start immediately with two waggons for the Zambesi, and wanted Frank Oates to accompany them. "I hardly think, however, that I shall do so," he writes, "as the season is so far advanced. I am principally afraid for my boys, who are far more likely to suffer than a white man is, who has a snug dry bed to lie on, and other comforts; and I distrust my old waggon, which has played me false once already."

On further discussing the subject with Stoffel and his companion, he found, moreover, that he had somewhat misunderstood their plan, which was only to be travelling towards the Zambesi now, and wait about upon the road till April or May, when they would go forward to the river. It was too late, they considered, to attempt to reach the Zambesi the present season. Though strongly tempted on some accounts to fall in with their proposal and accompany them, upon reflection he decided not to do so. It was the result, however, of what had passed with them upon the subject that led him to abandon, as intimated above, his projected trip to the Shashani, and accompany the trading party instead, as far upon the road towards the Zambesi as they meant to travel before coming to a stand. This would give him an opportunity of seeing an entirely fresh part of the country beyond the Makalakas, and he could return when it suited him. It is probable, too, that he still—if hardly acknowledging it to himself—may have entertained an ill-defined hope that travelling in the direction of the Zambesi he might even yet, through some unlooked-for turn of circumstances, find himself enabled to reach that river before the commencement of another year. That hope, assuming its existence, was one destined to be realized, little likely as it appeared to be at the time he left the settlement. It was the 3rd November when the united party started on their journey, and for the fourth time Frank Oates turned his face towards the Zambesi,

BLUE WILDEBEEST.—*Catoblepas taurina.*

Chapter XI

Final start from Tati—Bushman remains—A game-drive—Wild dogs—The Makalakas again—The Matengwe River—English hunters met with—The Nata River—The Pantamatenka—Christmas Day—Start on foot for the Zambesi—The goal at last.

THE country first passed through on leaving Tati was now fresh and green, with abundance of water along the road. Their first evening the party halted at "Mopani Pan", a small pond full of reeds and surrounded by tall mopani trees, a few miles from Tati. This pond is a favourite halting-place for travellers between the Tati and Ramaqueban Rivers, but soon becomes dry in the winter season. Here the party remained four days, hunting; troops of quagga, blue wildebeest, and waterbuck being met with. The veldt about here, though stony and for the most part very bare of vegetation, produced some fine white lilies, now in bloom.

Advancing again, on November 7th, to the Ramaqueban, they proceeded slowly up that river, and halted again for a short time four days afterwards, at the point where Frank Oates had stopped to hunt when here the previous August—the point at which the road for the Zambesi turns off from Ramaqueban again towards the Tati. Here the latter had now a hut of branches made by the boys for himself to lie in, as the heat in the waggon was insufferable. This was some relief from the usual state of things experienced about this time. "The flies," he writes one day at this encampment, "are perfectly maddening. One wakes early, when comparatively cool, looking forward without much pleasure to the coming day of heat and discomfort—no comfortable spot to retire to from the heat, and every place dirty and crowded. How different," he concludes, "from the luxuries experienced in some hot countries!" Here, on one occasion, his boys brought him some fine barbel, taken in the river, which proved delicious eating when rolled in meal and fried in fat and oil.

On the 13th, whilst still at the same point, Frank Oates's old ally, Van Roozen, arrived with Piet Jacobs, the Dutchman, from the direction of the Makalakas, the former of whom tried, it appears, to dissuade his late employer from attempting the Zambesi at the present season, a notion he was evidently by this time seriously entertaining.

Both these Dutchmen, as it chanced, were acquainted with the spot near the Ramaqueban River where the Bushmen, whose remains Frank Oates had already made more than one fruitless endeavour to obtain, had been massacred the year before. Still anxious, if possible, to secure some of them, and finding he was now within easy access of the spot, he entered into an arrangement with Jacobs to conduct him there; but again, as on former occasions, when the time arrived for setting off, his guide was not forthcoming. Jacobs, however, before leaving, had fortunately on this occasion found a substitute in the person of Van Roozen, through whose guidance the traveller was at last successful in his search, as thus related in his Journal:—

"*November 15th.*—Cloudy day. Old Piet left, having deputed Van Roozen to take me to the bones, but wanting to go shares in the profit. He left a boy with a sack; but Van Roozen seemed so lukewarm I let him send away the boy, and was nearly letting him go too, but Dorehill joined us, and at last we made a plan, persuading Van Roozen to take us to the place, whilst the waggons trekked to the big branch of the Tati, where Stoffel was to outspan. Van Roozen seemed a bit nervous; and, indeed, was rather perplexed to find the place, however, at last he did. It was a pretty spot. Some large trees, laden with yellow blossoms, growing in rich masses like laburnums, but in spikes, scented the air. Behind these rose a pretty rugged kopje, and in front of them were the old huts of the unfortunate Bushmen, and the screens from the sun which they erect. Heaps of ashes and game bones, broken pots, and other remains lay around, amongst which the skulls of the Bushmen appeared conspicuously. We found three here, and three more lay in the grass at some little distance[124]. We offsaddled and collected some bones, which I tied up, in order to carry on my saddle in front of me, and we again set off, but the sky was clouded over, and we were not sure of our road. However, we came out all right in the waggon-road. Van Roozen deposited his charge, and we rode forward to the waggons. Van Roozen shot a quagga just before we crossed the big spruit, and we soon arrived at the big branch of the Tati, where the waggons were outspanned, Van Roozen having decided to pass the night there with us. The following morning, early, Van Roozen took his departure, trekking south, whilst the rest of the party crossed over to the Tati, where, outspanning at the

---

[124] The skulls and other remains here obtained were brought to England, with the rest of the traveller's collections, after his decease.

'poort' (the pretty spot already noticed in the preceding chapter), they again stopped for two or three days to hunt, at which point the Journal thus continues:—

"*November 17th.*—Heavy shower early; pleasant, cloudy day. Out with two boys, shooting. ... During the ride I saw a big game-drive, made by the Makalakas, consisting of a long broad alley, the sides composed of large tree branches, forming a strong hedge. At the end were three pits side by side, walled round with stakes. On the top were placed light stakes, and long grass was laid over all. My boys say the Makalakas kill lots of quagga and other game in these traps."

CAMP IN THE VELDT.

"*November 18th.*—Cloudy morning; hot after-noon. Out to the right, amongst the kopjes; game very scarce. ... Rested, whilst out, under a large tree, with leaves something the shape and appearance of a poplar; the trunk smooth, thick, and of crooked growth. The fruit of this tree is small and green, and, when fresh dropped, useless; but the ground was strewn with last year's fruit, which contains, under a very hard shell, some kernel, not unlike walnut, but softer, and very nice, the only difficulty being the getting at it. Two goats of mine, which I had bought of Piet Jacobs, and had since been lost, turned up today, having been absent since Sunday afternoon (the 15th). They had come on alone, one having given birth to two kids."

The travellers on the 20th again moved slowly forward, and reached the first kraal of the Makalaka (Wankee's) on the 22nd, where they laid in a fresh supply of corn, the natives this time making but a very feeble show of attempting to stop their progress. The day before this Stoffel had fallen in with a large pack of wild dogs, a circumstance thus narrated in Frank Oates's Journal:—

"*November 20th*.—Cloudy morning, after a cold night; cool day. ... Stoffel rode when we trekked, and shot a quagga. He describes a pack of wild dogs he saw. Two pallah rushed past him pursued by dogs, which stopped when they saw him, and began to bark. They were all black, spotted with white, with thick bushy tails, and dog-like ears. They were the size of his dog 'Bob', larger than a pointer considerably—*i.e.* the males; females, he says, were less. They kept running and then stopping at near range, but he did not get any. He says he has seen a pack once beyond the King's, and once one at Gasuma, near the Zambesi, like these. A pack he once saw in the Free State were different colour (reddish or gray). That he saw to-day contained about fifty."

Leaving the kraal again upon the 24th, the Journal once more continues:—

"*November 24th*.—Hot, with a breeze. Started at 9.30 AM, and trekked till noon. Passed the kraal just beyond which my waggon broke before at a small spruit. We ride through mopani veldt, and soon come to another kraal. Pass lots of cultivated land, and then more kraals. The latter are small, and generally placed under a kopje, on which often grows one of the few striking and picturesque trees of the country. We crossed two other spruits during the trek, larger than the first mentioned, but not large.
"A rabbit got up close to the waggon directly after we outspanned, and the dogs set off. Dorehill lost one of his, and I lost 'Rock'. Our boys found the spoor, and as it turned out the dogs had been stolen by Makalakas. Stoffel, Dorehill, and I, with Jacob, rode with our guns and a lot of boys to two or three kraals, threatening them all with

punishment unless the dogs were given up. At night they were brought back by one of Stoffel's and one of Dorehill's boys, who had been to a kraal and demanded them. We decided to inspan and ride with the moon. Trekked through trees, thickly placed (mopani mostly), crossed several spruits, and outspanned at the Matengwe River; say three hours."

"*November 25th.*—Cloudy; heavy rain at night. Here we met a party of Griquas, who have been in Stoffel's employ before as hunters, and they are now willing to turn back their waggon and return with him. They tell sad tales of the Zambesi fever, of which many of them have died. They say it is comparatively healthy at Tamasancha[125], and they are willing to stand there till April or May, and then go on to the Zambesi. The old man tells me that a man gets a pain in his head and lies down, and next morning, if he is alive, he is 'salted'. Stoffel busy making arrangement with these people. Trekked through beautiful green veldt, road winding amongst a great number of kopjes; mopani, and other trees. Several large and rather bad spruits crossed. We kept near the Matengwe during this trek, and part of the time the road keeps along its bank. It is an extremely pretty river, and has a fine running stream in its sandy bed. I saw a plant quite new to me, with fine fan-shaped drooping leaves. Some pretty white lilies, delicately striped with lilac, grew close to the river's bank. I enjoyed the scene very much. Few kraals. Where we outspanned, I had a bathe in the river. People came to sell things."

"*November 26th.*—Cloudy day, but hot; shower at night. Went through mopani veldt, till we came to a big tree, where we stopped. My mare, who I noticed refused her corn, lay down, and on looking at her we found her panting, and that there was a running at her nose. When made to get up, she soon lay down again. Stoffel says it is horse-sickness. I ordered her to be driven slowly on behind us when we trekked. Went past Menon's kraal. Menon and some of his people came out. He was very civil, and appointed to come to us ahead, which he did, when we each gave him a present."

"*November 27th.*—Cloudy, threatening morning; a few drops of rain. Rain, thunder, and lightning in the evening. Started before daylight, and made a short trek through very heavy mopani to the drift of the Matengwe, where we outspanned. Some yellow matter was running from

---

[125] Tamasanka. DS

the mare's mouth and nose, but small in quantity. She pants and coughs but still eats a little. Stoffel, Dorehill, and Jacob rode to shoot, and Jacob shot a giraffe. I went on again a short distance with the waggons, through heavy mopani veldt, finally stopping on a 'sandbelt'[126] near a pan of water. Went out on foot in the evening, and saw some pallah, steinbok[127], and quagga, but they were too wild for me to get a shot."

"*November 28th.* — Cloudy morning. Heavy shower came on immediately after my return from an unsuccessful hunt on 'Bob'. Busy buying corn. The water lay deep all round my waggon. The mare lying down, every now and then getting up, but breathing very heavily, and, when last I saw her, making a 'roaring' sound. Nothing was running from her nose, but I found inside it a little bright yellow and black matter. I don't know that she ate anything to-day. She lay most of the time with her nose on the dirty ground. The skin of her back is all peeling off."

AFRICAN DWARF GOOSE.—*Nettapus auritus*.
(Length about 11 inches.)

---

[126] An arid ridge or zone of sand, of frequent occurrence in this district, extending sometimes a distance of many miles.

[127] A small antelope (*Raphicerus campestris*). DS

"*November 29th.* — Slightly cloudy day; very pleasant. Mare dead; froth like white sea foam on her nostrils and inside clear yellow liquid, a lot of which had run out. She was not perfectly cold when I saw her. All of them say it is horse-sickness. Dorehill afterwards opened her, and one of his boys found a great number of large fat grubs in her stomach, holding on to the inside. They seemed to have eaten the lining away, and indeed in places to have eaten through the walls of the stomach itself. This might account for the state of her back, and the fact of her slavering when she ate her corn, but I don't think they can have been the proximate cause of death. ... Out shooting to-day, but the game here is very wild."

"*November* 30th.—Cloudy morning; close, hot afternoon. ... On returning from the veldt in the evening, found every one who had been left at the waggons nearly drunk; the Griquas rushing about with loaded guns and fighting. Inspanned, to restore order, and went about four miles."

The following morning, some five miles again brought the party to the Matengwe Rive where a halt was made. At this point two English hunters, whom Frank Oates had met before during his wanderings—Messrs. Wood and Selous—came up on their way to Tati from the Zambesi. It was the result of this meeting which apparently determined Frank Oates's future plans; for, almost from the first day he left the Tati, the idea seems to have been present to his mind that he might yet make the Zambesi the present season, without waiting for the cessation of the rains. His own inclination was strongly in favour of this attempt, as saving him from the dilemma, otherwise presented, of either leaving the country with the river unvisited, or remaining there another season for the purpose; and the opinion and experience of the two hunters mentioned above, coincided, as it happened, with his wish and inclination. They both believed, and perhaps rightly, that the present was a safer time for the Zambesi than the month of April, when the rains would only just be over and the moisture not all dried up. Indeed Stoffel, who adhered to his present plan and waited to go on till April, himself took the fever when he reached the river, and died from its effects. The fact is that neither one plan nor the other was a good one, and between the two it was but a choice of evils. So anxious, however, was Frank Oates to reach the river that season, that, gladly catching at the moderate degree of encouragement he now chanced to receive from these two gentlemen, he resolved forthwith to push forward there at once, without intending, however, to make a lengthened stay, or do more on this occasion than merely see the Falls, and obtain a few specimens of natural history. And thus resolved, he again resumed his journey on December 3rd, and with no serious delay or hindrance succeeded in reaching the Zambesi. Before starting, however, he wrote home the following short letter, which Messrs. Wood and Selous undertook to convey as far as Tati :—

"MATENGWE RIVER, *December* 2d, *1874.*

"Again I report progress. I am past the obnoxious Makalakas, and am actually going to start for a hurried run to the Victoria Falls. I left Tati with the people I told you of, who were going on to a place about three days ahead of here on the Zambesi road, intending to wait there till April and then go on to the Zambesi. I intended to accompany them and turn back, as I did not wish to wait for another season, and did not think it advisable to make a hurried run to the Zambesi and back now. Indeed, you would infer from my letter it was not my intention to do so. However, things have so turned out that I think I am choosing the best course in going on now.

"In the first place, I have here met waggons coming from the Zambesi, those of Wood and Selous, two Englishmen, who hunt and know the country well. They both advise me to go once. They say they would rather go on now than stand all the time, and then go on in April. In fact it seems that April is too early; and all agree that it is infinitely better to go now that the rains are falling than it is to go too soon after they have ceased to fall. They say the risk of fever is not s great as long as the rains fall, and the really bad time is when they have ceased to fall. The traders, however, must wait, in order to avoid the really bad time, as they could not go there and trade and come back again; whereas in my case I have only to spend a fortnight in getting to the place where the waggons are left, and say ten days or a fortnight in going from there to the Falls and back (it can be walked in three days, I am told, easily), whilst another fortnight will bring me back in the waggons. So you may say six weeks will do it all, and it would not only be possible to be back in Tati before the end of January, but this would allow a lot of extra time. It is only three weeks from Tati to Daka, the standing-place and I am now a week's journey on the way.

"A man who knows the Falls and this road well has undertaken to conduct me to the Falls and back.[128] He is a coloured individual certainly,

---

[128] This was a native from the Cape, named John Mackenna, who, as well as Klaas the driver, remained with Frank Oates till his death.

but appears a very intelligent and capable fellow. He has been hunting for Wood and Selous, and it is thought he will prove very efficient. He has insisted on large relays of medicine and food, and I have been able to get nearly everything I wanted here. There were in fact eight waggons in all here yesterday. The trader, who lost his finger when coming on with me before, with his two waggons, and a partner of his with one waggon, went on last night. Another trader is turning back now with Wood and Selous, who are going back; and another waggon, belonging to a party of Griquas, has gone on with the traders.

"I expect to be back in Bamangwato in February, *en route* for home. ... I can scarcely fancy myself returning so soon from a successful visit to the Falls, having so often failed; but I think you will agree with me that I was not wrong in determining to make another attempt, as things turned out, and acting, as I am, on what I consider to be very competent advice. It is now the beginning of the rainy season, but very little rain has yet fallen; only a few heavy showers, with intervals of very hot weather between them."

The day after writing this letter—on the 3rd of December—Frank Oates started off again, as above mentioned, towards the Zambesi, and soon came up with Stoffel, who had left upon the 1st, in company with another trader who had joined him on the Matengwe. Dorehill had turned back with Wood and Selous. From this point to Tamasancha, a watering-place on the road to the Zambesi, where Stoffel and his companion intended standing till April, the road lay chiefly through heavy sand, and was traversed in about a week. Soon starting, the Matengwe River, which had now been kept near for some time, was left flowing towards the westward, and shortly afterwards the Nata River was crossed. From here to the Daka, a small river not far from the Zambesi, water can only be obtained along the road at the various 'pans', or small ponds, which occur at intervals throughout this the country, no other rivers intervening.

At Tamasancha, which was reached on December 10th, Frank Oates, after a short rest, parted from his companions, proceeding forward on the 14th alone towards the Zambesi. The country, from this point, is only varied from sand and thick bush by the occasional occurrence of these 'pans', or 'vleis', the favourite haunts of wading-birds and wildfowl. Soon after leaving Tamasancha one was passed (Flamakinyani) closely encircled by large trees, and a little later was another (Geruah), about the size of a duck-pond and extremely pretty, surrounded with the greenest of grass, whilst all around it extended the barren and sandy veldt. About here giraffe and other game was met with, including sable antelope, eland, and wild pig. Fresh elephant spoor was seen north of Tamasetsie, but the time now allowed of no delays for hunting. The 'poison-plant', growing low, and bearing a yellow plum-like fruit, was gathered on one occasion near the waggon-track.

The Daka River was reached upon the 21st, and the day after, some miles further on, two other small streams were reached and crossed, and then a third into which apparently the first two flowed. This last was a small river called the Pantamatenka, just beyond which is the place where waggons stand for travellers going to the Zambesi. These streams, it was evident, must all be very small, except during the rains. They were small indeed even now, though overflowing their banks and running quickly. Almost immediately after crossing the last-named, Frank Oates's waggon stuck in a very soft muddy place, but Mr. Blockley[129], who was in charge of the trading-station here, came with a span of oxen to help him out, and the following morning his waggon was taken up to where the store was built, on a little stony kopje above the watery flats. Mr. Blockley was here in capacity of agent for another trader, then absent—Mr. Westbeach[130]—and with him was a Dr. Bradshaw[131], who had been some time in the country. On the succeeding day, December 24th, the waggons of two other traders, Messrs. Trescott[132] and Wilmore[133], arrived from the Zambesi, the former of whom had been ill with fever, and was still very deaf and scarcely able to eat anything. He described their recent sufferings from fatigue, hunger, sickness, and the impossibility of keeping dry, as something truly wretched.

---

[129] George Blockley, an agent of the trader George Westbeech, who managed Westbeech's stores in the Zambesi valley for 16 years. Blockley and Westbeech were the first Europeans to ascend the upper Zambesi after Livingstone. DS

[130] George Westbeech. The best-known trader in the region; Westbeech enjoyed excellent relations with local rulers such as Lobengula, Sipopa and Lewanika, and regularly extended help to hunters and explorers in the area. DS

[131] Dr Benjamin Bradshaw was a peripatetic physician who travelled from the Diamond Fields in 1872 to join Westbeech's company as an assistant. After leaving because of his lack of interest in commerce, he remained in the area collecting zoological specimens. After a spell in Britain, Bradshaw returned to South Africa, serving as surgeon to the Bechuanaland Border Police before his death in 1883. DS

[132] James Truscott. DS

[133] Wilmore later had a store at Molepolole. DS

Christmas Day was celebrated at the store by the cooking and eating of a large plum-pudding worthy of the occasion, and the day following Frank Oates busied himself with preparing for his walk the Falls. This he intended to accomplish in company with Dr. Bradshaw, who had been there before, and volunteered to go with him. The 27th was the day fixed for the start, and before leaving he wrote home in high spirits the following letter to his mother which Messrs. Trescott and Wilmore were to take with them when they returned to Tati. It was the last he wrote:—

"PANDAMATENKA[134], *December 27th, 1874.*

"I am just about to set off, to walk to the Victoria Falls, which are only three days from here. This place is somewhere about fifteen miles to the north-westward of Daka, a place you will probably see in any recent map. Neither place is a town of any sort, but each is merely a river flowing to the Zambesi. At both rivers waggons stand, as they are both out of 'the fly.' The place where I now am is quite civilized, as it is a trading-station, and the man in charge here has a snug little house, well thatched, to keep out the rain. He has lived here three years, and is in the employ of Westbeach, who is at present at the residence of Sepopo[135], the Zambesi chief, some distance up the river. His man, Blockley, undertakes the charge of my effects whilst I proceed to the Falls.

"You will be delighted to hear that there is a *doctor* here, who is going to accompany me in my walk, and is a great stickler for comforts. He was, I think, doctor on a steamer, and at last got to the Diamond Fields, and thence came here with Westbeach, and has been here now two years. He spends a good portion of his time in collecting beetles, and is apparently very good-natured. He never loses an opportunity of telling you that a thing is very unwholesome, the next thing being its rapid disappearance into his own interior. There was a grand plum-pudding made here on Christmas Day. Besides Blockley and the doctor there are two traders, who arrived here after I did, on their way from the Zambesi. One has been ill and the doctor prohibited him plum-pudding, so there were four of us in all. We ate nothing but pudding on Christmas Day and the day following, with scarcely an exception. The men had another pudding. My man turns out to have been originally a cook, and when he likes can cook well. The doctor was found to be five pounds heavier after

---

[134] Pandamatenga, now the location of one of the border posts between Botswana and Zimbabwe. DS

[135] Also Sipopo. DS

dinner on Christmas Day. He strongly urged upon all of us the desirability of moderation, but no-one seemed to pay much attention to him, and he certainly did not practise what he preached. He has been to the Falls before, and in the rainy season too, so he knows what he is undertaking in going with me. I expect he will make very slow marches, but so much the better. I am going to take with me the identical tent I had with me in America, and which proved so effectual a shelter from the snows of the Rocky Mountains. There was a grand idea in the doctor's mind of taking a lot of cold plum-pudding with us on our walk, but the last morsel disappeared last night. However, we shall not be badly off for supplies.

"From Tamasancha, where I last wrote[136] to you, and where the traders were waiting till April, I was nine days in getting here. The waggon-road all the way goes through thick bush and heavy sand. There are no rivers, but abundance of pools in the rainy season. We have not had very much rain, but of course enough to fill the pools, and enough to make the road, where it goes through turf, as it does before reaching this place, extremely heavy. My waggon stuck the night of my arrival, but Blockley brought his oxen and helped me out; which, however, he failed to accomplish that night, though succeeding the morning following. He then brought my waggon up here on to the top of a little hill where his house is, close to which it is now drawn up.

"This must be a comparatively healthy spot, even in the most unhealthy time, as it overlooks the flat wet country around it, and the water will run from it. There appeared to me to be much more watery land, and more pools of water, about Daka than here. It is where so much land lies under water that, about the end of the rainy season, the fever is so bad. People may get it almost any time, but February, March, and April seem to be the worst months. I think Baines is said to have stated that he would rather be on the Zambesi in January, the height of the rainy season, than in May, a lovely month, but when the moisture is perhaps not all dried up. When it is dried up, it is then all right. Another thing seems to be, that people moving about are better off than those who have to remain stationary in one place.

"One of my goats was reported to have been killed by a leopard on Christmas Eve. We all went with our guns, and I took my dogs. We found the unfortunate goat lying dead, a live companion standing over it; and, also standing over it, and facing the live goat, an animal I thought

---

[136] This letter was not received in England.

was a dog. They told me it was the leopard, but I would not fire, still thinking it a dog. At last, however, I saw what it was, and we shot it. Two others ran away, and my dogs killed both of them gallantly, and in next to no time. They were cheetahs, a sort of leopard, very lanky, and a good deal like greyhounds in appearance. They were very thin, and probably hungry when they killed the goat; but the other goat must have kept them from eating it, as it had been killed a considerable time when we got to it.

"I must now get up and make ready to start. I am writing in the tent, having had a cup of coffee as usual, but not got up yet. I intended to have written this letter last night, and, having failed to do so, thought it best to make sure of its being written before I began anything else.

"I hope you are all spending a pleasant Christmas and New Year's time at home, or wherever you are; and wish every one a very happy New Year."

Starting upon their journey late that evening, the Journal resumes the narrative:—

"*December 27th*—Fine hot day, with a north-easterly breeze. Wrote letter home early, and made final preparations for the walk. As my own boys had all requested to accompany me, wishing to see 'Metse-a-tunya,' I took all (eight in number) except the Bushman, whom, with two Makalakas engaged for me at Pantamatenka by the doctor, I left with Klaas. The doctor had also got me another Makalaka, whom he handed over to me, as well as allowing me to pack one of his own three boys; so I had the benefit of ten, the doctor had two, and John had three boys. We were a party, in all, of two white men, one colonial boy (John Mackenna), and fifteen Kafirs, and left the Pantamatenka a little before sun-down; walked three miles up the river, and, crossing it, encamped for the night. During the walk I saw a fine tall palm—the first tall one I have seen. The leaves were fan-like and the tree extremely graceful."

"*December 28th.*—Beautiful day. Had coffee, and started soon after sunrise. Kept up the river, say five miles, then recrossed and left it, and went ten miles more, crossing a 'sandbelt,' I with two boys finding water in an open grassy space, or 'lichter.' The others missed the water, and I rejoined them in the long sandbelt, which extended beyond where we halted. Then went three miles more, passing some water, of which we were very glad, and at last reached a fine lichter, with a stream in it, running away to the east, into the Pantamatenka. On our left was a ridge, some two or three miles off, with palm on it, which the doctor says he passed on his right, when he went to the Falls last. Rose to opposite side of lichter, to high ground, and camped."

"*December 29th.* — Fine morning, but rather cloudy; a few drops of rain in the afternoon. Had coffee, and again started early. Immediately after starting crossed another stream, also running, they say, into the Pantamatenka. Giraffe and quagga spoor seen. We only went six miles to-day, as one of the boys had to be sent back for an axe, and we waited for him. Maclinwon, who had gone on alone, presently returned, having shot two rhinoceros, and we all went to the place and camped there."

"*December 30th.*—Cloudy; a shower in the afternoon. Walked ten miles to-day, crossing at two sandbelts, the last of which was stony, and with a very thin stratum of soil on it; the trees few and sparsely scattered. Some dry stony spruits here, and a fine view of the opposite sandbelt. Slept at a spruit in the hollow beneath us, where we had stopped to make tea in the afternoon, but where it looked so threatening we had pitched the tent. However, the rain was trifling. Some of Tibakai's Bushmen were seen and talked to. Whilst the boys were making the huts, the pointed out the cloud on the horizon to the northward from Metse-a-tunya. It keeps rising in a white puff, and passing away in little fleecy clouds. The others heard the Falls; I not sure I did."

"*December 31st*— Rather cloudy; heavy about sundown. Fine night. Went, roughly, say three miles further north across turf, to the river where I thought Tibakai was encamped, but found we were too much to the left, so after crossing the river kept down it about three-quarters of a mile to his camp. John was in front, hurrying on with one of his boys but when he came near the huts, stopped and hid behind a bush, from which he was peering when we joined him. Here he wanted to stay and send for Tibakai to talk, our object being to get two Bushmen from him to go with us to the Zambesi, for corn. I ordered him and the boys to march on to the huts, and stop at a distance now that they knew we were there. John was in a great funk, but found, with Tibakai, a hunter whom he knew. I left the boys and traps under a tree amongst the huts, and went with the doctor and John to have an interview with Tibakai. He is a Mungwato headman, with one or two of his own people, but all the rest are Bushmen, hunting for him, and staying with him with their families. Tibakai said we could not go to the Falls—he was captain here. Hearing, however, we did not come to hunt, he said we might go but must make our scherm here, and stay till tomorrow, when we might visit the Falls and return. He then conceded that we might have two Bushmen, whom he would give us to-night when they returned from hunting, but said we *must* sleep here to-night. I said we must go, and he could do as he pleased about the Bushmen. After this he again said we must stay to-night. This I flatly refused to do, and had already told him we should shoot elephants if we saw them. John wanted me to stay, and refused to come away. I ordered the boys to start, they having already told me they were willing, and again for the third time called John. We then started, all but him, and there was a great stir in the place; caps snapping, and one fellow running out with his gun. We moved on, I on the flank ready to fire; but it was not necessary. John remained behind, but, seeing us get away, joined us, and, when I upbraided him, said he was only waiting to see what they would do."

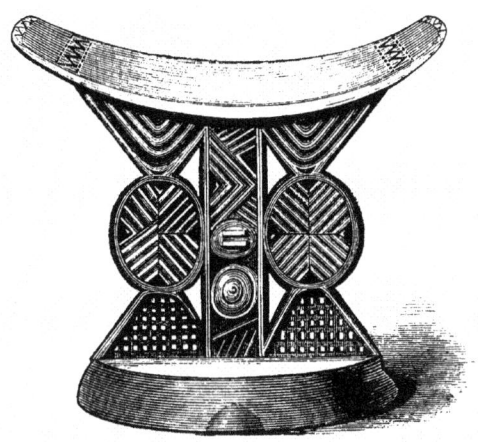

WOODEN PILLOW.

And now a walk of some twelve or fifteen miles brought them to the goal. The latter part—five miles or so—of this was over rolling ground, and here, as they advanced, they soon began to more clearly the distant clouds of vapour from Falls, and hear them more distinctly. The trees, before thinly scattered, were now fine and close together, and for a time obscured the view. Then shortly, through an opening in their midst, the columns of spray again were visible, now quite near, and the party pressed quickly on. The sun was about to set, and clouds were gathering, as if for an approaching storm. Stopping to shelter from a heavy shower just above the river, the first sight of Metse-a-tunya was here caught through the trees and a halt was ordered for the night.

Thus, the last day of 1874, the sun set on the fulfilment—after many hindrances—of the traveller's great desire!

Chapter XII

Main features of the Falls—The return commenced—Frank Oates attacked by fever — Course of the illness; improvement and relapse—His death—Dr. Bradshaw takes his effects to Bamangwato—His favourite dog—Arrival of W. Oates and Mr. Gilchrist in Natal—Conclusion.

VICTORIA FALLS, ZAMBESI (THE OUTLET).

IT is to be regretted that, from the time of his reaching the Zambesi till the date of his death five weeks afterwards, the entries in Frank Oates's Journal are of the scantiest description. Indeed, the whole time that he was actually at the Falls he made no entries in it whatever. This may have been partly owing to the depressing condition of the atmosphere near the river at that time, which would make any exertion—even that of writing—burthensome; and partly from his relying on his memory for a faithful recollection of a scene at once so novel and so impressive. "After breakfast," he writes on New Year's Day, 1875, "I visited the Falls—a day never to be forgotten." This is the sole entry in his Journal till the 14th of the month, when he was again back at the Pantamatenka.

And what gives especial cause for regret at the absence of any further entries in his Journal of the period is the fact that all the accounts of the Falls yet published have been given by those who visit the river in the dry season of the year. Of this number Edward Mohr may have suffered least from this disadvantage, for he was there in June 1870. Baines and Chapman were there together during parts of the months of July and August 1862; Livingstone was there, his first visit, in November 1855, his second in August 1860; and Baldwin at the time of Livingstone's second visit. On both occasions when Livingstone was at the Falls, the river, he remarks, was very low; and Chapman mentions that, when he and Baines were there, the water had recently fallen as much as seven feet. It remained for Frank Oates to visit the river at its fullest; at the very height, in fact, of the rainy season; but, unhappily, we are left without any results of his experience, except in the shape of a few pencil and two water-colour drawings he made on the spot. The two latter have been selected for representation in this volume—one of them coloured, the other in the form of a woodcut. Before offering any explanation regarding these, it may be well to recall to the memory of the reader the main features of the Falls as described by previous writers.

The river for some distance—at least two miles—above the Falls is of great width, and, flowing between hills some three or four hundred feet in height presents to the eye a smooth open surface, dotted over by a number of picturesque, tree covered islands. Where the Falls occur the river is upwards of a mile in width, and the Falls extend the whole of this distance, their line broken at intervals by dark projecting buttresses of rock, forming, some of them, small islands with trees upon their tops; whilst others, of much less size, present merely a bare and jagged surface. The Falls are occasioned by what appears to have been a rift in the original bed of the river— a rending asunder of the rock in the river-bed, over the edge of which the whole waters of the Zambesi are poured down into a deep, narrow gorge below, its width varying from something like eighty to a hundred yards. The water escapes from this deep abyss, where it boils and foams tumultuously after its descent, by a still narrower channel of from twenty to thirty yards in width, and apparently about the same depth as the fissure into which the water falls, the waters of the river being thus suddenly compressed into this narrow limit immediately after flowing through a bed upwards of a mile in breadth just above the Falls. The river after this proceeds by a zigzag course from east to west for about five miles, through a continuation of this narrow cutting, before it finally flows away in a more direct line eastwards. This outlet, Livingstone[137] informs us, is about 1170 yards from the western and 600 from the eastern end of the abyss, the river at the Falls flowing nearly due north and south, whilst the fissure which receives the water lies nearly east and west. At this point the rushing waters from either side unite after they have fallen. "The stream ..." writes Chapman, in his account of the Falls, referring to this portion of the river[138], "which here slackens its speed before the entrance, steals slowly round, at the solemn pace of a funeral procession, before it escapes from its confinement between the massive columns of rock". The water here is of "that sombre green", says Baines[139] in his description, "which indicates great depth; the moderate rapid formed in the narrow turn below the entrance rolling in that smooth, glassy swell almost destitute of foam, which seems so gentle and proves so overpowering when one tries to stem it".

It is the view from this point—"one of the prettiest and most comprehensive" that can be obtained of the Falls, says Chapman—that is represented in the preceding woodcut; in the foreground are seen the gliding waters flowing through the escape-channel, the spray of the falling cataract rising up beyond; whilst on the horizon, above that section of the Falls which is visible from here, extends the distant outline of one of the river's banks. "This point," writes Baines, "is the only spot, with the exception of the west end in calm weather, that is free enough from spray to allow the use of water-colours.

The remaining most characteristic feature of the Falls represented in this drawing is the rainbow spanning the abyss. The marvelous colouring of these rainbows, which are frequent here, has struck all who have beheld them; their "tints," says Baines, "more beautiful than in England's clouded climate one can ever dream of." Whenever the sun falls upon the clouds of spray these rainbows are always present, sometimes two, sometimes three in number, and the brilliancy of their colouring can scarcely be exaggerated. "Rainbows", writes Chapman in his description of the Falls, the first day he saw them, "so bright, so vivid, are never seen in the skies. The lower one in particular (on this occasion) probably from the contrast with the black-looking rocks below, was *too* vivid, nay, almost blinding, to look upon,

---

[137] *Narrative of an Expedition to the Zambesi*, p.254.

[138] *Travels in the Interior of South Africa*, vol. ii, p.130

[139] *Explorations in South West Africa*, p.499.

defying imitation by the most skilful artist and all the colours at his command, yet imparting its heavenly tints to every object over which it successively passed." So marked a characteristic of the spot are these rainbows that it appears, according to Livingstone, the early native name of the Falls was "Chongwe," signifying the Place of the Rainbow; a name, however, which has since given place to others. Frank Oates's boys spoke of the Falls as Metse-a-tunya, a compound word, signifying "water-sounding"; whilst the name which Livingstone received for them, as used by the Makalolo at the time of both his visits, was not dissimilar, viz., Mosi-oa-tunya, or "smoke-sounding," from the smoke-like appearance of the columns of spray which rise above the cataract.

With regard to the other general features of the Falls not referred to above but little remains to be added. Their actual height, as estimated by Livingstone, is about 360 feet from the top of the precipice to the surface of the water in the abyss; the columns which are driven upwards by the rush of air from the channel as the water descends into this narrow space, ascending to a height variously estimated by those who have seen them—and no doubt varying with the state of the atmosphere and the volume of water in the river at different times—from six to eight hundred feet, or something over.

It is these vapour clouds which, visible at a distance of upwards of twenty miles, as distinctly observed by Livingstone, mark the position of the Falls long before the traveller approaches them. Frank Oates, as seen in the preceding chapter, distinguished them at a distance of about eighteen miles, and his followers heard the roaring of the water at that distance, though he was not sure of doing so himself. Chapman, after he had left the Falls, heard them, he relates, "at a distance of fifteen miles on an elevated region in the south."

Comparing the Falls with those of Niagara, Livingstone points out that they are twice the height of the latter; whilst, "in the amount of water, Niagara," he says, "probably excels, though not during the months when the Zambesi is in flood."

It is unfortunate that no general view of the Falls, except a bird's-eye one from the high ground some miles distant, can be obtained, owing to the vegetation on the south side of the fissure and the dense clouds of spray rising from the chasm. "But for this," says Chapman, "the Victoria Falls, presenting one unobstructed view, would not alone have been the most magnificent, but the most stupendous, sight of the kind on the face of the globe."

And now, resuming our story, the remaining incidents are soon related, the material for its completion being somewhat scanty. From the time of his arrival at the Falls till the date of his return to the Pantamatenka, Frank Oates made, as has been stated, no entries in his Journal. Again at the Pantamatenka, however, on the 13th, he made a few brief notes, remaining there till the 19th of the month, when Mr. Westbeach, now back from the Zambesi, also started southwards, accompanied by Dr. Bradshaw. Two of Frank Oates's native servants were already by this time ill with fever, taken, no doubt, on the Zambesi, but the rest of the party so far continued well.

On the 25th, however, at the 'pan' called Geruah, the beauty of which had struck him on his journey north, Frank Oates himself complained to his companions—for his own waggon and that of Mr. Westbeach were never far apart as they advanced—of slight headache, the usual precursor and accompaniment of African fever. In a couple of days, however, he was better again, so that he even went out hunting. But this apparent improvement unhappily proved delusive, and it soon became evident that he was suffering from an attack of fever. And now he continued for some days, with slight fluctuations, better and worse till the 29th, when his condition became alarming. Throughout his entire journey up country from the Makalakas as far as the Pantamatenka he had been engaged in taking careful observations of the country, and noting the various watering-places along the road, and this he continued to do on his way back, to check his former notes. His regular Journal had been again discontinued on the 22nd, but he still made some brief jottings of the route until the 31st of the month, when, such was his condition, even these had also to be abandoned, and he continued very ill till the morning of the 5th of February, when there was a decided change in him for the better.

During the whole of this time Dr. Bradshaw had remained with or near him, and Mr. Westbeach had kindly lent him the services of one of his own boys, who could speak a little English. There was now every reason, so far as the traveller was himself concerned—and had been ever since he first showed signs of illness—for the party to make all speed upon their journey south. Once at Tati he would be in a place of comparative civilization, affording greater comfort for an invalid, and in a far better climate. Travelling is also usually found to be beneficial in most stages of this fever. They were, therefore, all now pushing forward to the Tati with the least possible delay.

On the morning of the 5th of February, as stated, Frank Oates's condition was much more favourable, and there may still presumably have been hope of his recovery, when, unfortunately, a point being reached during the day where some of his boys had to be paid off and discharged, the annoyance and excitement contingent on this circumstance—for at such times the boys always manage to be troublesome—brought on a relapse, and towards the afternoon of that day he again got worse. The party, as it chanced, were then in a part of country where there was no water for the oxen, and were travelling with all haste to reach a place where they could get some; yet so alarming were Frank Oates's symptoms, that towards evening Dr. Bradshaw, who was with his waggon, was obliged to order a halt. This occurred at a certain point in the journey, a little north of the same Makalaka kraal at which the traveller had already experienced so trouble. He was now much exhausted, and Dr. Bradshaw got him to take some soup and a little brandy, and then left him for a few minutes to go to the other waggon. He had not been gone, however, many minutes, when Mr. Westbeach's English-speaking boy, who had been left in charge, hurried after him, begging him to return at once, as a sudden change appeared to be taking place. This Dr. Bradshaw did—but only in time to find his companion sinking. Frank Oates tried to speak, but in so low a whisper that the other unhappily failed to catch his meaning, and a few minutes afterwards—about a quarter of an hour before sunset—the brave spirit sank peacefully.

At this point in the journey it so happened that the ground was very hard and stony, and, even had it been otherwise, there was no spade or other implement at either of the waggons with which a grave could have been made; so, hearing that Piet Jacobs, the Dutchman, was near at hand, having been at a neighbouring kraal that morning buying corn, Dr. Bradshaw sent to him for assistance. Several others of the party were by this time ill with fever, and the man who took this message—John Mackenna—was so reduced that he was scarcely able to sit the horse he rode upon.

Jacobs, in reply, sent back word for the others to come on further, where the ground was less stony, and that he would meantime find a place suitable for the grave. With this suggestion Dr. Bradshaw willingly complied, and, travelling in the night, met Jacobs early the following morning about an hour's journey at the other side of the kraal. Here the Dutchman, who was familiar with the country, had by this time found a spot well suited for the purpose. This was a disused game-trap, some eight feet in depth, at no great distance from the waggon-road so often traversed by the deceased, and placed by the side of a small stream or river flowing south. And here, in the deep repose of this silent spot, the traveller's remains were laid in their last resting-place. His was a burial which well became in its simplicity a true lover, like himself, of Nature and her wilds.

This ended, it now devolved on Dr. Bradshaw to convey the waggon and effects of the deceased to Bamangwato, where he left them in charge of the Rev. John Mackenzie, himself returning soon afterwards to the Zambesi district. His attentions to the deceased during the last days of his illness must have materially added to the latter's comfort, whose friends have reason to be thankful that he chanced thus accidentally to have been thrown into the company of a fellow-countryman at the close of his two years' wanderings. His interesting collections, moreover, of natural history, a part of which he now had with him, might readily have been dispersed, and his goods plundered, had his death occurred amongst unfriendly natives, with no one at hand to be responsible for their custody; whilst, as it was, all these with his waggon and outfit, and personal effects[140], were faithfully delivered by Dr. Bradshaw into the charge of Mr. Mackenzie at Bamangwato, there to await instructions from his relatives in England.

One incident of Dr. Bradshaw's journey should not be here omitted. It appears that many miles after they had left the grave, one of Frank Oates's pointers—his favourite, 'Rail'—was found to be missing, and boys were sent back in search of him. These men sought long and wandered far in vain, till at length in their pursuit they got back even to the grave, and there, patiently watching, they found the devoted creature laid. A little longer, and he must inevitably have fallen a prey to lions or other wild beasts, but now he was taken down with his companion to Bamangwato, whence they were subsequently conveyed to England. And thus it happened that, whilst Frank Oates's friends at home were rejoicing at the speedy prospect of his return, and wholly unsuspicious of the truth, this faithful dog was watching, the sole mourner, by his grave.[141]

The very day of Frank Oates's death his brother William—returned from his yachting trip to Spitzbergen—sailed from England for South Africa, to join him, accompanied by Mr. Gilchrist, the gentleman already mentioned in these pages, whom the brothers had met when they

---

[140] Dr. Bradshaw, since the above was written, has been down from the interior to the Cape, with considerable collections of birds and insects formed during his travels. Some of the former of these have reached the British Museum.

[141] Mr. Gilchrist, whose subsequent journey into the interior is related below, and who brought the particulars of this and other incidents connected with the narrative to England, understood the dog to have gone back to his master's grave the whole way from the Tati settlement—a distance of nearly eighty miles.

first reached Durban two years previously, and had afterwards travelled with in the interior, William Oates having returned with him to England. The day these two sailed from England—about an hour before the vessel left—letters were brought to them on board from Frank Oates, which had only just reached the country, giving a full account of all his plans, and of his wanderings up to the end of the October previous. The two friends reached Durban on the 15th of March, and at once commenced preparations for proceeding up country to meet the returning traveller. Mr. Selous, who had met Frank Oates at Tamasancha, as mentioned in the previous chapter, had now come down from the interior, and reported having seen him early in December, then on his way to the Zambesi and in perfect health. There was indeed just at this time, as it happened, a report at Pietermaritzburg that the traveller had died of fever in the interior, but—as subsequently proved by a comparison of dates—this report had certainly no foundation in the actual fact, and was found on enquiry at the time to be unsupported by any reliable evidence. The preparations already in progress for a speedy start into the interior, to meet him on his way back, were therefore still proceeded with, and waggons, oxen, and all the necessary outfit got ready for the purpose.

Another week and William Oates and his friend would have started on their way northwards, when—on the 1st of April, a fortnight only after their arrival—authentic intelligence reached them of Frank Oates's death in the interior. The object of proceeding on the Journey was now therefore completely changed, and, to enable William Oates to return at once to England and there offer to his bereaved mother such comfort as he might be able, his friend Mr. Gilchrist, in no common spirit of self-sacrifice, himself insisted on taking the sad journey alone into the interior—to bring down thence and convey to England all the deceased's effects; to hear such particulars as he could of his death, for the satisfaction of his friends at home; and if possible—a service attended with especial difficulties—to visit the grave, and place over it, to mark the spot, a stone prepared for this purpose in Pietermaritzburg.

Gratefully availing himself of this generous offer, William Oates sailed for England on April 22nd, having first seen Mr. Gilchrist leave Pietermaritzburg with two waggons, on his way up country; a sort of departure very different from that which either of them had anticipated. The journey undertaken by Mr. Gilchrist—under any circumstances a laborious and trying one enough—was rendered doubly so by the sad object with which he started; nor did he return till every purpose of the journey had been fulfilled. For not only did he bring safely to the coast— and subsequently to England—the large collections of natural history specimens and curiosities, and the notes and journals of his travels which Frank Oates had made, as well as his two pointers, 'Rail' and 'Rock', but, in spite of the obstacles opposed to his progress at the Tati, he even proceeded to the spot where the traveller's remains had been laid, and on his way back succeeded in obtaining an interview on the Ramaqueban River with Dr. Bradshaw, from whom he learnt the few additional particulars of his death which could be supplied, and which have been embodied in the preceding narrative.[142]

For this twofold purpose—of reaching the grave and seeing Dr. Bradshaw—Mr. Gilchrist, on reaching Bamangwato, had gone on thence with both his waggons as far as the Tati settlement, where he arrived on the 18th of July. There he found the same difficulty of proceeding further which Frank Oates himself had often previously encountered, a great fear still prevailing amongst the natives of 'red water'—the Natal cattle disease—being brought into their country, and Lobengula having recently sent strict orders to the kraals on the outskirts of his territory to keep all waggons from Natal from attempting to cross their boundaries. Fortunately, however, it happened that the Dutchman, Piet Jacobs, was now at Tati, who had not only selected the spot for the late traveller's grave, but was also intimately acquainted with the whole of the surrounding district, and who had, besides, a general permission from the king to enter his country when, and as often as, he pleased; for keeping, as he did, his oxen standing at Tati, when he was not out with them in the veldt himself, there was little fear of his introducing the dreaded disease into the country. With him therefore, as guide, Mr. Gilchrist was speedily enabled to make a start northwards; and, on the afternoon of the fifth day from the date of their leaving Tati, came to the point in the waggon-road where they had to leave it, in order to go down to the river's side to reach the grave. Mr. Gilchrist found it placed about six hundred yards to the left of the road, in a situation of much natural beauty, surrounded by low picturesque hills, and with trees of varied growth and foliage scattered at intervals over the grassy sward. The grave itself, over which a number of large stones had been placed when it was first made, was found quite undisturbed, and amongst these Mr. Gilchrist now

---

[142] By a singular coincidence, Frank Oates's devoted favourite, 'Rail'—for four years after reaching England the valued companion of his late master's relatives—died on the 5th of February 1880, the fifth anniversary of his master's death, followed but three weeks later by his companion, 'Rock'.

inserted at its foot the small white stone, neatly cut, which he had brought from Pietermaritzburg for the purpose, bearing this simple inscription—"Frank Oates, F.R.G.S., of Meanwoodside, Leeds, England; died 5th February 1875, aged 34 years." Then, the task of friendship faithfully performed, he returned without delay to England.

Nor had this journey, painful in its objects and associations, been entirely free, on Mr. Gilchrist's part, from privations and anxieties of a graver kind. Water upon the road had many times been scarce (on one occasion he was without any for his oxen—twenty-nine in number—for as much as seventy hours); the season was one of exceptional heat and drought, and the time occupied on the journey was unavoidably considerable.

And here, before concluding, it may be mentioned that at Tati, Bamangwato, or wherever he met those who had become acquainted with Frank Oates in this country, Mr. Gilchrist found but one opinion expressed concerning him. Many were the kindnesses treasured in men's minds and now related, which he had rendered to those he had encountered in his travels; whilst, on the other hand, he had himself apparently been no less fortunate in the kindly services he had received from others. Friends had arisen where he least expected them, beyond the pale of European civilization, from each of whom he parted in turn with a consciousness of mutual regret. Such was the way in which he drew all hearts towards him; and after his death, the good offices of those who loved or esteemed him in his lifetime were generously placed at the service of his family. Conspicuous amongst this number stood the Rev. John Mackenzie, of Bamangwato, and Mr. F. A. Hathorn, of the Standard Bank, Pietermaritzburg, the former of whom undertook the duties of executor for the arrangement of his affairs in the interior, whilst a like responsibility was accepted by the latter for the settlement of matters in Natal. Nor was it only what these two gentlemen did, but even more the manner of their doing it, which placed the traveller's relatives under a lasting sense of obligation to them, and served not a little to soothe the first bitterness of their affliction.

And now this brief history of the efforts and too early extinction of a devoted life, otherwise it may be conjectured destined to have rendered no mean service in the extension of scientific knowledge and research, may be concluded with a few words, written soon after his death by Mr. Mackenzie to one of his brothers with reference to the position of his grave. "Lonely the spot, no doubt," he writes, "is, in a certain sense; but, in another, your brother's grave is surrounded by all the activities of the great Creator and Father of all. Flowers will blossom around it, though not planted by mortal hand; birds will sing over it, and never weary in repeating the sweet notes which Nature has taught them. I have not been there myself, but I have no doubt the naturalist would not think your brother's grave a lonely spot; whilst to the Christian such a spot is the quiet resting-place to which the body sank when the spirit was called away by God the Father."

"RAIL."

BIBLIOGRAPHY

Works consulted for Introduction and footnotes:

Branch, B., *Field Guide to Snakes and other Reptiles of Southern Africa* (Cape Town, South Africa: Struik Publishers, 1998);

Byrnes, L. (ed) *Southern Africa Road Atlas* (Victoria, Australia: Lonely Planet, 2000);

Doke, C. M. *et al*, *English-Zulu/Zulu-English Dictionary* (Johannesburg, South Africa: Witwatersrand University Press, 1990);

Oates, F., (ed. Oates, C. G.), *Matabele Land and the Victoria Falls: A Naturalist's Wanderings in the Interior of Africa* (London: Kegan Paul, 1881);

Rasmussen, R. K., and Rupert, S. C., *Historical Dictionary of Zimbabwe* (Metuchen, NJ, USA: Scarecrow Press, 1990);

Rye, E. C., 'New Books', *Proceedings of the Royal Geographical Society and Monthly Record of Geography*, Vol. 3, No. 10. (Oct., 1881)

Stuart, C. and T., *Field Guide to the Mammals of Southern Africa* (Cape Town, South Africa: Struik Publishers, 1988);

Tabler, E., *Pioneers of Rhodesia* (Cape Town, South Africa: C. Struik, 1966)

————, 'Pioneers of Rhodesia', *Africana Notes & News*, Vol. 19, no. 5, March 1971;

van Wyk, B-E., Gericke, N., *People's Plants* (Pretoria, South Africa: Briza Publications, 2000).

Also available from Jeppestown Press:

Where the Lion Roars: An 1890 African Colonial Cookbook
Mrs A. R. Barnes

A reprint of one of Africa's earliest English-language cookery books, dating from 1890. Mrs Barnes' recipes for translucent, aromatic melon and ginger konfyt; fiery curries; and sweet peach chutney are as delicious now as they were a century ago; while instructions for making a canvas water cooler, and for treating snake-bite or fever, offer a fascinating insight into the domestic lives of southern Africa's Victorian colonists. ISBN: 0-9553936-1-2

For full details of our inventory, or to order direct, view our web site at **www.jeppestown.com**

JEPPESTOWN

The Bulawayo Cookery Book and
Household Guide
Edited by Mrs N. Chataway

This reprint of Zimbabwe's earliest cookery book is packed with recipes for Edwardian African delicacies: garnet-coloured tomato jam; fiery, home-made ginger beer and spicy bobotie. Packed with contemporary advertisements for companies like Puzey and Payne, Philpott and Collins and Haddon and Sly, the book even contains a section on veld cookery, contributed by Colonel Robert 'Boomerang' Gordon, D.S.O., O.B.E., who went on to raise and command the Northern Rhodesia Rifles at the outbreak of the First World War. ISBN: 0-9553936-2-0

For full details of our inventory, or to order direct, view our web site at **www.jeppestown.com**

The Anglo-African Who's Who 1907
Walter H. Wills (ed.)

A reprint of Walter Wills' quirky colonial reference book, containing the details of nearly 2,000 prominent men and women of Edwardian Africa. This astonishing work includes biographies of settlers, soldiers, explorers, politicians and traditional leaders from every corner of the continent. Invaluable for genealogists, historians, military researchers and medal enthusiasts, it offers details of over 1,200 separate medal awards, together with fascinating biographical sketches of colonial African celebrities—many of whom were known personally to the editor. ISBN: 0-9553936-3-9

For full details of our inventory, or to order direct, view our web site at **www.jeppestown.com**

The Rhodesia Medal Roll
David Saffery (ed)

Containing the names of over 12,000 recipients and revealing 2,300 previously unpublished decorations, this definitive book is the ultimate compendium of Rhodesian military and civilian honours and awards gazetted between 1970 and 1981. Fully indexed by surname, it is perfect for medal collectors and dealers, historians and genealogists—and a brilliant heirloom souvenir for recipients and their families. ISBN: 0-9553936-0-4

For full details of our inventory, or to order direct, view our web site at **www.jeppestown.com**

www.ingramcontent.com/pod-product-compliance
Lightning Source LLC
Chambersburg PA
CBHW070550160426
43199CB00014B/2448